BILINGUAL BEING

Bilingual Being

MY LIFE AS A HYPHEN

KATHLEEN SAINT-ONGE

McGill-Queen's University Press
Montreal & Kingston | London | Ithaca

Legal deposit first quarter 2013
Bibliothèque nationale du Québec

Printed in Canada on acid-free paper that is 100% ancient forest free
(100% post-consumer recycled), processed chlorine free

McGill-Queen's University Press acknowledges the support of the
Canada Council for the Arts for our publishing program. We also
acknowledge the financial support of the Government of Canada
through the Canada Book Fund for our publishing activities.

The epigraphs appearing on page 1 are from *Aesop's Fables* (trans.
Vernon Jones: Kahley Publishing, 2007) and Jacques Derrida's *Archive
Fever: A Freudian Impression* (trans. Eric Prenowitz: University of
Chicago Press, 1996).

Library and Archives Canada Cataloguing in Publication

Saint-Onge, Kathleen, 1957–
Bilingual being : my life as a hyphen / Kathleen Saint-Onge.
ISBN 978-0-7735-4119-1

1. Saint-Onge, Kathleen, 1957–.   2. Saint-Onge, Kathleen, 1957 –
Childhood and youth.   3. Adult child sexual abuse victims – Québec
(Province) – Québec – Biography.   4. Bilingualism – Québec
(Province) – Québec.   5. Catholic Church –Québec (Province) –
Québec.   6. Québec (Québec) – Social conditions – 20th century.
I. Title.

HV6570.4.C3S259 2013   362.76'4092   C2012-908045-4

Set in 11.5/14 Adobe Garamond Pro with Scala Sans
Book design & typesetting by Garet Markvoort, zijn digital

Pis c'est pour toé surtout, c'te liv'-là,
ma belle cousine Sonya.
Tu rêva' bin d'enseigner l'angla' itout un jour,
mais là, tu respire l'air fra' du ciel pour tou'es jours.
En haut, ousse que t'es, tu-vois-tu nos vra' pères là bas –
ceux qu'y ont mangé tant d'not'merde pour c't'affaire-là?
T'sais, t'as perdu ta voix binque trop jeune,
mais moé, j't'entends encore quand même.
C'fa'q'ej dédie c'te travail-là bin fort à ton honneur,
pis el maudit silence, on l'perce ensemb' astheure.

[And it's for you most of all, this book,
my beautiful cousin, Sonya.
You, too, dreamt of teaching English some day,
but now, you breathe the fresh air of heaven every day.
Up where you are, do you see our actual fathers there –
those who ate so much of our shit because of this mess?
You know, you lost your voice far too young,
but as for me, I still hear you anyhow.
So I dedicate the present work sincerely in your honour,
and the damned silence, we pierce it now, together.]

CONTENTS

POEMS

Letter

Dear Elder,

Did I make you nervous?
Or did you just happen to dislike me?
At parties, you didn't look me in the eye.
I never got a hug or smile, or conversation.
You were austere and unapproachable –
but why only with me?

Was my mother right?
Is this what I brought upon myself,
simply by becoming "so damned English" –
«mauditement froide pis indépendante»?*
Rejecting «ma patrie» for elsewhere,
and for this other tongue?

Or was my mother wrong?
Did you remember all along
what I'd forgotten until now?
Were you afraid my memory would trigger,
so you helped me move away from home,
by showing me I was already absent?

* Damned cold and independent (the latter being a very harsh criticism in French-Canadian culture, certainly not intended as a compliment).

Is that it, my dear Elder?
Because if it is, then I think history
will reveal that when our culture foundered,
and our folk abandoned distant shores,
it was too late for us to run, or hide.
The enemy was among us, deep inside.

Signed,
«Une p'tite fille d'l'famille»

Clockwork

«C'est l'temps qui passe
entre deux mains.»*
One, two: decade through.
Hands right on time.
Movements as regular
as clockwork.

One. 1963.
A crowd in here.
The dark red folding chairs
in the basement in the suburbs.
Family party. Too much champagne.
Miscellaneous uncles and male friends.
Two hands appear underneath my rump
under my dress, touch my frilly underwear.
That's precisely when the mechanism triggers,
the numbing switch. Controls skin, mind, soul.
Sensing fingers, as if anaesthetized but awake.
As if pressure pushes a perfectly frozen self,
looking at the girl sitting on the lap.
It is not necessary for someone
to intervene. Someone has.
I feel nothing
but time.

* "This is (the) time spent (passing) between two hands."

Two. 1973.
Alone down here.
The little orange couch
in the basement in the suburbs.
Weekend evening. Too much beer.
My date, a year older, already driving.
Two hands appear underneath my rump
under my jeans, touch my cotton underwear.
That's precisely when the mechanism triggers,
the numbing switch. Controls skin, mind, soul.
Sensing fingers, as if anaesthetized but awake.
As if pressure pushes a perfectly frozen self,
looking at the girl sitting on the lap.
It is not necessary for someone
to intervene. Someone has.
I feel nothing
but time.

Apologia: A formal defence of a position or belief

There's a classic French children's song, «Chère Élise,» about a girl who has a little hole in her bucket. It's famous, if that can be said about old songs and rhymes. I could hear it daily, weekly, in the songs of my mother, my grandmother, my great-grandmother – around my home, my street, my world, Quebec City. From the year I was born, 1957, a story from the knee, and after that, year by year. I hear it resonate in my head even as I write this.

In my mind, the voice is usually my mother's, and I try to join in, to echo the string of tricky phrases. There's a wave of tones, rising and falling, and some forgetting and laughing, and the comforting sensation that this Élise is at least a bit funny if not terribly smart – and that her song is a bit soothing though tiresome too. For me, Élise has many dimensions in French, complexity and depth. There's feeling wrapped up inside her – the smells and sounds of both ordinary and special days, remembrances of time past and moments never quite erased, however the years have unravelled their difficult scenarios.

In French, she's opaque, tangible, and sensual. And so her song has a place in the treasures of my childhood, a particular place of its own, like my soft cat with the plastic face and chewed-off ear. Or my favourite pink «jaquette en flannalette» [flannel nightie], as the language of home said then. A «jaquette de flanelle,» as the "reformed" language of home says now.

In English, the song's called "Dear Liza," but I don't know it half as well. I have a sense that not so many people sing it in English, but I'm told many do – anglo children. In English, there's no accompanying music in my head, no memories, no echoes, no presence of this material registering psychically in any way. But I can convert the words easily enough. In English, Liza is, becomes, a translation rather than a person. Transparent, constructed. A projection of Élise. Purely linguistic.

It's a classic children's round, its humour based on an interminably repetitive narrative. There's a hole in the bucket and Liza doesn't know how to fix it. What should she do? She needs straw to plug the hole. But the hay isn't cut. She needs a sickle. But the sickle isn't sharp enough. She needs a sharpening stone. But the stone isn't wet. She needs water. But the water hasn't been brought up from the well yet. She needs to fetch water. But there's a hole in the bucket.

Ah, poor Liza. She's a bit of a dunce, this girl, neither terribly autonomous nor independent. And quite illogical, too, no? Circular, even. As though everything she needs to do hinges on something before it, and that thing itself leans on something else that must be done before that … and when she backs up completely toward the past, step by step, she's right back where she started. We regard her with a kind of pity that we somehow don't feel.

Élise *and* Liza. Élise *or* Liza. We perceive our protagonist slightly differently in each of her languages, don't we? Her identity seems changed, and her personality is subject to reinterpretation, this way or that. Academics might say she has a presentation of self that varies with her languages as her bilingual identities play out like alters, fluctuating and flickering, influenced by the passions of affect, culture, and the primary allegiances of the soul. Our young multilingual, multicultural subject is quintessentially postmodern, multiple, fragmented, hybrid, liminal, fluid. A pin-up girl for the times. Chic split.

Is she a bilingual mess or a psychological virtuoso? It's hardly a question of interest to her. For all that she cares about other than that broken bucket is that she exists – she survives. The question of far greater value is how it feels for Élise-Liza to live like this, with a foot in each language. Is she comfortable? Happy? Does she enjoy playing in the wide space between her worlds – or does she feel lost between them? Does she belong everywhere, to everyone – or nowhere, to no one? And what's the impact of her shifting loyalties on those who love her and interact with her in one language or the other?

Now let's imagine that one day, as Élise-Liza is walking with her problematic bucket, she runs into a charming young woman her age who's also carrying a bucket, and they begin a cheerful conversation. The new friend, Jill, speaks only English. But Élise-Liza puts her bilingualism to good use in the months that follow, as they meet at the well each day. That's how Élise-Liza learns that Jill has a brother named Jack who's responsible for carrying water to the well, too. Some days Jack comes along with Jill, while on other days he runs out of the house and does it on his own. Élise-Liza is fascinated by this idea that a boy can do the well chore, while a girl can choose to avoid it.

When she returns home, the usual drips following behind her on the ground, she's still dreaming of her new friend, Jill, and this other world. Of course, she says nothing of what she's thinking, for it's her private world, too precious to share even with her own mother. So she feels herself becoming a bit distant from her family, with her own thoughts. And she looks forward to each day's trip to the well to learn more. Her mother watches her skip away into the distance and yells after her, «Erviens bin vite!» [Come back fast!] But Élise-Liza does not come back quickly. She lingers at the well as long as she can, delighted to think of new possibilities for her life, ignoring the dripping bucket.

Her encounter with a single child from another village has changed Élise-Liza forever. Our bilingual has realized that her new language is a passkey to another culture. Slowly, she's being transfigured, and her life will never be the same. Goodness knows, she was already a complicated girl, with her circular logic and that unfixable bucket. But she's now become incomprehensible to her family. For she's begun to imagine the impossible – and then, to consider it possible. Begun to know she's from «El Pays des vieilles chansons» [the Land of Old Songs], but that she could choose the Land of Nursery Rhymes instead.

And now a single thought: show me a bilingual person's autobiography, and I'll show you someone who's apologizing for something.

BILINGUAL
BEING

The moon once begged her mother to make her a gown.
"How can I?" replied she. "There's no fitting your figure.
At one time you're a new moon, and at another, you're a full moon,
And between whiles you're neither one nor the other."

Aesop

Nous ne sommes hommes et nous ne tenons les uns auz aultres
que par la parole. [We are but human, and we hold on to one
another but by our word.]

Michel de Montaigne

From this point on, a series of cleavages will incessantly divide
every atom of our lexicon.

Jacques Derrida, *Archive Fever*

Boxes

I seek out counselling in English:
describe my trauma as if I read it
or saw it on an evening newscast.
Yet in my mother tongue, pain is
embodied in a thick, bitter amber,
and I am closed, refusing therapy,
certain I wouldn't ever survive it.

The unconscious is a single field:
experience as an old French film
dubbed in English,where random
phrasing – long strings of lonely
echoes – erupt from thin fissures:
strange, haunted gaps in line-time
where it feels like I never existed.

But my consciousness is divided,
in its coding of inner talk (more
English than French) and its ego.
One voice is condemning, bleak,
abusive, self negating, critical;
another that is stronger is loving,
supportive, nurturing, confident.

Memory isn't bilingual either:
seems the brain has shifted the
responsibility for recording on
the psyche – so life's recalled
unevenly in duelling languages:
different readings of the past –
variant views of self and world.

Bilingual, it's hard to be consoled
or understood in one or the other.
Identities and ideas inhabit boxes
on separate inner shelves of mind.
Best to hang on to your languages,
or you'll need a dictionary one day
just to realize your own thoughts.

1

MY MOTHER TONGUE/MY MOTHER'S TONGUE

SANITIZED FRENCH

In September 2010, I found myself in a Grade 4 French immersion classroom in the Greater Toronto area. I'd already been a teacher for more than twenty-five years, so it was no surprise to find myself in a classroom. But it was my first year teaching French immersion since 1984.

I'd been underground as a francophone for a quarter century, nearly my whole career, teaching in English in English provinces – Manitoba, British Columbia, and Ontario. And that day I was handling a new problem, which is that one of my students, his parents also the product of French immersion programs, had shown me a note in his agenda telling me that «vidanges» – which I'd put on a word list – didn't exist.

What were they talking about? I use it all the time. «Vidanges» means "garbage" in my Quebec French – it's a real word. But according to the parents, who'd apparently been taught a sort of sanitized French devoid of cultural moorings, I should have used «ordures.»

I wasn't surprised at the comment, actually. We all know just what we know, and the boy's parents didn't mean any harm. I had a chat with my student about synonyms, with examples from English, and we called it a draw. I also stuck in some political commentary about the dominant francophone population in the country being from Quebec, so Quebec French matters.

But then a pattern developed with these agendas. The next week, another student, another note. I'd apparently erred in using the word «bicycle» instead of «bicyclette,» according to this parent. Again, «bicycle» is perfectly acceptable in my Quebec French. Some days the notes broached the absurd. One parent wrote a long message asking me to double-check the verb «gaspiller» [to waste], which I'd given the students the previous week, because she was sure that the word is «gaspiyer» instead. It's not. But by now my French was being corrected randomly, continuously, by individuals who had the best intentions but who couldn't help the fact that they'd apparently acquired a sort of sterile French from standard texts and a few teachers who were short on synonyms.

And so the ironies kept flying. After more than thirty years of drifting across this country to separate myself from my French heritage, deliberately and incidentally, and trying until only recently to stay mum about my French origins, I found myself half-defending French culture and French expressions. I also had to run to the dictionary daily on the sly to check that I was right about things, like the verb being «gaspiller» and not «gaspiyer,» because the sad truth is that I wasn't sure – even though I'm a francophone by birth, by baptism, and by any other way you want to measure it. French is my mother tongue, my mother's tongue.

LIKE MME X

These days, in the halls before and after school, the few parents who are native francophones (one in a typical class here) reach for my elbow, grab me for a quick chat. They're hungry for word from home, literally, and not afraid to seek and emit a human connection. But a quick comment about the weather, a digression into the day's plans, and I make sure we're both off again on our separate ways. That's all the French food there is to eat today. It's enough for me. Almost too much. I'm afraid they'll catch me out, discover that I don't have a French husband, French children, French friends, favourite French authors, television shows, movies, or music – or a French lifestyle of any kind outside of school. Thankful for cautions about fraternizing too much with parents, I take my sturdy English legs down the hall, smiling as we part. Another day, another escape.

It's the same fear reflex with staff. The only other teacher who claims French as her birthright (again, one in a typical school here) finds me in the photocopy room, bemoans some new grammar error in a colleague's classroom, gender misagreement on signs and handouts – «*le* fenêtre, franchement» [honestly]! She articulates her familiar complaint: «Pis après, c'est moi qui 'es a l'année prochaine, pis leu' français est d'ja plein d'erreurs.» [And after, it's me who has them next year, and their French is already full of errors.]

She's funny, generous, artistic, and hard-working. Still, she seems to have a bit of trouble maintaining allies in the staff room, among the other dual-track teachers at this school – mostly anglophones, and a few who are certified, with mixed confidence, as "French qualified." Maybe it's the judgment calls coming from her end, or maybe it's the anti-Quebec backlash coming from theirs. Hard to say. Even among bilinguals here, the identity tension is anything but dissipated. It's okay to speak French – "good to *have*," everyone says, some gritting their teeth a bit obviously, for FI is a lucrative pass into the slowing teacher's job market. But to *be* French Canadian – now, that's another thing altogether.

Their acquired French, in almost every case, comes from urban Ontario language education programs in bilingual schools and a quick summer in Europe – or, more rarely, part of a life spent in Egypt, Algeria, or the Ivory Coast. "I just don't get Quebec at all": that's the summative opinion here, expressed daily, weekly, monthly. Some have never even been. It's only a few hours away, I say, and historically stunning, I tell them – in English, of course. "Maybe next summer," they say. "Or maybe the south coast of France."

But I'm different. And the jury's out, apparently, on whether it's in a "good way" or a "bad way." "You speak French just like Mme x," some Grade 3s pointed out to me recently. Even with only a handful of French words and two years of FSL under their belts, they can spot dialects. "Real French," the kids call it. "Like on the videos," they say. So, of course, from where Mme x stands in the teacher's workroom today, I'm a rare find, an ex-pat – «J'toujours la seule, t'sais. Mais là, on'est deux. J'contente.» [I'm always the only (native French) teacher (at schools I'm placed at). But now, there are two of us. I'm happy.] She's articulating her fundamental allegiance with me. As if a shared accent is all it takes to form a sisterhood, hold a secret society tight. Note that

I say "articulating" instead of "trying to negotiate," because my loyalty to her, and to French, is naturally assumed, taken for granted, thanks to my "authentic" speech.

But that's precisely what I'm afraid of, my speech, because I know this type of conversation all too well. It stirs up trauma from the deep: a dangerously worn, mixed bag of not belonging yet wanting to belong, and of being afraid – entirely unable, in fact – to do either. So I try to change the topic, not because of some high, solid moral ground against gossip – in truth, ground of any kind rarely holds still for me – but because I haven't been educated in French, like Mme x has, and the subject of grammar is as dangerous for me as it is for the colleagues she's currently critiquing. I know – or at least, I profoundly believe – that if I don't find the stapler or the hole punch soon, and make my way out of here back to the safety of my classroom, it's only a matter of time before I'll be found in error myself, queried on some technical issue or, God forbid, be asked to proofread something of hers in French. That's when I'll blow my fragile cover. Shatter my thinly held illusion of safety.

So what's happened to keep me away from French, then draw me back when I'm past fifty? To make me leave it, and now promote it? For it to be the language of my heart, yet a language I can't put onto paper without a dictionary? For me to be embraced in my profession as a native speaker, yet rendered suspicious for the same reason? And why am I teaching children to do what I've never done myself, and what I've never wanted my own children to do – attend school in French? Why, too, is it that after a lifetime as an "anglophone Canadian," it's still Quebec's folk songs, tales, reels, and rivers that bring me to tears, that evoke a sense of belonging, whereas the English landscapes of earth and mind never do? My emotions are completely entangled in French rather than in English – a connection of first language and inner being that is potent, even gut-wrenching.

LES BONS PIS LES MAUVA' CÔTÉS

These are the thoughts that engage me as stories come pouring out of the fissures left by «les bons pis les mauva' côtés d'la vie» [the good and bad sides of life], as they say in the «joual» of my native city, Quebec.

My trauma is twice lived. Once, in multiple incidents five decades ago. And recently, in the "confirmation" of this difficult knowledge.

My truth starts to crawl out of its tomb one ordinary day in early July 2010, when some elderly females of my French «tribu» share expensive champagne to celebrate their longevity. Working its usual alchemy, alcohol begins to transform the essential properties of original identities. On this day, it dilutes the fragile boundaries of a pact of secrecy left vulnerable by the intervening decades and the ravages of age. It is but a simple bit of slippage in an otherwise pleasant afternoon of «p'tites crudités» and reminiscences. One who mistakenly thinks everyone knows something about the subject says a few things too many, and too loudly, to one who knows for certain. The knowledge is received haphazardly by the others – denied, disguised, refused – in clashes of silences and outbursts in the bathroom that quickly turn the mood sour. Seems an ill wind has blown into the otherwise charming summer interlude.

Naturally, one might have tried – and so it was apparently attempted – to forget it altogether. To annul the comment and its sequelae, to stuff things back into the bottle and cap it really tightly once more. After all, what are a few faults in the course of a life? What good is it to worry about water under the bridge? What right does anyone have to speak thus of the dead? Isn't it true that «on a bin toutes nos bons pis nos mauva' côtés» [we surely all have our good and bad sides]? Tears are exchanged, traded from one to the other, as personal grief is weighed in the service of justice. Seems an ancient tactic is being redeployed to forge a new deal. But for the sake of whom, now? Hard to say, but I'm told there was a concerted effort to restore the «joie de vivre» of the innocent afternoon.

Yet it is too late. I'm less than fifty days away now from a startling affirmation that the human lot is full of very pleasant people without any sense of honour. The critical information has been released by one of those ugly old brass keys that looks like a mutated claw – a cold, twisted skeleton. The kind that jingles in a rusty metal noose from an old man's dirty pants pocket. In the weeks to come, the secret will make its way steadily towards me like a brave little worm, guided by emails begun separately – serendipitously – between a sister and brother giving their shared origins one more try. There are pointed questions from me – and intriguing replies from him – about obnoxious scents, rooms with double entrances, men with particular traits, and windows of time. Slowly, reluctantly, the past begins to yield itself up to the light of the present, as words run furiously behind the scenes between my brother, sister-in-law, mother, and various aunts. At issue is what, exactly, was said in July – and how it strangely matches some of the garbled shreds of my memory. History's translatability. Unsurprisingly, I'm miles away while it all unfolds.

That's how my great "revelation" – the "confirmation" I've been waiting for, on and off, all of my life – finally arrives on 29 August 2010 as a simple phone call from my mother. «T'es-tu assis?» [Are you sitting down?] she asks. «Garde, c'ta …» [Look, it was …] And almost without a pause, she gives up the name of a close family elder – just like that. «Vois-tu, c'ta pas ton daddy. J'te l'ava' bin dit.» [See, it wasn't your father. I told you so.]

That's it. No tears. No apologies. She demonstrates only relief that the mystery can finally "close" with excuses to one paternal ghost while another takes centre stage. «Eh oui. C'ta' un pédophile,» she says, as if we're diagnosing an ordinary illness. «Dans l'temps, on parla' pas d'ces choses-là.» [Back then, we didn't speak of these things.] So a non-story then becomes even less of a story now. «P't-êt' binque, maint'nant, tu vas p'voir final'ment tourner a'page,» she adds optimistically. [Maybe now you can finally turn the page.] Trouble is, my book's just been opened. And it's silence itself that's the fable here.

A few days later, I get another phone call, this one from a maternal aunt. I can ask her questions about this affair she says, but only this once. Words as a limited-time offer. And yet there's a wall in her voice too, an impenetrable fortress of aggressive joy that allows nothing to come at her. She speaks about the art of moving forward «dans vie,» of living «sans regrets,» and of the importance «d'pas perd' une minute.» Then, she says flatly that she isn't willing to spend her last years thinking about it. Besides, as far as the elder's character is concerned, «dans l'monde des problèmes, c'ta' pas grand chose» [it wasn't such a huge thing]. Family and cultural myths invoked like lullabies. Ssshhh.

In the end, it's quite an unremarkable tale, then. There's nothing special here. It's about a French family elder who was known to be a pedophile and whose power was taken for granted. He kept regular company with a second perpetrator, a Roman Catholic priest – enjoyed shared interests, one might say – safe inside a social and cultural space that had more than a tolerance for incest, child molestation, and child pornography. «Dans l'temps» – in that time, and in time – this environment of permissiveness would invite more aggressors. How could it not?

Enter number three, a male cousin on my mother's side in his late teens who was apparently my babysitter from 1957 to 1961, and who enlisted me in his covert experiments with sexuality. «Ah, y t'aima' donc bin» [Oh, he loved you so much], my mother recalls. Indeed. And later, number four, a francophone teen neighbour at our new suburban home who happened onto a preschool girl preconditioned by her preexisting family drama – just another boy on a lucky street, I guess – with whom I played far too easily (and often) the games of «docteur» and «marié.» In turn, their eyeballs, noses, and hands would partly fuse in the odd record I've kept inside myself all these years, blurring the vestiges of some ghost(s) who took illicit photographs in at least two locations. And a few bit players who may or may not have participated, each in their own way, perhaps just by looking.

It'll turn out that I'm correct about many things. But I'm completely wrong about the first offender, the primary cause. Over the years, a ménagerie of potential perpetrators will offer itself for consideration: employees of my father's, other neighbours, family friends. But never this elder – *never* him. I could sense his powerful presence, but I couldn't materialize it in the least. Like a black hole, it was evident only because of a devastating emptiness, an inexplicable absence in my mental layout. He took me on one-way journeys: odd trajectories going into things but never coming out. I imagine he started small, with a touch. Then, with years ahead of him, he intensified slowly and prudently. So I got used to him when I didn't even have any words at all – not one. And then he taught me so well to keep quiet about it that I didn't even speak of it to myself. "Recovered memories," they call them. Trouble is, I never knew they were lost.

It is 1961 or '62. Turning left through the huge, carved doors to the grate that guards the balcony, the Elder grabs a skeleton key from the ring on the long string tied to his pants. His left hand holds my right, tight. We turn left, south, walk a bit. I think: «Ça encore? Pas ça encore.» [This again? Not this again.] Then up some stairs, turn north, up a few more, reach another door, and walk directly east across the dark polished wood floor. I see the golden top of the altar on my left, way down on the main floor, and the big organ next to me on my right, that disgusting metal monster. Small brown birds live in the rafters further on the right, just before the squat brown door at the southeast corner. «Viens-t-en, ma belle.» We open that little door and walk into the bell tower. I get to try to reach for the wide horsetail with my fingers. I look up at the huge brown-black bell, and down into the well of darkness. Through the arches, I see blue sky, some bigger white birds flying by. A coat's on the ground now. «Tiens. Assis-toi.» [Here. Sit down.] Scratchy wool on bare legs. A little brown glass bottle, like dark caramel. Pressed-in sides make it flat, a black cap. It's a picnic in the sky. I think, this is what it feels like to be a princess.

The record stops.

It's 1964 or '65. A cousin my age who's an altar boy prepares for mass. I see him fussing about with the vestments as we exchange a look of recognition – a "You too?" or "You – here?" Inmates crossing paths. But holding the Elder's hand, I walk right past him in my shiny black shoes, through the sacristy, to the door that opens onto the rectory at the back. We walk up the stairs at the northwest corner, then down a long white hallway lined with lots of square windows on the left, facing north, every few steps. I see the tops of trees, the grey sky. There are doors up and down the right side. When we reach one near the end, we knock softly. «Ah, bonjour, ma belle.» «Bonjour, mon père.» I curtsy. It's a narrow room, not well lit. A desk and chair are to the right, and a bed is to the left. There's a white wall ahead with a picture of Jesus, and a blackish rosary on the same nail. The Elder and I sit on the bed. The Priest sits on the chair and offers us «des petits biscuits» with a glass of something pink. My hands are in the lap of my short frilly dress.

The record stops.

Yet everyone's so close by, right across the street. My father is downstairs at his store, smoking and fixing. My mother's with him, counting and phoning. And Bébé is upstairs there, eating and sleeping. But here I am on another errand with the Elder to a weird world I'll never (be able to) tell them about. And we reach the part of this story I'd have rather *not* shared: that I didn't do enough to stop it. That I let myself get hurt again and again – I failed to protect. Rationally, I know the odds. But I still can't excuse my stupidity.

ON S'COMPREND PAS

At any rate, around the age of twelve, puberty – by which time I viewed myself as a little anglo girl stuck inside a French world – something inside me began to shift, like a turning over. I don't know how else to describe it. By then I remembered only gaps in time, bodily discomfort and pressure, pretending to sleep, distinctive odours, and a bizarre collection of pictures – bits of body detached from the rest of the owner. That, and a lost clown who had a story he'd eventually tell. The one certainty I had, though, was that the "troubles" had gone on, and on, and on. Not a one-shot deal, that's for sure. A matter of years, as recalled by my height relative to furniture, the colour of a dress, the position of a bed in regards to a window, the pet we had at the time – that sort of thing. So it was right around then, equipped with the fine logic of a teenager in full hormonal bloom, that I began obsessing with the question of who could possibly have had access to me over the course of so many years.

Unsurprisingly, that's when I made a decision to make my father my number-one suspect – the one who'd done the most, or the worst. It was a position I'd hold, on and off, beyond his death. I thought it would explain why we never got along and why I more than anyone triggered the dangerous anguish that marked his later life – his trademark stress that slid quickly into emotional and verbal violence. Sadly, the frequency of his lethal moods did much to obscure «ses si bonnes qualités,» as my mother puts it. For he was an animal whisperer who could fix or build anything, and his work ethic left men half his age in its dust. But over time, he experienced a downward spiral that defied both his daily medication and his occasional psychiatrist. So while I lived with him, I never said a word to anyone about suspecting him of the abuse. My silence was routine, organic – entirely embodied. Thus it was that the Elder remained successfully hidden deep within my psyche all my life. Under his inspiration or their own, my aggressors took me when and where they could: in the back rooms of family parties where little ones are laid to rest; in cars on drives from A to B; in the brand-new tunnel car washes; and during countless afternoons, evenings, and weekends of babysitting. Eyes, hands, tongues, penises, promises, and threats where they definitely should not have been. Knowledge rammed hard into the psyche.

The extent to which I've collapsed several incidents into one in memory, or taken one incident and remembered it as multiple, remains an enigma. But in all, the troubles I endured at «leur discretion» would span the first nine or so years of my life, beginning prior to my first birthday. Their rights to me had apparently been granted «à 'source» – at the head waters, the point of origin of my personal geography – long before I was born. It had nothing to do with me, in a way. But it would come to have everything to do with me.

The indelible marks these "troubles" left in my mind gave rise to some strange coincidences where my life seems to be a bitter echo of the times. For example, precisely as «La Grande Noirceur» [the Great Darkness]* was ending in my province, my own great «noirceur» was just beginning. The subtext of my life would become a hidden shadow as I was subjected to a pathological secrecy that took my voice and then my tongue. The whole experience left me completely «décrochée pis déracinée» [unhooked and unrooted]. I remained essentially mute on these troubles for more than forty years, other than a half a conjecture or a weakly formulated question every decade or so. The story of my troubles lived entirely in the dark, where I even hushed it myself. I ciphered scraps of sense strictly on the walls inside my own head. I learned to move on.

Finding out for certain in 2010 was surreal – a corroboration *half a century* after the fact. If I sound curiously abstract and impersonal in relating this, rather than justifiably enraged, it's because that's precisely what, and who, I became. That's the dominant personality that's emerged through years of internal struggles during which the attached

---

* The "Great Darkness" was the complex postwar period from 1945 to 1959 marked by social upheavals and also by the illegal confinement to mental institutions of countless orphans who are known in the collective memory as «Les orphelins de Duplessis» (Duplessis's Orphans), after the reigning premier. The children endured physical and sexual abuse at the hands of religious administrators and other staff.

affect, images, smells, and sounds remained largely indecipherable, like hazy bits of evidence. A trail of breadcrumbs in my psyche concretized by a few anomalies and some scars I've learned to ignore. Learning that I was right all along delivered a strange sort of relief, a reduction in the pressure compressing so many memories. Well, if that's right, then this is right too. The domino effect, the unravelling, began this story, made it possible. But it also triggered a colossal rupture that provoked me to revise and reinterpret my whole life – to self-edit the countless moments by which I've come to, and through, such a profoundly uncomfortable tangle of crime and denial. It was, in short, the unsettling of everything. Paradigms started to rumble hard under my feet. Knowledge became an emergency.

I freely admit that I'd like to just relax and live well instead – pursue happiness and experience life fully. But that's where the sticky business of my languages comes in. It arises in the fact that, reacting on instinct for my psychological survival, I fled French into the waiting arms of English. It resides in the conflict between English and French that's framed my life and the life of my family as a result. And it remains in the confession that I've used both of my languages to survive – for better and sometimes for worse. So as I witness the bilingual spectacle around me in my new teaching roles in French Immersion, I can't help but be aware of the bilingual spectacle that's *in* me, that *is* me. What is this conversation about bilingualism it's drawing me into? And am I its subject, its object, or both?

I'm a French-Canadian female, a child of the 1950s, of eligible age just in time for the election of the PQ to provincial power in 1976, the first election in which I ever voted – but too far gone towards the edge of the world, in every way, to come back to Quebec from Victoria, British Columbia, twenty years later, to vote in the critical provincial referendum of 1995.* And in another one of those metaphorical echoes of self and state, just as Quebec passed its famous Charter of Human

---

* The Parti Québécois: a political party in Quebec advocating separation from Canada and the revisioning of Quebec as a nation with a distinct society. Supporters are commonly referred to as «péquistes.» The 1995 referendum was to decide whether or not Quebec should officially separate from Canada to form a distinct nation.

Rights and Freedoms,* I used my own freedom to flee, joining the exodus of anglos who dispersed into other provinces.

I'm «une fille d'la souche» [a girl of the root], descending along several lines from the first French arrivals to Quebec four hundred years ago. The regional patois is actually derived from a language called Saintongeais, originating in the former French province of Saintonge.† And my family crest is three yellow fleurs de lys and a white bishop's mitre on a blue background. You can't get much more French than this. Yet I've not spent more than five days in a row in Quebec in thirty years. Aimless wandering around is what happens when you lose your bearings – emotionally, psychologically, and geographically. Then again, my aristocratic French heritage ironically comes courtesy of my bilingual father and what I came to know as the "English side" of my family – from a father raised by a British immigrant, my beloved Granny. A father who'd speak exclusively English to his mother and siblings. And who'd read, write, and watch television in English rather than French. His non-news favourite? *The Flintstones*. Clearly the confusion runs deeper than just me.

A QUIET REVOLUTION

«On s'comprend pas, ma fille» [We don't understand each other, my daughter], my mother states so clearly, so perfectly, early last year on one of my visits home. «T'as raison, on s'comprend pas. Mais on peut essayer,» I say. [You're right, we don't understand each other. But we can try.] «Eh oui,» she sighs, the difficult possibility of understanding one another suddenly laid out before us like the gulch that it is – that it's always been.

There is, in fact, compelling evidence that French was the first language to my ears – and my heart still reverberates with French children's

---

* Le Charte des droits et libertés de la personne was passed in 1975 and came into effect in 1976.

† The patois known as Saintongeais is referenced widely online and in print as originating in northwestern France in regions formerly known as Saintonge, Aunis, and Angoumois – and as being the tongue that has fundamentally shaped the current dialect of Quebec, while also influencing both Cajun and Acadian.

songs like «Alouette» and «Frère Jacques.» My mother is a hereditary francophone whose family has lived in Quebec without exceptions or departures for four centuries, and who speaks English with a heavy «haccent.» She once gave her neighbour, a white South African who was the only anglophone friend she'd ever have, a birthday card that said, "May the bluebird of happiness crap all over your birthday cake." She bought it because the bird was pretty and she assumed "crap" was a synonym for "swoon."

Her innocence was genuine. And the more excited she became, the worse her English got, conversations sprinkled with asides – «Ah, comment qu'on dit ça?» [Darn, how do you say that?] These questions were purely rhetorical, and they'd inevitably bring their own responses in minor excuses, "Ah, you know me an-my-Hanglish." More canapés, a bit of champagne, no problem.

Meanwhile, I became an academic, counting four university degrees and still enrolled – a teacher who earned her living with «les étrangers» [strangers, foreigners] in ESL for fifteen years and made friends inside cultures my mother looks upon with grave suspicion. I then drifted further into the realm of the Other, learning about Islam and wearing a hijab for seven years. I felt at peace with the desexualized self in the mirror in those years. Comfortable fading into incomprehensible tongues, a barrier of silence. Not only that, but at prayer times I was oddly reminded of the haunting rhythms of the equally incomprehensible ecclesiastical Latin mass of my youth.

Besides, the hijab made my life so much easier. I finally had the visible difference that had been screaming inside me for decades, submerged and invisible. A marker that could be discussed – instead of one that wasn't admitted. And when people didn't like me, I could console myself easily: they were simply being racist. Not like being rejected without a hijab. That was pure, stabbing pain, confirmation that I was unwelcome in someone's heart. A reminder I wasn't good enough – dirty and damaged. I couldn't even blame them, because I was sure that if anyone ever knew my secret, they wouldn't want to have anything to do with me. In hijab, I was humanely identified and disguised all at once. A handy solution. Without it, I had to behave so impeccably, make sure I was entirely above criticism and irreproachable, just to avoid rejection. With it, I could at least relax a bit.

I started wearing the hijab right after 9/11. Back then, I was just another disaffected Catholic, spiritually drifting. Under this banner I'd married a moderate Muslim some months before. I had a general interest in faith anyhow, so I took to reading and finding out more from him and his friends who lived nearby, and from their wives and children.* At the same time, I was teaching night school English in Toronto, to groups where at least two or three students in every class were in hijab. I remember sitting at home on September 11th, 2001, watching the horrible tragedy unfold on television. Riveted like millions of viewers, I recall one single feeling piercing my being – that the world had suddenly become much more dangerous. Not just for those poor victims and for North Americans in general, but for all those women I knew in hijab who'd be blamed in reactive racism.

Wouldn't it make a great act of feminist solidarity, I thought, if all kinds of women put on scarves? That way, Muslim females would be safer in anonymity. As soon as I had the idea, it seemed hypocritical not to act on it. After all, I was already on a cultural bridge myself. So I bought one and put it on during the weekends for a couple of months. It was uncomfortable at first, but it grew on me. And by Ramadan that year, I wasn't just wearing it full time, even at work, but I began fasting too. Exalted anorexia – another a good fit with the pre-existing, troubled self. Religion as pure emotion, as raw sensation.

Over the years to come, I'd be ignored at shop counters while people addressed my husband (who *was* a language learner), assuming I spoke little or no English. I'd be yelled at through the open windows of passing cars and spoken about derisively in English or French in bank lineups. As I entered a grocery store after work one day, someone exiting accidentally triggered the theft alarm. "Shoot her!" a man in the produce section yelled, pointing at me. "She's a terrorist!" Fortunately, everyone ignored him.

I was in hijab in the summer of 2004 when I visited a new museum in Place Royale honouring the Saintonge region and the Sieur de

---

* In the years that followed, I'd contribute articles and editorial support to a small Turkish-American publisher, and I even wrote a book, *Bridge to Light* (The Light, 2006), about Islam in an interfaith context.

Champlain de Saintonge, who built the first settlement in New France and the first Catholic church on the continent. I kept silent about my name that day, paradoxes crashing, but months later I told my Grade 7 students in Toronto about the exhibit. A student asked me, "Was Champlain a Muslim too?"

«On voit p'us tes beaux ch'feux» [We don't see your pretty hair anymore], my mother said, grieving inside and out in those years. My scarf made it impossible for her to give me the highest compliment she ever gave any female: «A'est-tu belle un peu, mon Dieu!» [Isn't she beautiful, my God!] It seems my valuation had become immeasurable, been lost. The span grew. Few relatives came onto my horizon through it all, and my mother kept «c't'affaire-là» [that business] underground as mounting evidence that I was not only estranged but strange. Yet symbolic of my origins again, I'd conducted my own «Révolution tranquille» [Quiet Revolution],* effectively removing myself from the purview of the Roman Catholic Church and using English to enter another faith. I was engaging in what was viewed at the family and community level as a grave act of cultural heresy.

So we remain, French mother and English daughter, with a void of misapprehension between us. Such is the life we've co-created. «C'pas d'ma faute si j'ta' n'bonne élève pis j'ai bin appris l'anglais. J'aime bin l'école, t'sais,» I tell her in my own defence. [It's not my fault that I was such a good student and I learned English well. I love school, you know.] «Eh oui,» she whispers, her voice breaking.

And so it was, and is. The damage done, fifty years lived. Two women at a kitchen table, both past their prime, and it's nearly midnight now. The moment lingers. Silence again. A life spent in linguistic tension. A love spent in psychological tension. One history erasing another. Talk about trouble – «En veux-tu, en v'là,» as they say. [You want some? Here's some.] Traumas too thickly knotted to separate – or to solve.

---

* A period that began with the death of Maurice Duplessis in 1959 and continued throughout the 1960s, wherein Quebec society shifted towards secularization, most notably with the provincial government taking control of health and education away from the French Roman Catholic Church.

Landslide

Between the erosion of my faith
and a few males' «dégorgement,»*
I lost my foothold in my culture –
suffered a quick slip of the tongue
and fell hard into English.

But it was a good-enough landing,
so I was able to steady my feet,
head off in a different direction,
and reinvent myself as someone
born on solid ground.

---

* First, to release water under pressure (such as that held back by a dam); second, in making wine, the process of removing the cork to let out the air pressure; third, to remove the water from a fruit or vegetable.

2

UN BOUBOU

FLY FISHING

The year is 1967 and I'm almost ten. I'm on a lake in a rowboat with my parents. My brother is in another boat accompanying some family guests this weekend because, even though he's not quite eight, he's good at this stuff. I'm the one you have to take along because everyone will be out all day, after all, and there are bears around, you never know. Near my feet there's a cooler with a couple of Molson or O'Keefe beers for my father, some egg or tomato sandwiches with the crusts cut off, some celery and carrot sticks in Saran Wrap, a store package of chocolate cookies, a Coke for my mother, and a 7-Up for me. Next to it, an old cane fish basket with leather straps my father's owned since his youth, and a short-armed green fish net with a tear near the metal rim.

My parents are both proud of the fact that they're fly fishers, not trollers «comme 'es touristes pis 'es américains.» My father stands at the stern, casting his fly line way, way off. Tall and thin with a cigarette hanging out of his mouth, he's an oversized boy right out of a Norman Rockwell painting. He's got a timeless look on his face, and sometimes I wonder what he's looking at, what he's thinking. But I'm shut out already – his choice or mine. Hard to say by then. Once in a while, he shoos away a mosquito with his other hand or pees over the edge. Mostly, he just stares, neither smiling nor serious. This is happiness for him, I can tell. Being far away – gone.

My mother is seated in the middle of the boat, casting in the opposite direction. They have to coordinate quite a lot and watch the wind if they cast at the same time so the lines won't get tangled. If they do, my father's fury is unleashed with the most menacing surprise. But my mother's very good at this sport – an award-winner among their friends for being able to land a fly inside a target – and she knows my father better than anyone. Besides, she's learned from the lessons of her heritage to negotiate the difficulties of men and survive on her own terms. So most of the afternoon is pleasant enough. Of course, unlike my father, who wears a sensible checkered shirt with the sleeves rolled up and a fishing vest pricked with lures, my mother is topless. «Pourquoi pas?» she says. «El Bon Dieu a d'ja vu toute ça.» [God's already seen it all.] No doubt her breasts do much to prevent my father's fury, to tame him like a savage baby. But like I said, she's an expert, much better at this game than I'll ever be.

Unlike my father, my mother's hardly silent as she chit-chats with the fish, calling them silly or handsome, luring them with her promises, «Viens-t'en, gard' donc si c'-tu une belle mouche, ça!» [Come on, look at what a beautiful fly this is!] It is, like all things for her, an opportunity for festiveness. And she thinks nothing of the mosquitoes that land on her. «Y m'ont tellement piqué d'ja qu'ej goûte p'us bon. J'ai d'l'immunité.» [They've stung me so much in the past that I don't taste good (to them) anymore. I have immunity.] I actually think she's right about her hard-won immunity – and that there's a dark truth here.

For myself, I have a disgusting sense of those big breasts. My poor mother. She's got a beautiful body – generously top-ended, in the style of her rivals for my father's admiration, Brigitte Bardot and Sophia Loren. In town, her look is surprisingly like my Barbies, with identical proportions and hair-dos. And here she is just being free and sexy, after all, a real woman of the Sixties. Yet all I care about is that those breasts won't come near me, that they won't accidentally touch me. I try to keep my face turned away so I won't notice when my father touches them "accidentally" when he reaches for the tackle next time. The giggles give the gesture away, though.

Meanwhile, here I am with my knees crunched up at the bow, keeping company with the Javel container, top cut off and filled with cement, that I can barely see twenty feet below us at the end of a long horsetail rope. I'm reading again – Nancy Drew, teaching myself to be a detective. Or else I'm running my fingers in the water to make rows of tiny vs. By this point the Elder has moved to the country, the Priest and the Cousin are living near Montreal, and my neighbour has left for post-secondary studies. But it really doesn't matter to me what they're doing because I've already forgotten almost all of it – or else given up thinking about it. And as the years pass, what faint hold this material has on my reality slips further into the watery depths of my unconscious. Nothing comes of it except at the absolute back of my mind and in my dreams. Then, from about eighteen to forty-two, I'll recall *nothing* – not a thing – about being younger than nine or ten. I'll become a quiet girl, withdrawn and studious, as the true self recedes and goes to sleep somewhere deep inside. Sleeping Beauty with no prince.

My job in the boat today is to unhook the fish as humanely as possible. I think I'm pretty good at it, though the fish might say otherwise. Later, it'll also be my job to slice them open with a sharp knife, like my father taught me, and empty out the stringy mess onto a newspaper to throw into the fire. They're for supper tonight or breakfast tomorrow, to be fried up with «des oreilles de crisse» ["Christ's ears," cubes of salt pork about half an inch square]. My tasks are limited, it's true. I don't even have responsibility for the special black tackle box positioned between my parents, nor for the truces they negotiate:

FATHER: Ça mord' pas bin fort. Passes-moi donc un Royal Coachman.
MOTHER: Es-tu sûr? Moi, j'ai un Dusty Miller, pis ça mord' pas pire.
FATHER: Ah p't-êt' bin. Mais pas el Professor. El p'tit maudit d'seize pouces la s'maine passée m'en a volé deux, t'rappeles-tu? Pis là, c'ma dernière. Gard' p'-êt' bin, donne-moi donc el March Brown. On va essayer ça ... [It's not biting too much. Pass me a Royal Coachman. Are you sure? I have a Dusty Miller and it's biting not too badly. Oh, okay, maybe then. But don't pass me my beautiful Professor. That damned sixteen-inch last week stole two, remember, and that's my last one. Actually, maybe you could just give me the March Brown. I'll try that one ...]

Their business dealings, as my mother co-managed them, sounded much the same – «en bon frangla'.»* My mother's supportive input, my father's final decisions. English breaking into French as necessary technology. Bilingualism on the fly, one might say.

My father makes these flies painstakingly by hand at his basement work bench, with slender metal vices clinging by their teeth to the edge, tiny drawers full of feathers, beads, variously sized hooks, and spools of thread mostly in black, silver, and gold. He'll sit here on weeknights hunched over the tiny carcasses of flies, following his Anglo-American do-it-yourself tackle manuals, just as he hunches over carcasses of televisions during the day, using his Anglo-American do-it-yourself electronics manuals. He's not to be disturbed, cardinal rule. Never mind, because we'll hear it upstairs if something goes wrong. But it rarely does during this activity. Making flies soothes him, and his creations are masterpieces.

His hobby stretches over decades, well into the 1970s and '80s. With all those lovely craft supplies, you'd think it would be natural for me to hang around him, to make small suggestions to improve this or that fly, or to play with a few turquoise feathers. But I can't watch him. It makes me ill. I can't bear to see or smell his yellow-tipped fingers, his narrow yellow fingernails, that close up. Just like I'll confuse his sweaty polyester shirts with the Elder's, I'll get the nicotined hands mixed up too. So he becomes, over the curious course of my life, the enemy within. And I become, over the curious course of his life, the same thing. The object you throw your madness at.

My father, with whom I'll engage in a lifelong match for horribleness. After some crisis of his own, he'll talk not a word directly to me from 1969 to 1976 – not one, not even "hello" – unless guests are around. So in 1971 or '72, on another fishing trip, I'll refuse to sing and play guitar for his important business buddies, and never sing again, ever. Children's banter at meals causes him to be virulently nauseous – the infectious power of words again, I guess. Most nights my brother and I

* «Franglais»: an expression denoting the liberal mixing of French and English that was so common prior to the provincial language initiatives begun in the 1970s, and is still recognized locally as an idiom for bilingual slang.

eat without making a sound as my mother echoes his tense comments about «el maudit commerce.» She issues her daily cautions to me right before supper. Pleas for my abiding muteness no matter the provocation, no matter the insult, his fishing for a fight – «J't'el demande. J't'en supplie. A'soir, pas un mot. Pas un. Pour moi.» [I'm asking you. I'm begging you. Tonight, not a word. Not one. For me.] Seems that trusty weapon, silence, is still the only one we've got. And there are timely kicks under the table to remind me to ignore the aggressive taunts he aims across the busy ashtray that separates us. He keeps a cigarette lit through the meal, inhales between courses. What demons of his own is he fighting? What do I embody for him? This'll be my other difficult thinking project.

I'll learn to fear his footsteps and the sound of the front door. And to be especially vigilant about quick pitch changes in his voice. There's no immunity to be had here. But in recent months, I've begun to wonder about his crisis of 1969. Had he learned something about what happened to me? Seen a photo? Heard some dirty story during a disagreement with someone? Or did it, like most things with my father, have nothing to do with me at all?

My first year at McGill, he'd mail me pipe cleaners and feathers – as if he woke up one day and noticed his loss. And I'd hurry to throw them all out. My father, with whom I remember collecting hazelnuts by the roadside in Saint-Férréol-les-Neiges when I was ten, and «des agathes» on the beach in Kamouraska the following year – two hours of my life that stick out from the rest. Then, the record stops. My father, for whom I felt something good and real *once upon a time*, before I took a last breath of him on a day I can't recall at all and then let go forever.

UNE CANADIENNE ERRANTE

"You always speak of your language as being French, and English as being *other* – this thing from outside that you migrated to. But you always had a choice. You had two languages in your home, French and English – your mother's and your father's. It's just that your preference for English was motivated by the trauma, by your need to escape."

My friend and colleague is an insightful listener, and I'm left to ponder her comment for days, locked in an inability to articulate how

French has always been on the inside and English on the outside. And why I never considered it a choice at all – at least, not until I began to deconstruct my personal history from my professional perspective as a linguist and educator.

My mother was French and my homeland was French – and that just seems to say it all. And my father's tongue? His English was my doorway out. Perhaps this was because he was so psychologically absent from our home and so far from me in particular – pointing to the exit, one might say. Perhaps it was because he skewed his own language ways over time until he was, on his deathbed, a French-dominant bilingual, knee-deep in patois as much as the next «bon bonhomme,» speaking English to only his "mum" and brothers, his mother tongue now become his holiday tongue. Most likely, it was because I so badly needed his language, this other language, any other language I could grab onto from the dirt around me to feel like the language of outsiders – a language that could take me beyond my context, far and away. Up the narrow rope ladder out of my crater.

The funny thing, though, is that in all the opportunities I had to learn other languages over the years, especially Turkish and Arabic, I never wanted to – refused to. It always seemed like English was enough of a separation between my inner and outer worlds, a sufficiently hard journey to travel, relentlessly carrying and hiding my secret self, this tiny bundle, dark and fragile. I could go no further. Not unlike the good-enough mother, English became a good-enough stepmother.

But as for choices, the only one I ever had was to leave. The mother's tongue is the language of home. And to be a stranger in your own home is a sorrow far harder to bear than the pain of departure. Migration often begins with a language choice – a necessary escape. And this choice sets off dominoes in the bilingual's life about attitude, affect, loyalty, home, friends, culture, society, faith, worldview, and goals – all triggering unique possibilities on every level. One language becomes a shelter from another, a vehicle for a variant self.

That's how it's come to pass that a person like me, so deeply entrenched in a French lineage, has lived her entire life without saying «Je t'aime» (though I say "I love you" every day). I can't even write it in a card. And up to now, I've had a firm resolution to date only anglo or Other men, males my parents would often dislike and to whom I'd never have to speak of love in French. «Je t'aime»: like and love as the same word. Too much commitment for someone who trusts no one? An expression tarred by my aggressors? I can't know for sure. But its inarticulability has been my most consistent symptom.

What I do know is that I am, technically speaking, the product of a mother's francophone hearth and a father's anglophone hearth – a daughter of two solitudes. I've changed my name twelve times in my life: from unofficial shifts in my first name lasting seven to ten years (Kathé, Katheleen, Kat, Katie, Kathy, Kathleen) to legally assuming the surnames of my first two husbands, taking an Islamic first name (Nur) with the third, and then back again to St-Onge after each divorce, to the latest change to Saint-Onge. In word and deed I'm «une Canadienne errante» [a Canadian wanderer], like the famous song says, forever in search of identity. A paradox and a tragedy. A poster child for the language debate.

In the school where I taught in 2010, students assembled in the gym for Remembrance Day and sang "O Canada" in English, four hundred voices from junior kindergarten to Grade 6. Staff, myself among them, looked on in approval and sang with them. But what happened next was something I'd never witnessed before, as it was my first French immersion school in Ontario. The majority, some 250 in the alternate program, then began singing "O Canada" in French. The sound reverberated through the space, filling every corner to the ceiling and back, again and again, entering my veins with a flush that made my ears hot. I found myself shaking, my voice cracking as I worked hard to catch the tears that formed, then fell, from my eyes. It was among the most beautiful songs I'd ever heard, as mystical and piercing as a Gregorian chant.

And I was entirely swept away by my love of a memory, by a resonance locked in the soul of the child that was, is, me. I saw then what I should have seen so long ago: that I'm scripted into the songs and histories of others, in the daily acts of the times in which I live, and have lived. I exist inside a larger narrative even before I begin to write, or tell, or live, my own tale. Can a story I tell about myself, then, ever really be all that I am?

THE BOOK IN THE CLOSET

In 1961, aged four, I owned one book, Dr Seuss's *The Cat in the Hat.* I still have it after a complicated life in which I've liquidated just about everything, including people, and moved dozens of times across provinces. My family also owned an English dictionary that was kept in the linen closet and became crucial to my personal project of language conquest.

As for *The Cat in the Hat,* it was apparently the first issue of a series being promoted by a door-to-door salesman who was turned away on that first book drop, for my father was notorious for resisting long-term financing arrangements. The book lived in my brother's closet for a decade, on the single shelf. It sat there, alone, next to a woodburning kit, some children's shirts, and stuffed animals that were no one's favourites.

I don't know why the book wasn't in my room except that it didn't fit, evidently, with the French provincial décor. Besides, my closet shelves were full of my mother's stored purses and bags in boxes, and fancy lacy things between sheets of white tissue paper. When I got older and needed to use encyclopedias for research, I had to visit my mother's friend who'd married a Protestant and was raising her children in an anglo style, speaking English to them and pushing their education. She had a set of *World Book* encyclopedias in her home in the same place in the living room where my father kept his collection of hunting guns (locks deemed unnecessary in those years) and my mother displayed family photographs and souvenirs from various trips. Knick-knacks on display, books in closets: it was a proper French-Canadian home in the 1950s.

But true to that first book, *The Cat in the Hat,* the two languages in my life were about to become Thing One and Thing Two – bizarre creatures that would make an even bigger mess of our home and of our lives, and certainly threatened to, and did, completely upset my mother. And whereas the cat let Thing One and Thing Two in by the front door, it was my mother herself who took me to the front door by which these creatures would come to deal their chaos, upsetting the pretty plans of mothers everywhere: that a daughter will be close to her mother, follow her mother, love her mother expressly. I would disappoint grievously.

MAMIE AND DADDY

The front door in our case was that of my new school, Marymount College, a private English Catholic school for girls in Sainte-Foy, run by an order of sisters from upper New York State. It was located across the back fence from my house, through a tiny stretch of wooded bliss, but accessed by a mother and daughter walking hand in hand by road that cool September morning in 1961. At the ripe age of four, I was delivered for the first day of kindergarten in pulled-up hair ringed by pink and white fabric daisies, tiny patent leather oxfords, ankle socks, a tidy white shirt, and the pleated blue tartan skirt and navy blazer of the school.

The clothing was handed down from the encyclopedia friend, who was two years ahead in this ritual with her own daughter and would always be, ensuring that I lived in hand-me-downs from start to finish, from shirts to books. Nothing would be the same for us from that day forward. But unlike Seuss, we lacked the all-purpose contraptions to tidy up the works. Our mess would be much harder, nearly impossible, to clean, to fix. And it would take a lifetime for us to even have the opportunity to try.

I don't remember feeling different from anyone else that first day of school. I only recall the beautifully clean kindergarten classroom with the ballet barre and the big mirror in the back corner along the south wall, where I'd begin my efforts to be a dancer. It would be a fantasy I'd hold until about age twelve, when my feet would not form into points and my jetés became obviously hopeless, even by my own estimation.

In terms of academics, I was apparently a star pupil from the beginning, perhaps because I'd been playing schoolteacher on a card table in my front yard – literally feet away from my kindergarten desk – for the entire summer. In any event, I was spared the hardship of being a second language learner in school. I was, instead, simply an over-ready four year old with an early love of school. It was an eagerness that my mother, to her demise, initially admired – and that my father, true to his opinions on books, schooling, and authoritarian systems in general, completely ignored.

I was, after all, the child of a one-parent-one-language mentality, though no one called it that then. The difference was felt in their names: one English, "Daddy," and one French, «Mamie.» Day-to-day life involved "talking English with Daddy," and «on parle français a'ec Mamie» [we speak French with Mum]. That was how my brother and I were raised and then sent to school in English, so that we'd spend our entire lives henceforth with me speaking in English to my father and brother (unless my mother was present) but French to my mother – and my brother speaking English to me (unless my mother was present), but French to both of our parents. It was complicated, hanging on my brother having stayed back far longer than me in the 1970s and learning to live in French, to love in French, and to make Quebec his home – while I took to school, then more school, then further schools, anglo partners and husbands they hated, cities too far for a weekend trip, making my life in English and rarely looking back.

But in that summer of 1961, our linguistic trials appeared to be nothing more than the most superficial confusions. We learned, bit by bit, that you had your "head in the clouds" in English instead of «dans' lune» [on the moon]; that you had a "frog in your throat" instead of «un chat dans'gorge» [a cat in your throat]; that "goosebumps" were identical to «d'la chaire de poule» [chicken skin]; that if an idea was any good, it had to be "able to fly" instead of «s't'nir d'bout» [stand still]; that you should treat some people "with kid gloves" in English instead of «des gants d'soie» [silk ones]; or that in English, you needed to completely "clear your head" to relax, whereas in French, you could just «t'changer 'es idées», change the ideas that were in it.

One day we were loading the car for a trip and a francophone neighbour, a girl my age, was helping out. My brother, two years younger than us, found himself with a free hand while our friend carried more than she could manage. This prompted my father to tell him to "give her a hand." My brother heard the English and translated it into French, his own internal language. The idiom in French, though, is quite literally, «Vas donc y donner un coup d'main.» [Go and give her a hit of the hand.] And so my brother walked right up to our young neighbour and, dutiful son that he was, struck her across the face.

Needless to say, the next hand flying was my father's. And that's how my brother and I both acquired the precious knowledge that a «boubou» [error] can easily turn into a «bobo» [a small hurt in French, yet still just an error in English]. Rather than a good laugh at the expense of our bilingualism, the memory is etched in my mind as a dire warning of the trouble that would lie ahead, as our brains tried hard to do what our hearts could only achieve with difficulty – to be divided within and among ourselves.

MOTHERESE

That «boubou-bobo» confusion was an early symbol – one might even say a symptom – of a major complication in our lives. We just didn't know it yet. Of course, every language has its own special way of addressing children. There's even a name for the language we use to talk to the very youngest: "motherese," or baby talk. Each tongue has its own ways of cooing, and its usual "first word," normally the one for "mother," or baby's approximation of it. That's how the mother tongue starts, with a word for "mother." And it seems the point where a baby knows his own language, through rhythm and intonation, is as early as a handful of days. So a baby who's barely two weeks old can tell the sound not just of his mother but of his mother tongue.

We can't imagine the questions on a bilingual baby's mind, about the kind of weird world he's been born into. I don't mean anything at all about potential trauma or hardship: I mean an odd universe of sound patterns where wavelengths and amplitudes are a difficult business. A curious sensory space where vocalizations that are so similar to one another – "words" – represent entirely different things. Like «boubou» and «bobo.»

But it can get even trickier than that for a bilingual baby. There's a natural confusion between my two languages, for instance, between «doudou» in French and "doodoo" in English. How can a baby tell them apart? By articulation? Impossible. By tone? Perhaps. By meaning? Of course, he must. In French, this «doudou» is a lovely, soft thing that you sleep with, the transitional object of modern psychology, the special "stuffy" on the bed, the "blankie" you drag around. One «doudou» I personally loved is still in my possession, in a fancy hat box where I keep my most precious curios. It's a white rabbit about the size of an eggplant, and you'll have to trust me that it's a rabbit because it doesn't look much like one these days. It's a rabbit shape, but that's about it. Along the way, I ate the whiskers – thick, tasty plastic. The tail is falling off, and both eyes are gone. Its dirty feet used to be pink, and one of its filthy pink felt ears is torn away. To top it off, it's almost bald, worn down to the real rabbit skin it was made from. I apparently inhaled the fur right off its body, especially along its back.

It's still with me today because it was special not just to me but to my mother, who sheltered it for forty-five years in plastic shrink-wrap until she shipped it out one day when she was cleaning the basement. That's the way it is with a «doudou.» You hang onto it unless you lose it. You never wash it. It has a busy life because it goes everywhere with you. And it's called a «doudou» in French because, quite plainly, it's «doux-doux» [very soft].

The etymology of the English "doodoo" is something else entirely: it's a childish term for excrement, simple as that. Not something you want to hang onto. Something you do wash off. It's true that it can be soft, but most people don't talk about their bowel movements openly like that. It's something that's highly unlikely to be spoken of as beloved – quite often, just the opposite.

So the bilingual baby hears the same word being used, by one or both parents, to mean either the most precious thing in the world or the mess in the diaper. Freud could not have anticipated his own accuracy any better than this single word dangling between French and English. A psychological bonanza. And the child's polar feelings towards the French «doudou» and away from the English "doodoo"? A psychological yoyo.

Yet another example is the matter of the French «dodo» and the English "dodo." In French, it's a reference to sleep, made from a simplification of the verb for sleep, «dormir.» Some of the most common expressions in any French-speaking household with children include being enjoined to much-needed sleep, «fait un beau dodo» – and the promise that something will happen after this sleep, «après ton dodo.»

In an English-speaking household (other than the scientific reference to a dodo bird, which surely isn't that common), "dodo" is slang for someone who's intellectually incompetent, forgetful, error prone.

When you'd hear it, you wouldn't be encouraged to do it, or to be it. In other words, in French, you'd want to move towards this word in your affect, while in English, you'd want to move far away from it. Emotions torn in opposite directions once again. Not just a plain word, but a conundrum.

I don't even want to consider the confusion stemming from "doodoo" and "dodo" taken together. Similar enough in sound. Agreed, the vowel sounds are different, but vowels are the most unstable between people and dialects, moving like oil slicks inside an accent. Can a vowel be trusted? What can you make of a childhood where a single *sound* made with lips and tongues not even touching means everything from your favourite toy to feces to sleep to an insult? Of a world where your feelings hang on fine discernments of context and pragmatics? All this when you're barely able to take in the limits of your own body?

Of course, babies get used to sounds quickly through their pre-school years, sort it all out, and become abled in many tongues. But what a curious few years they must spend while they're exposed to conflicting input but can't even formulate a question yet. Was that «doudou» or doodoo? «Dodo» or dodo? A bilingual baby's small, centred world easily becomes a wide, complicated communicative space, a domain of double meanings.

INÉGAL

On a visit home to Quebec in summer 2011, I woke up to find *Le Soleil*, as usual, in my mother's mailbox. It's been delivered to her every day since we moved to this house in 1961, a kind of fifty-year anniversary. My mother likes her routines, prefers the least change necessary. Of course, the paper has been altered considerably over the years. Like most dailies, it used to be on huge paper, but now it's the size of a tabloid – much like the *Toronto Star* has shrunk. It's one of the common points in recent cultural history, perhaps one of the few, this superficial commonality in the appearance of the most influential language dailies.

Yet the covers are entirely dissimilar. While the *Toronto Star* has a mix of international and national news, a veritable collage of images and headlines on a dozen stories or more, *Le Soleil* typically has one huge colour photograph with a single, overpowering headline, along with a handful of sub-headlines pertaining only to local or provincial issues. A different audience, with different needs and interests, is assumed and served. Inside the writing of the two "official" languages, then, it seems that there are variant unwritten codes about values, concerns, and ideologies. You can't walk between the two languages, or even meander inside them, without noticing. Trouble is, once you know that – once you have a kind of objectivity about each linguistic community, a bit of distance, and your own perspective – you'll have acquired, well, distance.

I never read *Le Soleil* as a child. It seemed it was crucial not to disturb the perfect alignment of the pages for its adult readers. So I approached it that morning as I do all things before my first morning coffee – lightly, without much commitment, as I might glance into the refrigerator for breakfast ideas. The massive headline read "Ben Harper inégal." It was a reference to a concert that was part of the annual «Festival d'été» the previous night, the one I missed as we were just driving into town.

My brain had not quite adjusted to the surroundings, I guess, so I read it in French and filtered it into English. I worked with the words as they wormed their way through my second language, the conduit of my cognition. As a result, I concluded that the performer's show was "unequalled," in short, amazing. I'd never heard of him before, but it sounded like it would have been well worth the crowds. "Too bad," I said to my kids, "we should have tried to get here a bit earlier. We could have caught the show."

I flipped a few more pages. In Ontario, the "Will and Kate" visit to Canada had been ridiculously big news for days, consuming the print and television media. But not here. Here, there was a small photo with a three-line caption buried inside the paper – maybe a tenth of a page in all – of the newlyweds at the Calgary Stampede, and no story whatsoever. It seemed the royal visit did not register on the public radar. There was a complete absence of information about what was billed in Ontario as the most significant national current event.

It spoke volumes about the gap between the perception of the world in my mother's kitchen in Ste-Foy at that moment and in my own kitchen in Toronto less than twenty-four hours before. Somewhere around Cornwall, it seems, between the "Ontario Welcomes You" and the "Bienvenue à Québec" signs, something unseen snaps in the public consciousness – on or off, depending on your viewpoint, depending on the issue. The provincial border isn't just the halfway point between Toronto and Quebec City. It's a sociological fulcrum, a powerful pivot. Something changes dramatically. Something is different here. Or something is different there. Take your pick.

I flipped a few more pages and eventually found my way to the story about the concert, a full page. That's when I realized my colossal error, my embarrassing lack of comprehension. I'd seen the right word but that bilingual engine of input and output had let me down, again. The word "inégal" technically *does* mean "unequal." But it turned out that the show had been "unequal" as in "uneven." It was a sense I hadn't thought of. The exact translation had popped up first in my head, like a dictionary entry, secondary meanings further down the list, perhaps after my second cup of coffee.

So having been home for less than twelve hours, and on reading my first word in French on this trip (other than road signs), I was reminded of the crux of my problem: I think in English. I hear or read my first language and process it through my second language first. Does that even make sense? My languages become like one of those reversible figures where it's so easy to ignore one image, to get completely stuck on one view and miss the other. To see the profile and miss the chalice. And if I can make that much of an error with one word, what harm might I do to a whole sentence? A whole conversation? A whole culture?

It was meagre comfort that I could still read the *Toronto Star* online every day from here. I didn't. I'd come face to face with the hard evidence that I was *not* a good audience for words that reached me in my own tongue. It wasn't just that I'd lost my voice in French because of my curious life trajectory, compromised my capacity to produce in my mother tongue. I'd also lost my eyes and my ears, my capacity to comprehend, to receive information accurately. Never mind that I could still translate easily back and forth: I wasn't engaging real meanings. I was at a communicative impasse of my own creation. How had I got here?

Pirouette

«Pirouette en salopette*
petit merli, merlot!†
À la galipotte, à la galipotte,
plus haut, plus haut, plus haut!

«Champignons, cornichons,
alli alli oop, là là!
Petit merlot, petit merlot,
vas-t-en pas!!

«Pirouette de cacaouette,
Pirli, pirli, pou,
Sauvignon, petit cochon,
mange-en pas!»

That's one of the pretty songs I lost
when I came out of the cultural ocean
of my great-great-grandmothers.

They use different words on land.
Instead, they talk about a Golden Goose and
some birds of a feather that flock together.

---

*   First verse: Pirouette in overalls; merlot (repeated as a play on sound); off on an
    adventure (repeat); higher, higher, higher. Second verse: mushrooms, pickles;
    [nonsense line for sound effect]; little bird (repeat); don't go away. Third verse:
    Pirouette of cashews; [nonsense line for sound effect]; sauvignon, little pig; "Don't
    eat it!" – in other words, this wine is not fit for pigs. It's a classic children's rhyme I
    was taught in my earliest days, I believe by my grand-grandmaman Blais dit Raisin. It
    has a loose ABAB rhyme scheme, the sort a child would skip rope to.
†   The same word designates a small bird and a type of wine.

So it is when you learn another tongue:
you trade the lovely bird in your right hand
for strange species in a linguistic bush.

3

A NEW LINGUISTIC LANDSCAPE

LIBRARIES

In that first kindergarten classroom, as in every classroom, I discovered an easy rule for my orientation in this new linguistic terrain: the SRA box* with its cards and multiple-choice questions. It was my North Star, and I wanted to sit by it in every class. I was lucky because, as a good student, I was seated at the back of the classroom, the closest you can get to an SRA box since it's never put on window ledges (the sun, after all) but always on the back shelves. Perfectly aligned in their crisp, pretty-coloured covers, the readers were organized by increasing difficulty, with accompanying checklists – everything a competitive little social climber like me could want. I admit I was greedy for cultural currency in this foreign territory of sentence parsing and spelling bees.

Then, as if this building wasn't already my version of heaven, my school opened a tiny store in the basement, in the locker room across from the chapel. It sold pencils and pens and proper school notebooks, and there was a revolving black metal rack about four feet high where a relatively new author was being featured: Charles Schultz. I turned into a *Peanuts* junkie on the spot – orange cover, brown, green, yellow – looking forward to each new issue and becoming, as much as my small savings permitted, a book addict then and there.

---

* The SRA box was a "reading lab" produced by Science Research Associates.

More and more, school served as my private refuge, my sanctuary, nurturing my love of the English language. It was a marvellous place where I could be successful and forget what was troubling me outside of school, where my so-called private life was becoming ridiculously public thanks to my sexual predators, whose game was far too complex for me to grasp or stop.

Tellingly, I was caught hiding at school twice after hours, refusing to go home. Once I was found in the closet of my Grade 3 classroom, sleeping on the top shelf after a strategic climb over boxes of supplies and a winter coat on a hanger. Another time I was found in the library, sleeping along a lower shelf by the big front window, my head propped against some books, and my knees bent, fetal-like, to fit. I don't know if my parents were told at the time because nothing more was said of it. I arrived home late from school those days, that's all. Not so odd in those years when children walked outside on their own and often played far from home.

Through later years my additions to my English library – never French, no, thank you – would only grow. I'd go about collecting the *My Old Bookhouse* series from the 1920s that had been scattered amongst my English relatives, one book at a time, until I had them all. I'd keep them through every move over the next two decades until the late 1980s when they were consumed by mould and insects and I was forced to part with them.

I became a discard sale expert, lining up two hours before opening time at Victoria Public Library's biannual book sales, with a floor plan and a strategy, amassing enough children's books to supply a small town library – forty-two boxes at last count. Friends who helped me move joked that they'd circulate my photo and have me banned from the sales. Then, to my delight, I discovered online bookstores, everything at my fingertips. My personal library grew and grew until books surrounded my walls, ideas filling the empty spaces in my life and thoughts. When every wall was covered with Ikea shelves full from top to bottom, I was finally able to sleep with the lights off.

From books to safety – a familiar journey. That's something I should make clear about myself before we go any further with these disclosures, with this telling of how it is that my story becomes my work and my work becomes my story. My mother's hope for the past few years was that I'd take to painting or drawing again, to «t'changer d'esprit» [change your spirit]. My own hope was somewhat less ambitious: that I'd survive, perhaps even continue in the recovery of a strength I'd lost so much of through some dangerously close contacts with despair. Such close brushes with the edges of things, reality and sanity, were not a new thing for me. But then again, neither was – nor is – my willingness and my ability to survive.

QUELQU'UN D'DIFFÉRENT

I've always been known as a "troubled person" of sorts, «quelqu'un d'différent» [someone different], my mother puts it somewhat diplomatically. Successful on the outside but problematic on the inside. «Toé, tu s'ras jama' heureuse» [You, you'll never be happy], my mother announced one day when I was about twelve, more prophetic than harsh. And so it was that a girl who believed and claimed she'd been sexually abused as a child became a drifter – spiritually, geographically, and linguistically – never finding answers or lasting peace. «Tu cours tout l'temps» [You're always running], my mother observed on so many occasions. «Oui,» I agreed, «mais j'attéris t'jours su' mes pieds» [but I always land on my feet]. «Eh, oui,» she sighed.

I did land on my feet, across four provinces, always making ends meet, successfully married and then even more successfully divorced, three times now. Yet her forecast lingered as a painful truth. I wasn't really happy except when I was with my children. In every other way, I was often fragile, insistently a loner at heart, «mauditement indépendante» [damned independent], as my mother termed it, not intended as a compliment. «Toé tu cherches t'jours queq' chose, mais t'sais pas quoi» [You're always looking for something, but you don't know what]: my sister-in-law's verdict, as astute as my mother's. A cut of the same cloth.

I certainly had been looking for something. And, right again, I didn't know what. Spending my life trying to remember something essential I felt I'd forgotten. I don't know quite how to describe this sensation, and I know it's logically absurd. If you remember, it isn't forgotten. And if you've really forgotten, then you can't remember you've done that. Yet, so it was. For it seems this curious sense of having, and not having, a memory was directly connected to the bizarre timing of my aggressors.

They first began their machinations in my infancy, when I existed prior to formal language, when the solitary means I had to record things was primitive. So the body kept track below consciousness, as it's capable of doing. Down but not out, one might say. And as I was moved from place to place, pushed and squeezed, inhaling the associated smells of danger – mould, nicotine, sweaty polyester, latex gloves, dental solvents, dry-cleaning fluid, dirty metal, wood dust, and pine and coal tar – circuits and chemicals pulsed in the hypothalamus and amygdala, old brain matter that nurtures the early senses on which survival hangs: smell, affect, body position, instinct. Meanwhile, the rest of my mind – cortical structures through which I'd later perform the more complex functions of life, including my bilingualism – lay dormant, still developing.

If my perpretrators had stopped then, I suppose I'd have merely been a child with an overly kindled unconscious. But they kept on going, so that new traumatic material became tethered to my reptilian brain, from which it could occasionally erupt into conscious space when triggered. Fifty years of vague thoughts and waking dreams that couldn't be erased by the passage of time. Memories that were untouchable and undiminishable precisely because they were pre-experience, pre-language, pre-self. And that muddle of mine between what was and was not – the boundaries of language and thought – would have huge repercussions for my way of looking at the world and my way of thinking about myself. Profoundly confused, I'd end up looking on the outside for what was lost on the inside.

MOTHERS' WORK

That's how, during the first week of May 2010, when I'd just finished two years of course work for my master's degree and needed to come up with a research topic for my final paper, I took myself where I often go when I'm trying to hide or to think: a public library. I paused a few minutes to flip through the discards in the pile by the front door, three for a dollar. There's always something useful.

I was eminently comfortable in my home away from home that day, calm behind the countless shelves, my barricades, and anonymous among random readers, hoping for inspiration. Four hours in, I'd read the front pages of the dailies and given up on doodling. I meditated, staring at the walls, and let myself fall into emptiness. It was then that I heard it – the conversation that gave me standing whiplash.

It was between a Chinese mother and a boy aged four or five. "What book you want?" she asked him in a sweet voice, in slightly hesitant English. No answer. "Ah, you like ah-the book like this one?" No answer. She continued in English, "How 'bout video? You want some ah-video? You want some this one? Look, it's 'Solly –'"

But she couldn't finish the sentence, couldn't name the video, because the child spoke out suddenly, in almost perfect English, rude, loud, and impatient. "Mom, it's not 'Solly,' it's 'Sally.'" There was clear disdain in his voice. "Oh, okay, 'Sally,'" the mother agreed, hurt and pride weaving a sorry cloth. I shuddered. "Run!" I wanted to say, "Run! Take this child with you and never look back! Speak Mandarin to him today and every day until he's yours to keep! You're losing him, losing him. I know, because I'm him!"

Yet I stayed silent. Don't I always? I tried to go back to my own thoughts, mind my own business. But there was more and I couldn't help but listen, here in the public soup that is the library. A few feet away, a Russian grandmother read a dual-language book to her grandson, around seven years old. She sounded out the words, beautifully, lovingly, the Russian rolling from her tongue like soft currents.

The child was looking at the other page, the one in English, and blurted out "birthday party!" She replied in Russian, calling him back. "I don't like this book," he spat and hopped off her lap. She sighed.

"Run!" I wanted to say to the grandmother, too. "Run, run, run!" And all of that. But she was too old to run fast. And I was too weak to speak. I was caught between what I justified as a gesture of privacy but what was actually a colossal failure of courage on my part. For I knew something that needed telling.

Instead, I said nothing. Again. I felt furious, torn, but I kept my panic to myself. I've learned how to do that. There are stories no one wants to hear. And there are times when too much has been lost already – a child who'll never be as close to his family as he could have been in his own tongue. I know: I'm living proof of how a mother's work, of her place in a child's life, will forever be compromised, lessened.

In the social sciences this kind of listening in harmlessly to sample the field is sometimes called "botanizing." It's a term that sounds earthy and good, but I felt like I was touching thistles, then falling head-long into them. For here were mothers and grandmothers – and, I'm sure, fathers and grandfathers, too – caring enough for their children to bring them to the library, to the door of the language they'd need to be successful here – the mainstream, dominant tongue. Witnessing their children's linguistic gains, their investments, in the new language. But also witnessing their own and their culture's losses, and the child's diminished loyalty, in the old language. For losses these surely would become. Learning a new language is a gamble.

WE DON'T TALK LIKE THAT HERE

Among the circle of newcomers to Canada I was close to for years through work and personal preference, there were so many examples of language risks that I could pick a day at random and relate at least one. Mothers telling their children that dinner was ready, in the mother tongue, to have their words returned by "Yeah, whatever, lemme finish. I need to beat the level." It's muttered so fast that the mother misses it and innocently asks, "What's that, honey?" Another day a parent calls for help with a daily chore as the child whispers under her breath in perfect English, "Shut the hell up."

I witnessed much in those years that I never shared with these parents either. It seemed too hurtful and hit too close to home. But I *did* speak, off to the side, to those numerous sixteen, fourteen, twelve, ten, eight, and even six year olds. "You shouldn't talk to your mother like that," I reproached. "It isn't right. You shouldn't use your English like that, to be sneaky and rude to your parents." "So sorry, Abla [sister, a common greeting]. I won't do it again," they replied, contrite for a few minutes. Caught out. The outsider – me – now deep within their halls, kitchens, and living rooms, monitoring a dangerous game of power reversal inside the household. A difficult play where the new tongue is used to engage independence, as the mother tongue, slowly diminishing, struggles to maintain the appearance of normal relations.

In these situations, the mother typically failed to register the impolite remark, asking innocently, "What?" She knew she'd heard a string of sounds, but it was too quick, too speckled with colloquialisms the child had picked up organically and she'd never encountered. And as she tended to assume the best intentions from that incomprehensible utterance, English became the secret code of children, idioms flying past parents at dazzling speed – the source of transitory humour soon becoming an instrument of distance, then defiance. If monolingual, long-settled parents think their adolescents are slipping away from them, they should try spending a day in an immigrant's shoes.

The examples need not be so brutal. There's ample evidence, even among the young, that language is a barrier, a breach between worlds, one you cross at your own peril. My textbook example of this dates back to a dinner event I attended in 2003 or 2004. I sat with the women in a large living room, while my much loved then-husband sat with the men in a front sitting room. The conversational flow throughout the home was in Turkish, and a few women were becoming quite bilingual. As I chatted with one on the couch, her four-year-old son came out of the men's area to ask her if he could have another cola. His mum gently indicated with her hand that he should wait until I finished my sentence.

I watched him out of the corner of my eye as I talked to his mum in English. His face turned from me to her, and back again, several times. Then he interrupted me, matter of factly, as if he urgently needed to instruct me about something substantial, to correct me about a meaningful oversight about which he had critical knowledge and I, quite evidently, did not. "We don't talk like that here," he said. He then repeated what I'd just said. "Here we talk like this": he then gave a sample utterance in Turkish of about the same length, perhaps a direct translation.

In other words, this was not the right place, or person, to be speaking English to, he was kindly explaining. As he properly understood it, this was a home, an occasion, and a listener for which I should have been speaking in Turkish. Trouble was, while his mum was doing her best to learn my language, I was entirely failing at learning hers. She was seeking to acquire my tongue, presumably for better economic opportunities for the next generation of her family. But I was actually seeking the opportunity to hide inside hers, to *not* learn it so that I could let its prosody alone be my safe shelter, a songlike sea of voices where I was, and was not, addressed. Where I could be both present and absent, engaging and withdrawing at once.

I didn't say all that, of course. I just looked at him in amazement. For he'd crossed a bit of a breach himself, bringing linguistic theory right into my face over baklava and chai. "You're right," I said to him. "I should be speaking Turkish to your mother, but I don't know Turkish. Your mother's English is getting pretty good, so we're speaking English to each other."

"Oh," he replied, pensively. A bit more silence, then a smile. "Well, you should learn it. It's easy." He made his request to his mother, in Turkish, and skipped away to get his drink from the refrigerator. And why wouldn't he see it that way? After all, he was fluently bilingual, years before and more perfectly than his parents would ever be. It was just one more symbolic snapshot of how easily children play in linguistic fields and then run quickly beyond view.

While his mother had been a bit embarrassed at his rudeness, his interruption, I frankly thought he was a genius. In fact, though, he was a fairly typical immigrant child. Using expert English acquired from six months of pre-school television programs and community daycare – while his newly arrived parents struggled in LINC classes* as they tried to recertify their professional credentials – he'd figured out that language is a system deeply connected to context.

He'd understood that there's such a thing as a mother tongue: that's what you speak to parents. That there are places where you speak only the mother tongue because outside tongues belong, well, outside. And that you can switch between these different communicative systems as a straightforward choice, each having its own meaning and purpose. Not even five himself, and before even entering the school system, he

---

* Language Instruction for Newcomers to Canada, a federally funded, country-wide initiative administered by Citizenship and Immigration Canada that provides free English (or in Quebec, French) language instruction.

understood that language demarcates space and time, self and other, inner world and outer world. That language divides.

UNE P'TITE RÉVOLUTION

I've always believed so strongly that language can break a family apart that I'd trust my own children to no language other than the one they were born into: English. The father of all three is an Anglo-Canadian originally from the Toronto area. We met in Manitoba and throughout our married life lived on the West Coast as best friends and isolates. Sufficiently distant from my francophone roots that it was easy to accomplish an English focus from the start, I taught myself English lullabies and songs to expose my children to literacy in ways I'd never known. The growing collection of *My Old Bookhouse* was pressed into use, as were recycled English picture books, courtesy of the discard sales.

I endeavoured in every way to give my children the childhood I never had: a conservative, child-centred world of play dates, parks, and storybooks. And while it can be argued that childhood is necessarily an imagined community – a play-driven place where the currency is games, sleep, snacks, and fictional characters – my children's world became my own imagined ideal, a reliving of youth as innocence. I found genuine healing in this reinvention as I watched my children become what I understood to be English-Canadian youngsters – children who knew nothing of French other than the fact that their mother occasionally talked on the phone in a strange tongue.

As they grew, I chose to home-school them, their education becoming another personal act of resistance. I was determined that they'd learn to read before I sent them to school so that they could be critically distant, reflective, independent. I was living out an instinct that the odds are much better in this life if you can stay alert and keep a mindful eye on what and who's around you. And I wanted them, above all, to hold foremost the values of home. I was unwilling to let the language and visions of school get between me and my children, or between each of them. I'd seen the damage in my own life, in the abyss between my family and me.

Of course, home-schooling was a radical move that infuriated my family in Quebec: children first being denied their heritage and then schooled like hippies! But we were, thankfully, in a community of like-minded souls, wounded Easterners reacting to our separate histories, all gathered on the edge of the country living out alternatives, grounded in a kind of neo-Pagan-Buddhist worldview. Across this expanse of geography, in an English-only context, I felt strangely safe – far from all that was French, «mon enfance» [my childhood], and everyone familiar. It would take fifteen years of this deep healing, nursed by the smell of the ocean and the Douglas firs, before I had the courage to come back East in 2001.

That's how I came to be lost along the timeline that is my curious bilingual life, and I remain so. All of my life I've run from my mother tongue and from my heritage, seeking shelter in English. I'm able to teach other people's children in French these days because the French I work in at school is a pleasant, neutered, decultured French spoken only on some days, with some students, for some purposes – and shared with colleagues whose fluency is not always assured and who are distant from its heritage. A tongue stripped of emotional saliency and discharged of affective ties, like a stale image of a poignant scene that can be observed safely, detachedly.

But on that Saturday in May, while I tried to hide in the safest place I know, a room full of books, my deepest fears found me. Rattled me to my depths, laid bare my linguistic wounds. So how does someone who loves libraries and learning so much take half her known linguistic knowledge and deliberately put it on a shelf high out of reach for thirty years? And how does a girl who finds so much comfort in words and texts become a linguistic runaway?

Mouse House

We're the victims of
forgotten birthdays, you and I:
Cousine A, Cousine B, Cousine C,
Cousine D, Cousine E, and how many
others among us? We were there, they
tell us, these mums of ours, these
ones who passed through their
own forgotten birthdays too.

Apparently, we played "pin
the tail on the donkey," where we
stumbled blind in the dark, and other
pleasant games – like "musical chairs,"
moving our butts from place to place,
never knowing when things would
ever stop, and "pass the parcel,"
shifting prizes hand to hand.

We ate cake and candy in
profusion, accompanied by pop
and handmade sandwiches stuffed
with eggs and ham, pickled onions,
radishes shaped like roses, and countless
visions for every oral desire – our bellies
always filled up to the brim, packed
tight like Cousin Gretel's.

We wore our Saturday best,
pretty dresses, cute and short, as
we posed for all those men with their
cameras, and for the Elder. And that's
how we know now that we were there – the
photographs – because we've forgotten
countless parties. Seems like only the
boys there remember them well.

That's all right. Never mind.
I have a party to invite you to at my
new friend's house – Sarah M. I met her
in Grade 5, when her father (a reporter) was
transferred here from Ottawa, and her lovely
parents are making bread and soup, and
have invited us for a mouse party
today at 4. Can you make it?

What's a mouse party? That's
when we play house with Sarah's fourteen
mice, "little cousins," she calls them, who
live in the huge doll house that her father made
for her, with the sweetest cotton beds her mum
sewed for them, munch bits of cheese on tiny
tables, climb up and down the elfin stairs,
fast and free, and even eat the walls.

It's hilarious, pure delight, to watch
their Lilliputian selves run around their
own house, doing what they please, eating
when and what they want, making up their own
games, escaping easily. Plus there's not a single
frilly dress or camera in sight. Imagine! And
when their spirits die, at least someone takes
the time to bury them outside with dignity.

4

CULTURAL BORDERLANDS

LINGUISTIC JOINT CUSTODY

I don't remember learning English. I don't remember learning French. The years went by with both my languages alternating like a game of leapfrog. Logistically speaking, there was one parent for English – my bilingual father who wanted (or felt obliged) to make it possible for his children to interact with his culturally anglophone family and his English "mum." And there was one parent for French – my virtually monolingual mother who believed in children being natural extensions of their mothers, as she herself was, and as her own mother was, and so on. But since my father was a workaholic who withdrew psychologically even when he was home, and spoke only French with my mother or in her presence, our entire household effectively ran on French «essence.»

Besides, all the neighbours, local clerks, servicemen, and salesmen spoke French – everyone from the whistling milk delivery man, to the pop delivery man with his big tins of «des chips au vinaig',» to the bread man who brought green and pink loaves sliced horizontally for our party sandwiches, to the Chinese food delivery man who came on so many Friday nights with his local version of «des nouilles chinoises, pis du chow mein, pis des egg rolls, pis des p'tits spareribs.» Everything one needed was brought to the door. The mothers I knew seldom left home except to visit family, see the doctor, or buy a gift – and most

French mothers, including mine, didn't drive a car. Groceries, medicine, dry cleaning, and everything else just showed up. Fathers went to work early and came back late. As a result, there was usually one place for English – school – and one place for French – home. This also meant that there were typical days for English: Monday to Friday, business hours. And days for French: Saturdays, Sundays, weekday evenings, and summers. The whole thing, in retrospect, sounds more like a cell phone plan than a family.

There was one family for English, the St-Onge side – and one family for French, the Dumont side. As a result, the yearly calendar was also divided. Christmas Eve was spent with the French side at an aunt's house, rotating from aunt to aunt each year, including midnight mass and the «réveillon,» the party after the mass, lasting until four or five in the morning, featuring pork in every conceivable dish, egg and tomato sandwiches, sweet onions, jellied salads, «des têtes de violons» [fiddlehead greens], and too much champagne.

In turn, Christmas night was spent with the English side, at my English granny's home, complete with turkey dinner and "all the trimmings," an expression for which I have no French equivalent. «El jour de l'an» – New Year's Day – was spent with the French side, at my French grandmaman's home, with more pork, more sandwiches, more champagne, and a special treat, buckets and buckets of strawberries, kept frozen from the previous summer. The children were allowed to drink the juice in the emptied plastic bowls, my favourite treat. Thanksgiving Day, not properly celebrated by French Canadians, or so the story went, was spent with the English side, at one uncle's or another, rotating year by year. And then there was «les Pâques» [Easter], which it was generally agreed was not adequately celebrated by the English side, or so the story went, so that after prayers on Holy Thursday, Good Friday, and abstinence through Lent, Easter was spent with the French side at my French grandmaman's.

If you do the math carefully, you can see the French side coming out ahead by one holiday. This was offset, however, by the fact that other than sharing in my mother's family's birthdays, births, deaths, and marriages – an additional twenty days a year or so – it was to my English granny's we went every Sunday for dinner, bringing the English side ahead by about twenty days a year. It was an excusable breakdown of arrangements in a decade where it was understood that «l'homme est l'roi d'la maison» [the man is the king of the house]. By any definition, then, French and English enjoyed an arrangement with our family not unlike that of joint custody. And like any such custodial settlement, each side vied for my preferences.

Of the greatest importance to me was that the English side honoured my scholastic achievements. They patted me on the head and smiled, praising me and speaking about me so that I felt like a prize myself. I'd been designated "intellectually gifted," which seemed to matter to them. On the French side, academics were virtually ignored: «Y a bin des choses qui sont bin plus importantes dans'vie qu'ça, t'sais.» [There are many things in life that are more important than that, you know.]

That's how my mother explains how she attended as few parent nights at my school as she could get away with, happy to pop her head in to hear "Everything is fine," and hurry back home. My father never entered the building except for one Christmas performance in my Grade 1 year, where I was the Blessed Virgin holding a doll in wraps and was kissed by Joseph – my Jewish neighbour and best friend for three years – to the *oohs* and *aahs* of an auditorium full of parents. I look back to find so many contradictions and irreconcilable paradigms in that minor holiday performance, as I played the virgin getting her first kiss, my Joseph and I already outsiders. But when your life is a confusion of truths and secrets – a discordant blending of what is open and hidden – you become suited to life in the borderlands, accustomed to, and expecting, incongruity.

JE'L SAIS, JE'L SAIS

Unlike his anglo siblings, who took it upon themselves to support my English cousins' schooling, my father was an inherently pragmatic man who was too busy to care about such matters. He had, after all, done extremely well for himself without schooling past Grade 8. And so it was that I attended, one year, the father-daughter breakfast unaccompanied, at my mother's command: «Ça va êt' correc'. Y va y en avoir d'aut' qui sont là toute seule aussi. C'est pour les p'tites filles ça. Tu vas voir.» [It's going to be okay. There are going to be others who are there alone, too. It's for the young girls, this event. You'll see.] There weren't.

Witnessing every other girl there with her dad, I vowed to do my best never to bring memos home about school events again. Father-and-daughter days were really for the fathers, not the daughters. But in my mother's world there was plainly no reference point. Imagine a father minding the children's schoolwork! Or a group of men invited to spend the afternoon at a convent! Unthinkable! My mother's misunderstanding was in fact completely reasonable. It was up to me to become more vigilant.

And it would have been a good plan except for my mother's best friend, the encyclopedia woman again, a dynamic spirit, unstoppable even today nearing eighty. She was one of the key school volunteers, working on her English and energetically supporting her three daughters. And she'd fill in my mother about the goings-on at school. I'd have to work hard to counteract her efforts. Why hadn't she informed my mother about the logistics of the father-daughter breakfast? Likely she'd been too busy setting the tables, ordering flowers, sending out the invitations. Besides, within a few years, both women figured out exactly where my father stood in relation to school, this one or any other, and I was spared further incidents of this sort.

We moved into a phase where interest in my schoolwork became a cursory practice, a glance at a row of marks while my mother ground up beef by hand, turning the crank, never pausing. Straight As. What else was new? «Je'l sais, je'l sais» [I know, I know], she'd say, and ask me for the salt or the milk. How could she be expected to take an interest? Wasn't this school changing everything between us? How did her daughter being so good at it make any of that better? It only made it worse.

I was learning English too well, too fast, and it was churning our lives over as surely as that meat-grinder handle. She could feel what I could not and feared what I entered into fearlessly: that learning English was making me into the disconnected daughter who'd break her heart, while it turned her into the marginal mother who'd become less influential as the English side battled for my head and began winning.

My report cards from those years, kept in a file by my very organized mother until the end of Grade 8, speak to my quick progression, my lightning advance. In Grade 1, there's a steady row of 80s and 90s, 82 per cent in English and 98 per cent in "application." Within one year,

I have a 98 per cent in English, a mark I'd hold virtually undiminished even in Grade 4, a peak of my troubles, when my "application" hit a C+. I was a bit distracted, I suppose. I note, though, that other than that "low effort" mark – ironic, to say the least – nothing registers on the social landscape in the way of help or intervention. By Grade 5, a teacher commends my spirit for refusing concessions, though I "missed class discussions" and "missed tests." And by Grade 8, through more spotty absences, I record A+ straight down every column, through every term.

By age thirteen my report cards were no longer kept. It seems that in my mother's eyes I'd reached the end of the line, achieved a destiny that she wasn't sure she wanted to keep witnessing. But as for me, I wasn't done at all – barely beginning. I'd bury myself in a book every night, every moment I was home. I studied and over-studied. I looked forward to essays and projects the way others might anticipate a new piece of clothing or a toy. Through my English school, I'd found a perfectly convenient outlet not just for my identity but for my powerful anxiety too.

A COMPLETE WRAPPING OF THE SELF

On the other side of my linguistic custodial arrangement, the French half continued to do what it had always done – vie for my senses, for my intuitive self, trying to bring me into its domain with a direct appeal to the visceral core of my being. There was the cooking, obviously, especially the baking: desserts at every meal, cakes and pastries for every occasion, mouth-watering smells filling every recess of our house in testament to my mother's outstanding skill and versatility, and to that of her mother, grandmother, and sisters. Their tables stood like tapestries of colour thrown up against the drabness of "roast beef Sundays" and "turkey holidays" on the English side, identical each time. Tasty, of course, but sameness glorified nonetheless.

In my French universe, everything was colour and smell and whimsy. Cakes in springtime were shaped like butterflies; breads shaped like dollar bills celebrated a new job. Sandwich loaves were coloured like art, and gingerbread men had painted faces and clothing. Unrecognizable things floating in jellied salad didn't need to be explained – people just laughed at the novelty. And in all of those years, on all of those long buffets improvised on pingpong tables and plywood propped between ironing boards, I don't remember a single straight celery stick or carrot stick (they curl into ribbons, you know) or any round radishes (they were all roses, of course).

Even ordinary dinners took on something of the magic when my father's absence released my mother's spontaneous charm: Kraft slices made into cheese eyes and smiles on mashed potatoes to get us to eat our vegetables – «Y sourit parce qu'y veut qu'tu l'manges.» [He's smiling because he wants you to eat him.] I happily became a potato predator.

The appeal to my senses went beyond the food to a complete wrapping of the self in an image that withstood time and has remained firm in my psyche despite all I've done and lost since then. During «el temps des sucres» [maple sugar season], kids ran through the woods to check the pails, the giant pots boiling on wall-to-wall wood stoves until we could finally roll the taffy in the snow, as adults in «la cabane à suc'» [a log cabin deep in maple country] sang and drank too much wine in the thick maple-scented vapour.

On fishing trips to «el camp d'pêche» [a log cabin or fishing camp], though I hated fishing – too sad for the fish – I made crafts for myself with sticks and bark, and learned to draw insects, dragonflies especially. Best of all was rowing alone, slow waves hitting the bottom of the boat. At night, the parents gathered to play spoons – with much beer and wine, it's true – but there was honest laughter and the smell of the wood smoke climbing to the rafters of the massive fishing lodge. A dozen children pretended to sleep as they whispered ghost stories to the movement of flashlights on the log roof, the sound of bears scraping away the bark on the log walls, and, if we were really lucky, the rain on the thick tin roof overhead.

My favourite nights of all were the sleigh rides around Carnaval, when my mother and her extended family, everyone from «mon'onc' Henri» and his clan from «la campagne» [the country], to «ma tante Yvette» from Montreal, manager of what some would have called "a gentleman's service," would descend on Quebec. We'd rent a huge horse-driven sleigh for a ride through the woods at dusk, finishing off, of course, with another party. Among my mother's treasures is a photograph of one such event, a black-and-white image about three inches square on thick Kodak paper. I remember how the older folk pinched our cheeks when they greeted us, and the smell of the bear skin tucked around my face, its comforting prickliness and warmth, as we were bundled for the dark ride through six-foot snowdrifts. It was 30 or 40 degrees below zero, but we were warm to our souls.

Inside, while the adults revelled, we were put down here and there on beds covered with aunties' wolfskin coats, to fall asleep to the sound of fiddles and spoons, an old aunt on the accordion, loud bawdy songs, and feet hard on the wooden floors, through the winter night. It was a celebration of cultural and temporal isolation, sensual and lyrical, just as that icon of Québécois society, Gilles Vigneault, once described it in a song that became an unofficial anthem: «Mon pays ce n'est pas un pays, c'est l'hiver.» [My country is not a country, it's winter.]

I hate the cold now, dread life below zero degrees, but I still adore the look and feel of winter, especially the nights when gigantic, slow snow-flakes fall quietly against the black sky. When you stand by a street light and look up, it seems as if they're splitting their trajectory right above your head, parting gently just so they can pile up lightly on either side of you. You're a little boundary for them, standing there against the night. And all around, the world is softened. Every sharp edge and bit of dirt is erased, muted by an aesthetically perfect layer that grows right before your eyes.

DES MUGUETS

If I move even further back in time from those cold nights of old songs and slow snowflakes, I can recede even deeper into my cultural border-lands. My guide for that part of the journey is my baby book, mailed to me during another of my mother's basement cleanups. It indicates that I began life as a sturdy female, nine pounds, and was baptized as a Roman Catholic on the seventh day of my life. My mother rec-ords with meticulous care the «cadeaux et visiteurs» [gifts and visitors], numbering them to an impressive seventy-four.

I note the instructions from Hôpital St-François D'Assise that my mother feed me every four hours, not through the night, and for no more than thirty minutes each time. I also read that at eight months I was taken off heated Carnation evaporated milk, thick and syrupy, and put onto cold, thin, regular milk. Seriously? Carnation milk? In a baby bottle? Like so much else, its application as infant formula becomes another signature of the peculiar times, the commodification of pleasure.

In fact, modernity was branding everything – including children – in the name of happiness, endorsing unrestrained frivolity. Santa smoked his Lucky Strikes or Camels – and drank beer, or most often, Coke. Over there, the "miracle of Marlboro" baby encouraged his parents to light up and relax before punishing him, while other babies promoted everything from coffee to dog food. Toddlers pushed "barbiturate therapies" such as Nembutal, and the "sleep fairy" championed Valmid – each with their convenient calming effects. Children were even used to boost thalidomide sales, with Distaval and its companion products touted as convenient sedatives "without side effects." Soporifics for children became critical aids in this age of adult exuberance, alcohol and chloroform standard ingredients in children's syrups for coughs or sore throats. And everywhere, the Coppertone Girl flaunted suntan oil, showing her naked bottom as a little dog mischievously pulled down her swimsuit (she had no top, of course). She came into the world in 1959, drawn to look three, blond, blue-eyed, and naive. On mechanical billboards, the dog stripped her again and again, fine entertainment. Putting her fictive birthday in 1956, Coppertone Girl was my senior by barely one year in this market, and widely considered «une p'tite bonne femme adorab'.» Not just an icon, but a model.

It was par for the course, then, when an amateur photographer my mother knew took a shot of me in a ritual that would become familiar – and later, far murkier in my mind. It's a black-and-white Kodak print in which I'm on a blanket, on a table of some kind, up against a wall. I'm wearing a short baby dress, and my feet are bare. I have a toothless smile, and both of my arms are slightly elevated in a delicate startle motion. My expression suggests I was perhaps midway into a round of peek-a-boo. It's paper-clipped to the page titled "La première photographe de bébé."

My mother has written «Mr x est un photographe amateur et il a pris cette photo de Kathy sans préparation, alors qu'elle était a jouer. Elle a 8 mois. N'est-ce pas un amour de bonne femme?» [Mr x is an amateur photographer. He took this picture of Kathy without preparation, while she was just playing. She's eight months old. Isn't she a dear, good woman?] A few pages later I'm recorded as being a child who's «bonne et ne veut jamais faire de peine» [good and never wants to hurt anyone], who likes «les jeux calmes et tranquilles» [quiet, calm games].

It would turn out to be a problematic combination, my calm compliance and this playful photographer. My brother shared in an email once, "I bumped into him a few times in the last twenty or so years, but it always seemed weird because he was asking about you the way someone who knew us very well would, while he was actually more of a stranger to our household." Weird, it was.

Nonetheless, in my brother's letter, there's an essential truth about my first language: his patent literacy in English endures despite the predominance of French for all fifty-two years of his daily life. It seems the mother tongue's power has its *limit*. But in my mother's description, there's an opposite linguistic truth, that the mother tongue's power is *limitless*. For in her neatly scripted caption, the local flavour of spoken French and its norms of conduct are neutralized, standardized. Its grammar is dressed up for company, just like me. So Mr x's contribution to my young life actually sounds civilized, hiding its darker meaning as the earliest recording of a small girl seen through the eyes of men who love looking at small girls. Not only innocence but guilt is inaudible here. My baby book is easily the scariest book I own.

And my already complex world would thicken still. Within a few days of that Kodak print, I'd be found floating upside down, naked, in a splash pool on a lovely July afternoon, behind the home of the Elder, who was an associate of the photographer's. I was saved by the quick actions of an aunt with a knack, even today, for serendipitous timing, who suddenly arrived by car. Apparently, I'd been left in the care of «une bin bonne femme» [a really good woman] while my parents were away for a day or a weekend – the details are not well recalled. It's been, like many things, politely hushed.

My mother records the incident in the baby book as follows: «Bains de soleil, observations: juillet 58, joue dans un bain d'eau au soleil.» [Sunbathing observations: July 1958, plays in a water bath in the sun.] She isn't overtly hiding the truth – she truly believes there's no sense in remembering, or discussing, the bad. Life's hard enough, and we don't need to stew over negative things. Turn the page, let it go. Best foot forward. After all, only the choicest adjectives will do for the grand narrative.

OPENING MY EYES

I guess I wasn't as intuitive about mathematics as I was about language, because I didn't put two and two together until far too recently. I spent my life, from adolescence onward, unable to open my eyes for flash photographs, a reflex that foiled even the most expert professionals. I was afraid of swimming and uninterested in physical games, unplayful. My mother noticed it by my seventh year, for under «les sports,» she's written «ne semble pas très sportive» [doesn't seem very athletic]. My physical inhibitions were a mark of the past on the present, a kind of neurotic haunting I learned to live with, work around, and move beyond. Why these problems waited for adolescence to surface, though, I can only muse about. Some sort of hormonal reboot, the psychological deck being reshuffled.

«Ah! Mon Dieu! Tes yeux sont ouverts!» [Ah! My God! Your eyes are open!], my mother and sister-in-law exclaim together in reference to a recent photograph. It's the first time in more than forty years that I've managed to do that. Every other indoor photo they have of me has slits in the middle of my face. Open ears, then open mouth, then open mind, then open eyes: that's been the sheer power of knowing about the abuse. Of making it conscious.

At any rate, it's evident from that baby book that by eight months, the engines of my social construction as a French-Canadian «bonne femme» of the 1950s and '60s were already set in motion. I was well on my way to hosting my own fancy parties with curly vegetables. The question remaining was, which sort of «bonne femme» would I turn out to be? The docile games player? The coy doll on show? The well-intentioned, absent-minded female? The most popular prototypes were continuously paraded and rehearsed. But I don't remember making a conscious decision about it one way or another. What I *do* remember was my definite realization at the age of four, a few days into the first school year at my English school, that there were two entirely different worlds in the world. At school, I didn't have to be a «bonne femme.» It wasn't even something anyone there wanted.

In the years of progressive anglicization that followed, I would become increasingly academic and decreasingly sensual, securing the highest grades every year despite borderline anorexia and an ever-evolving list of allergies and psychosomatic issues. But as I headed off to school in those early years, through the woods between my mother's kitchen and my classroom, I journeyed from my sensory world to my intellectual world easily still. I remember breathing deeply, checking on beloved patches of «muguets» [lily of the valley], and searching for treasures. I once found an ox skull, perfectly preserved. Who knows how old it was – fifty years? A hundred? It was about the size of a man's large shoe, whitish-grey with a long snout and two huge eye sockets. I thought it was spectacular, and it gave me an early desire to be an archaeologist. It's a wonder to me now that I had such a childhood in «la banlieu» [the suburbs], walking deep into swamp grass full of frogs, past trees with mushrooms up and down their bark like silver shelves, to the special place where there was a small clearing with wild strawberries. It was the most perfect consolation, and it entirely satisfied my need for goodness and grace.

Not only that, but I was able to do it all on my own. For in this age of ignorance-as-innocence, there were fewer concerns for the safety of children, and little was suspected or spoken about the sexual crimes of random men – least of all, of those men close to us. The invaluable solitude left my daily canvas beautifully blank for fantasy, fairy worlds, and happy endings. So I delighted in it each morning, taking in all its possibilities before entering the tidy yard that led me towards my school. Almost always, I was seated at the same back corner of the classroom, so that not only were the SRAs close by me but the window was beside me, beckoning. A few hours and I'd be walking there again …Would a squirrel have taken the nut I left for him? Would the pretty design of stones I built still be in its place? What story would be waiting for me today?

My English school was my professed destination – my home the prior limit of my origins. But it was in the woods on the borders between my languages, and between the forces that pulled me, that I talked to myself in a timeless language that nurtured my core. It was an instinctive language beyond words, beyond French and English, where there was always peace. And that core self spoke decisively about survival – assured it, in fact. So I believed it willingly and fully.

Sacrilege

I run my hands on the well-worn wood.
I go along the edges with my tiny fingers:
up, left, right, up, down, right, left, down,
back to the bottom, where I started from.
I touch the cool metal body all over,
so smooth, and hard, and golden, and
feel across the undulated chest to the face –
the long hair, spiked crown – down each arm
to the spread hands with the holes in them,
then past the short, wrinkled loincloth
to the lanky legs and punctured feet.

I feel the four brass tips, like scallop shells.
Then I turn it over and open its back door.
I slowly pull out the «rameaux»* from Jerusalem,
about four inches high, yellow-green and dry,
and move my fingers carefully along each
fine, sharp, vertical edge – crisp petite blades;
touch the shred of prayer in blue hand-written ink
that's not allowed to come out at all – «jamais»!
And I slide the little wooden door shut.
Sliding, I open and close it, again, again.
Grand-maman wouldn't take it down like this,
that's for certain! She'd never let me fondle the
armpits of Jésus Christ with my sticky fingers.
This is a treat that only the Elder allows
because, he says, I am «une fille très sage.»†

---

*   A palm frond, of special value in Roman Catholicism, in particular during rites
     around Easter; my grandparents had apparently obtained it from a priest, a family
     friend who'd been on a pilgrimage to Jerusalem.
†   A very well-behaved girl.

Where did that cross go when the house where it all
began and ended was flattened into a bank parking lot?
It used to hang right over the main entrance to the
living room – the fancy «salon» with two ways in,
plastic on the chairs, a piano, and peculiar games.
I asked my mother last year, but she had no idea.
Funny, but I could never imagine forgetting it myself –
invaluable, encrypted consolation – my coded message:
a naked man lying dead, covert doorways in and out,
obscure treasures hidden deep within a private casket.
Jesus with the confounding secret I always kept.

5

SAINTS AND SINNERS

PENETRATING THE HOLY OF HOLIES

My parents' first home, where I lived until the age of four, was an apartment on St-Cyrille Avenue in Quebec City, a street now renamed Boulevard René Lévesque courtesy of some politically inspired rebranding. It was at the corner of Holland Avenue, a ten-minute walk from l'Église du Très-Saint-Sacrement, under whose auspices my brother and I were baptized – a huge Roman Catholic church poised atop the second most dangerous hill in town (the other is in the walled city itself), overlooking the vast expanse of land and people it dominated.

Across from the church was the three-storey my grandparents owned, with a commercial space and bedrooms in the basement, a kitchen, living room, and bedrooms on the main floor, and an upper floor of guest rooms. My grand-maman Dumont ran a boarding house here for priests and Laval University students. She went to mass every morning, spoke in muted tones, and hung images of priests in every room. For his part, my grand-papa was a carpenter who specialized in repairing church bells.

By all accounts, my mother's family was poor. My grand-maman was raised on a farm in St-Isidore de Dorchester, one of thirteen children of a single mother. Her father died in the Rivière Chaudière one cold November day. A tall man, he'd stood to work his way along the river's edge and tipped his «chaloupe» [wooden rowboat], turning his wife into a survivor, a family legend.

Emilie Blais née Brochu dit Raisin – Gran'man Raisin, as we called her – was everyone's favourite. She gathered up the children after dinner, when the other older people at the event were being «bin ennuyant» [very boring], she said, to play «Poisson» [Fish] with us around a metal folding table with a burgundy leatherette cover. We gambled dangerously with wooden matches while she sipped brandy, the same kind she kept under her pillow in the care home along the Chaudière where she spent her last months at eighty-five. My grand-papa, for his part, was also raised by a single woman – his sister Blanche – when his mother, Amanda, died birthing her fourteenth child. The first stepmother, Célamire, also died in childbirth, and his father forged a new life with a third wife and more children still, leaving young Gérard in the care of his eldest sibling.

My sense of religion evolved and merged with my languages. I often walked through the church with my grand-papa, up to the bell tower or through the «sacristie» – the Catholic version of the Holy of Holies – to visit priests in the adjoining residences. On other days, drives that stretched from sunrise to sunset, I went to the monastery at Oka where they make that world-famous cheese we always had on the table, to bring small gifts to priests my grand-maman had befriended. She worked until the 1980s, her five children sometimes sharing a room or sleeping in bathtubs. Such was the way «d'arriver» [to make ends meet] during the Depression, and the good habits of industry and frugality stuck.

I was christened with her name, Cécile, as one of my middle names. My other, Marie, was automatically given to every French Roman Catholic girl of the era. In hindsight, it strikes me a bit like Jane Doe, a generic name stripped of identity, ominous even. I passed much of my early youth in my grand-maman's calm company, watching her cook, bake, and clean for the boarders. My favourite object in her home was a heavy wooden cross about a foot high, with a hidden compartment behind it. It hung over an entranceway as a kind of door within a door. It was my important clue about a secret world, and a useful reminder of the constant surveillance. After all, grand-maman always said, «El Bon Dieu y veille su' tout l'monde.» [God watches over everyone.]

A BLESSER OF CHICKENS

My grand-maman Dumont spoke not a word of English other than "hello." She could certainly not get past hello to "glad to meet you." But then there was no need to. Her world, her universe, was unilaterally francophone, and she moved in small circles from the butcher next door to the drugstore. Milk was delivered, produce was delivered, and «la messe» was barely one hundred feet away, in full-blown Latin every day. It was a self-contained world in which she contented herself dutifully, fully, religiously.

The only hint that there was ever any other side to her comes in an anecdote my mother shared with me just last summer, which I never actually witnessed. It was a Friday, apparently, and «l'Église» – a general catchall word for religious authority in Quebec – had fairly recently decreed that everyone should eat fish on Fridays. «Ah ça,» she said, «c'ta'in arrangement a'ec les maudits commerçants d'poissons pis 'es syndics, laisse-moi t'el dire.» [Ah, that was some shady arrangement with damned businesses and the union bosses, let me tell you.]

It must be said that a true Québécois is always willing to tell you the truth about the church, and my grand-maman was no exception. Everyone knew and believed the corruption. And yet they went to mass nonetheless, they gave nonetheless, and it held them together in ways they couldn't verbalize, beyond the priesthood and «les maudits prêt'» [damned priests] and – except for the years of John Paul II who was, in their books, «un ange» [an angel] – all the other «maudits papes» [damned popes].

It was a funny, awkward, irreconcilable matter to have a boarding house full of priests, to frame and promote «el bon monde» [the good people] among them, all the while being cognizant and resentful of most of the others as «une gang de fous» [a gang of idiots]. And their hierarchy in general was otherwise known, in the streets and bars, as «les vra' voleurs» [the real thieves], in contrast to the local politicians, who were deemed «des amateurs» by comparison.

Such was my grand-maman's context one Friday when, unable to find a fish in her house for dinner, she pulled a chicken from the fridge and pronounced, with utmost solemnity, «Je te bénie au nom du Père, du Fils, et du Saint-Esprit. Tu es maintenant un poisson» [I bless you

in the name of the Father, Son, and Holy Spirit. You are now a fish].
With a muffled giggle, she served chicken that night. It was evidently
an evening when the priests had gone to some retreat, as they tended to
do, for such lightness would never have passed otherwise.

Such was my grand-maman Dumont, all six feet of her, skin and
bones, «une bonne femme qui a tellement aidé l'Église» [a good woman
who helped the church so much] and who was, quite rightfully, eulogized as a near saint one wet day in April, when she was prayed for in
the same church where she'd sat, veiled and humble, every morning of
her life. A woman-saint. A blesser of chickens.

I remember her lying in her coffin as I walked past, near the end
of a long visiting line that lasted for days. She was clothed in something loose and plain – I remember only the saintliness of the outfit.
Her eyes were closed, her stern serenity permanently installed. Her face
was immobilized by embalming fluid so that her smooth, white cheeks
seemed fixed in wax. And her fingers, straight and firm, almost translucent, were placed humbly over a tiny cross. It wasn't in the least a
horrifying scene, more a comforting one. She looked like a statue in
the church she loved so much. The most beautiful one of all. One that
would have made the priests pray to her, for a change.

EL P'TIT JÉSUS

In fact, a casual relationship with the church in Quebec, with «el p'tit
Jésus» and «la bonne Vierge,» was commonplace and even a matter
of ethnic pride. «Nous aut', on vient pas fous pour la religion.» [We
(French Canadians) don't get/go crazy for religion.] «Pas comme 'es
anglais.» [Not like the English.] It was a typical belief that the English could turn to madness given the right religious fervour, and the
French could, at any moment, depose a pope or ignore a saint, or put
some priest in his place just because he was «un maudit écœurant» [a
damned annoying/sickening person]. The French could handle their
religion, make it or shape it, but keep the ground firmly under their
feet, while the English tended to «exagérer» in all things religious. Or
so the story went.

We have a huge reproduction of a poignant black-and-white photograph that my mother displays and her sisters hide, where the five chil-

dren – four girls and a boy – pose behind their house on an ordinary day, the photographer invisible to the purpose or time. The hem on one skirt is loose, socks are rolled up, and shoes are too large for various feet and heavily scuffed. A clothesline dominates the background, and there's a corrugated metal shed and more rundown walk-ups through the dusty alleyway.

Inside, my grand-maman scrambled to make meals for a half-dozen capricious priests and maintain her pristine demeanour, which she did impeccably. I have no memories of any humour or lightness in her, only common sense and good cautions. Drink warm water before bed, it's good for you. Study hard. She'd once been an apprentice French grammar teacher through a professional course following high school. She was «une femme sérieuse.»

So when my mother fell down one hundred stairs, from the top "porch" – a metal railing leading from the back door of the kitchen to that alley – down, down, down to the hard ground below, following a small lapse in one of the older sisters' responsibility for locking the gate, my grand-maman took it stoically as with all things. She took my mother's blindness in one eye from age four, and her being «coq l'œil» (slang for "cross-eyed") as a result, as just another test – another way to «gagner ton ciel» [earn your way to heaven].

This idea of needing hardship to earn your salvation would become a permanent installation in my psyche. It was as if you had to have trials and tribulations to be saved, quite literally. A day without a problem was a day to be worried about: God forbid you should die that day. So you made inquiries among sick relations, double-checked bank accounts, mused on small bodily changes. Where would hardship come from next? You asked the question not despairingly but with genuine interest and curiosity. For you were ready, armed with «prévoyance» [planning ahead], a particular type of optimism and preparedness by which you could face the new problem – a problem without which you were quite effectively doomed.

Faced with a difficulty, then, you could afford to be stoic – «bin, qu'est-ce-tu veux» [well, what can you do] – since it was your ticket to heaven. So when my mother reproached me in adolescence because «tu cherches t'jours du troub' toé, t'aimes donc bin el conflit» [you're always looking for trouble, you love conflict so much] – irony, for sure – she should have been happy with me rather than upset. Comforted that I had, in fact, absorbed the lessons that were put before me and the enduring philosophical edifice on which they rested.

Never mind how this periscopic search for harm, evil, and pain played into my chronic anxiety, my conviction (with good evidence) that danger was, in fact, waiting for me in the backroom darkness of family parties, unfortunate choices of babysitters, and quick car rides from here to there. If this worldview is correct – and perhaps I should hope it is, given my circumstances – then I should have a front row seat when I get up there.

J'AI MENTI DEUX FOIS ET D'MI

As I grew and we moved to the suburbs, I began frequenting the modern Roman Catholic church on the corner, St-Louis de France, where, tellingly, within less than a decade, my friends and I would hold beer parties among the trees behind the most prominent stained-glass window. But in the early days, going to church was something I often did on my own, in keeping with my father's profound atheism and my mother's avowed obedience to him. We went there together, mother and children, only on holidays.

Otherwise, I was normally there alone, making my way to confession every time. And being careful to be precise, too: «J'ai menti deux fois et d'mi.» [I lied two and a half times.] It's possible, you know: a half for the mere thought of it, yet not doing it, or so the rule went as I understood it. In retrospect, I find it fascinating that it never occurred to me to confess anything about the darker side of my life, acts too vulgar for this lovely chamber of carved wood and polished brass. This, even though some priests were pretty nosy: «Dis-moi, ma belle, qu'est-ce que tu fais avec les garçons ...» [Tell me, pretty girl, what do you do with the boys ...] I remained the perfect Catholic: trained to acknowledge small, polite, excusable offences and hold my silence on the large, unmanageable ones. Keeping one priest's sin from another.

After confession I'd sit on benches polished with lemon oil, sucking in the frankincense from the air, saying my rosary as ordered over the fragile, white plastic beads I still have, a gift from my grand-maman. I loved the peace I found there, the pretty colours on the windows and the tapestries, and the miles of shiny floor. But even when young, I was sceptical of the saints and their cover charges, $2 for this one, $5, $10. «Celui-là, y est-tu meilleur? Y a-tu plus d'pouvoir?» I'd ask my mother. [Is this (expensive) one better? Does he have more power?] «Ssshhh!» she said tensely. And there was something I couldn't get at all: since a host was «el corps du Christ» [the body of Christ], why were we eating it? I once ventured, honestly trying to understand, «Comme 'es cannibales?» [Like what cannibals do (too)?] «Ssshhh! Mon Dieu!» and a hard gulp, as if we were about to be struck by lightning.

Today the church in Quebec is selling off properties, trying to stall parish bankruptcies, and coping with mounting sexual abuse lawsuits – which paradoxically exclude more than they include, neglecting the thousands violated outside institutional contexts (like me*) by those who claimed immunity by association or upheld self-serving perversions of ideology. And there's universal agreement on the streets and in the «brasseries» [local pub-type restaurants] of Quebec that the current pontiff, Benedict, is «un maudit pape, p't'êt même el diab' lui-même, on sait pas» [a damned pope, maybe even the devil himself, you never know].

Yet the candle-lighting business and a belief in «Notre Dame,» saints, and angels still thrives among the province's women at least, including me, their husbands notwithstanding. And religious artifacts are hot sellers at second-hand stores around the city. Recently I saw a cross just like the one at my grand-maman's at a Value Village store in Quebec, for only $4.99. The sad truth is, I almost bought it.

Saints among us and angels as lifelines: these cornerstones of faith far outlast «Monsieur l'Évêque» [the average bishop]. These days, of course, saints ask for different things, such as beer to be poured down the sink. My sister-in-law inquires of my mother with a grin, "Why not just drink it? After all, who'd know?" My mother loves her a lot so she mutes her comment that this is frighteningly sacrilegious. But another beer goes down the drain, this time for my sister-in-law.

---

* Both my main perpetrators are deceased, and the timetable for legal intervention has long passed; information on the high rate of incidence of sexual abuse cases involving the Roman Catholic Church, both within and outside of residential facilities, is widely available.

DES 'ERTAILLES D'HOSTIES

At holiday time, for a special treat, my mother and I headed downtown to buy «des 'ertailles d'hosties» [communion wafer cut-outs] – thin, flat sheets the size of computer paper with holes where the hosts have been cut out for the prayer service. Made only of flour and water, and pressed thin, they taste like unsalted matzoh, my favourite breakfast food for the past five years. The sisters had a budding business making communion hosts, delivering them to the priests each week, and then selling the cut-out sheets in handmade packages wrapped in brown butcher's paper with a tidy knot of cotton twine.

We often went to the Augustine sisters on Grande-Allée, though the sisters selling these changed over time. We lined up in front of a plain white wall with a small wooden sliding door about chest height for an adult, a foot square, with a ledge under it about ten inches deep. A little sign told visitors about the preferred manner of knocking softly – once, twice, three times – to call a cloistered sister to her post. Within a few minutes, so discreetly, the sliding door would open, my mother would put her coins on the ledge, the sister would put out the corresponding number of packages, and the sliding door would close. Not a word was exchanged, for the sisters were sworn to honour silence and invisibility as the essence of their vows. And so it was that at a «guichet» not entirely unlike those at racetracks and casinos, we traded our silver, nickel, and copper for the currency of faith.

They charged twenty-five cents a package but we always gave more, a few dollars, since the «bonnes sœurs» [good sisters] were fundraising for «leurs missions.» Alongside their sale of «'es 'ertailles d'hosties,» volunteers managed a little shop in the main entrance that was open to the general public. There were a few glass cases with historical artifacts, such as the order's original property decree, or a page from the founding mother superior's diary, or a piece of the cross that had been erected atop their initial facility before its first devastating fire, and so on. There were also tidy tables set up with pictures of current charitable projects where direct donations were invited. And there were impeccable handmade socks, baby sweaters, and doilies for sale, most made by the volunteers, and pictures of saints ornamented by the sisters: $2,

$5, $10 again. But at least this time I could see the reason for the cost difference – the frames.

Since the church business has taken a big hit in recent decades, host cut-outs are now being sold at the «dépanneurs» [corner stores] for two dollars a pack, with holes punched out where we're supposed to imagine the hosts used to be. They're displayed right alongside the beer and wine – a kind of do-it-yourself communion. These fake church snacks are the relics of an era, its language degraded to an illicit trade in swear words. People use religion on the streets now to talk about everything from «une hostie d'belle fille» [a host of a beautiful girl] to «un hostie d'trou d'cul» [a host of an asshole].

I actually received some «'ertailles d'hosties» as part of a "Christmas box" when I was living in British Columbia, my universe of complete disconnection. A neighbour, a high-functioning heroin addict and former English Catholic, looked at me as if I were the devil incarnate, eating host clippings like chips. Maybe I am. Then again, perhaps I'm French after all, a bit irreverent, whimsical towards faith, appropriating it for my own ends.

My mother still makes sure to pick up «des 'crtailles d'hosties» at the dépanneur every Christmas. There's one package for every family member, from herself down to the grandchildren, each bearing our names. «Ah, mais c'est binque trop cher astheure» [but it's too expensive now, overpriced], my mother says. «Pis el gout, c'pas pareille» [and the taste isn't the same]. I have to agree with her on this, absolutely. We all miss the sisters' authentic homemade ones. They tasted like crisp flatbread that had picked up some of the fragrance of the ovens they were cooked in, the careful hands they were bundled by, and the sincerity of purpose for which they were made. These new ones are like thinly crafted styrofoam sheets with unpredictable hole sizes – oftentimes far too large – as if correlating them to the original is not even meaningful anymore, a token undertaking.

We eat a few sheets, almost superstitiously, like making sure to have a bite of someone's birthday or wedding cake just to avoid damning the moment. Perhaps we're still hoping for more of these Christmas seasons together. Then we throw out the rest. As for the dépanneur, it keeps them stocked pretty much year-round, though sales are briskest around the holidays, I hear. I guess that's when nostalgia for church symbols, and for church as a communal memory, comes back to grab even the most cynical souls as they head off to the dépanneur for a pack of gum and a bottle of wine.

My sarcasm notwithstanding, I always considered an empty church to be my refuge. I could have harboured a sense of duplicity, I suppose. I was not a virgin, after all, and thus contaminated, or so the priests would tell us all from the pulpit every week, hypocritically extolling purity. But I remember my conviction that they often had no idea what they were talking about, and so I remained a young girl who enjoyed faith no matter what they – or those whose secrets I kept – ever said. As often as I could, I snuck off to the chapel of our school, downstairs, the same place where I was confirmed in 1965 at age eight.

I've continued to hide in empty churches whenever I don't want to be found or need to feel safe in a dangerous world. I understand the irony of my doing this, given that my perpetrators were pretentiously religious men, but the self exists somewhere beyond the mere words of men. And more than my tongue in those years, my silence spoke my culture. In fact, the Quiet Revolution was a non-violent rebellion not *in* silence but *against* it. It was a flat refusal to continue the vow of obedience the church had imposed on everyone by controlling everything from undersized children in their beds to oversized business contracts. So it's hardly surprising that in my personal revolution against the mutism imposed on and around me, I'd seek my voice elsewhere.

Undershirt

Please.
Not here. Not now.
Not today, in this pretty place.
I feel sand tickling underneath my feet,
the sun in my long hair, a soft breeze on my walking legs.
A sense of peace begins to hold me, an unfamiliar fragrance,
a thread of self connects with new sensations, infuses hope.
It's such a lovely, different sort of day from life in town:
sweet cottages nestled up against the edges to our left,
open water on the right, waves teasing as we walk
along the beach: mother, brother, female,
her friendly son my age and size,
and me. Lac St-Joseph,
Quebec, summer,
1961 or '60.

Toxic cognitions
infect me long after
that day has passed:
I can't get a break.
It always ends like this.
Nothing ever changes.
Experienced in French,
but installed in English.
Thoughts I can't escape.

A big wave,
and the boy is wet,
but surely he's not cold – it's hot.
It's true I have an undershirt to share, and
we're both three or four, so it's bound to fit.
But I don't want to strip half naked in this open space.
Am I really so ridiculous to care, like you say, as you insist,
and I comply as always? What you don't know is that I do this
elsewhere, other times and spaces. (How come you don't know?)
Cold and grey outside now – the ocean, cottages seem distant,
faded. Feels like town again. If seagulls fly, I don't hear.
Just the sound of inner pleading, pointless:
not here, not in this pretty place,
not today, not now.
Please.

6

THE VIEW FROM HERE

THE WORLD IN COLOUR

My grand-maman's attachment to the French Roman Catholic Church was either an encouragement or an obligation, depending on whom you ask, of my grand-papa's own piety. That's why at twenty-seven years of age, after five children and her many illnesses, he attended a closed retreat at Jésus Ouvrier [Jesus the Worker] seminary outside Quebec, where he summarily took a vow of chastity which he was deemed to have kept all of his remaining years, of which there were almost sixty.

He spoke in solemn whispers, priest-like, his head low even when he pronounced the annual «bénédiction» over all of us every New Year at midday, as we knelt on the floor before him and he did the sign of the cross over our heads. A self-made craftsman, my grand-papa also repaired small tools, appliances, and miscellaneous things. This explains why he was willing, even eager, to encourage my father into what was then the cutting edge of technology, the "television business," with himself and his only son, Roger, when my father married my mother.

The television store was located on the lower floor of the family's boarding house, and the first television programs to be broadcast in Canada were viewed in black-and-white on heavy, tube-based wooden consoles with a tiny screen. Later, my family would be the first on our block in the suburbs to have a colour television set, thanks to my father's burgeoning trade, and among the first to see *Bugs Bunny* in colour.

I remember musing how ridiculous it was that we'd someday be able to see even the news in colour. Who'd ever care about the colour of the suit some man wore while reporting? Ah, my narrow lens, never imagining the graphics of war in full colour.

I was dazzled by the display of colours that came on every morning when stations came back on the air, just before a graphic of a stereotypical "Mohawk head" with an official notification that the day was beginning. In those early days, there wasn't much to see. Three channels, one in English and two in French, were on air from 6 AM to 11 PM. The English channel mostly had news and animation. *Looney Tunes* cartoons weren't classics then, just shows. The Roadrunner getting smashed again and again. Hilarious. The only French character, Pépé, a smelly skunk. Still funny.

My father watched the English news on CBC, but in those days I watched to laugh. I saw flat black images moving fast, even the original Mickey Mouse strips with the off-key music. Meanwhile, in French, instead of animation there were people dressed up and puppets of all kinds, mostly hand puppets but huge ones on strings, too. I learned songs and stories with Marie Quatre-Poches and Bobino and became a major fan. My mother was partial to the French news on the local radio station. And there it was again: two parents connecting with the world on opposing channels.

In my baby book, my mother kindly observes that in my first years in front of a television as a toddler, I liked *Rin-tin-tin* and *Télé-Popeye* best of all. I realize now that both were mythological hero stories. The first was about a German Shepherd who saved people (mostly children) in distress – the second about a cartoon character who became miraculously strong eating spinach and saved one particular female, Olive Oil, every time she came to harm, which was often. Was I deliberately choosing imaginary rescue scenarios? Or did these shows just happen to be on when I was allowed to watch? Who knows. The contrast between reality and fantasy was pretty thin for me in those days. And television played right into the final blurring of whatever boundary there might have been.

Yet as I got older, I *did* notice more and more the contrast between languages, between the variant worldviews emerging on television. On the English news channel, soldiers died in Vietnam; Parliament in Ottawa was in session; there had been a flood in Alberta. Absent was the local, the here, the now. On the French news channels, a local business had had a roof cave in after the last storm; a new highway was opening soon linking two communities; and some provincial politician had died. Absent was the national, the elsewhere, the other.

I also remember the first commercials on television. First in black-and-white. Then in colour. A famous one on the French channel featured a woman, Mme St-Onge, tired and in a plain house dress. She was having trouble cleaning her kitchen floor until she discovered Spic and Span cleaner. Since we were one of the only families in the phone book with that last name at the time – the others being my uncles – we got a lot of crank calls on our black dial telephone. «Oui, allô? Bonjour, Mme St-Onge. Est-ce que vos planchers sont propres?» [Yes, hello? Good day, Mme St-Onge. Are your floors clean?] Then laughter, giggling. My mother hung up, a bit angry, but never furious. Not my mother.

EL MAGASIN D'TÉVÉ

On special occasions, we children sat along the stairs from «el magasin d'tévé» [the television store] to grand-maman's kitchen, a few on each step, peering at dozens of televisions, feeling privileged. And then there was one peculiar day: Sunday, 24 November 1963. We gathered that day for one specific reason, to watch television together. Here we were, inundated by the horror on two dozen screens, as John F. Kennedy's body was taken to lie in state. Adults sat and stood, up and down those stairs, in aprons and sobs, as the events of the past forty-eight hours were retold and replayed. Murder in colour in a way my dim vision hadn't foreseen. Little did I realize then, nor for forty years forward, the symbolism of that day and place in the rupture of my innocence. Such is the magic of television. The illusion that crime happens only in other spaces. It would be an expensive delusion, one that began on the stairs of my grand-papa's television store.

My father bought out my maternal uncle when I was about six, and edged out my grand-papa when I was about ten. As he moved the shop to the suburbs, this Grade 8 graduate would make ample money for my mother to be «bin comfortab'» [very comfortable] in perpetuity, even after he'd sold the whole works to a firm in Toronto around 1980, retired, and passed on. He plied his limited education for the greatest imaginable gain, not an easy thing to do on one lung. The other he lost to tuberculosis at age sixteen when he spent eleven months bedridden, hovering near death, followed by a year of incapacitation as water kept refilling the remaining lung. When he was given only days to live, his family consented to his being a guinea pig for an experimental drug called streptomycin.* The rest, as they say, is history.

In recovery, he ordered a self-study kit on home electronics in English, which he completed in lieu of formal schooling at St Patrick's High School. Incomprehensibly, his mother had visited only once during that hospital year, and his father and brothers, never. My father was sustained by only one regular visitor – a female neighbour roughly his own age – and his ward-mate, Jean-Paul Desbiens, aka Frère Pierre-Jérôme, aka Frère Untel, with whom he had daily philosophical discussions.†

Sickly as my father was, he began to appreciate the potential of remote control devices to allow patients to have access to televisions in their rooms and manage them on their own, switching channels and adjusting the volume without the assistance of orderlies or nurses, just to pass away the hours. After his release, he used his new knowledge to design, patent, and produce hand-held "controllers" wired to televisions

---

* The first clinical trials for streptomycin were launched by the British Medical Research Council in 1947. My father was hospitalized at Laval University's research hospital, which apparently served as a satellite test site.

† Frère Untel [Brother Such-and-Such] achieved popular acclaim (and clerical wrath) for eleven letters he wrote anonymously to Le Devoir in 1959–60 which insolently but patriotically took on the clerical hierarchy and education standards, and then became the linchpin for the Quiet Revolution. He and my father both lay dying in the isolation ward in 1946–47, aged nineteen and sixteen, respectively, and it's hard to say who affected whom more. But the good brother would end up longingly wishing for a Québécois Chesterton (his letter 7); and his letters 8 to 11 sound precisely like my father's daily diatribes against the church hierarchy and the incapacity of the average man (Desbiens, 1959–60; republished by Les Presses de l'Université Laval, 2010). My father was apparently released before him and spoke of him often to my mother when they were courting.

he began installing in care facilities. Gradually he acquired television contracts for every hospital but one in Quebec City, and many hotels.

I remember countless visits to that television store, the family business – daily from infancy to school age, then weekly – as my mother occupied herself «à faire les comptes» [doing the books, the accounting] and my father sat hunched over metal carcasses on a workbench, smoke from the nearest ashtray wafting past his face, while he expertly fixed wires and tried to jump back quickly when tubes exploded. That's how our household moved from lower class to middle class within a decade.

The materials for assembling the remote controls were kept in our basement in the suburbs for many years. As soon as he was manually skilled enough, my brother made his pocket money putting them together. He painstakingly assembled the speakers on a metal plaque, then added wiring and plastic dials. The next step was to put the works into a plastic shell in hospital colours – white, beige, pale yellow, pale pink, grey, or black – add a curly telephone-type cord of the same colour to the bottom, screw the gadget shut, and glue on the company logo.

I can't remember how much money my brother earned for each, but it was more than I made ironing every week. I could have joined him, for my father was non-discriminatory in his hiring practices. But he was exceedingly fussy about the soldering, and I couldn't maintain his high standards with that frightening tool. So I stuck to making polyester shirts steamy and hot, a smell that induced a deep funk for no reason I could remember. And that's how my brother and I both ended up with a bit of loose change for candy at the «tabagie» [tobacco store] up the hill.

For my brother, those riches were always spent on Aero, Coffee Crisp, and Caramilk bars. For me, the preferred logos were MacIntosh Toffee, Cherry Blossom, and Kit Kat – my father's nickname for me. Candy labels were in English. I remember thinking that was weird. Why was there no French candy? No matter. At ten cents for a small one and twenty-five cents for a large one, we ate a lot. The candy almost made up for the fact that when that assembly business moved in, my brother and I (then aged about five and seven) had to give up our favourite room, our precious «sous-marin»: a half-finished space at the back of the basement where we randomly nailed things into two-by-fours.

From here, we planned to attack the known world and then, fully submerged in our high-tech submarine, cruise far away together.

CURLY BOWS AND CHIVAS

This would all be irrelevant to this story of bilingualism and biculturalism were it not for the fact that my anglo father couldn't have obtained permission for any hospital set-up – the foundation of his modest corporate empire – without my mother's family pulling strings, lots of strings, with the sisters. The French Roman Catholic Church establishment ran the hospitals in Quebec in those days, as it had for almost three hundred years in one form or another.

Negotiating these partnerships, business and church, allowed my father to route wires behind x-ray rooms and open up ceilings in high-security areas. This took a strategic amount of alcohol, which religious administrators politely accepted, certain brands only – «pas d'la cochonnerie» [not the junkie kinds (literal meaning: what's for the pigs)]. I wrapped the bottles myself, a prestigious task to which I assigned great personal honour because I was handy with small scissors and curly bows. Curly bows and Chivas for «les bonnes sœurs»: it wouldn't have been Christmas without that.

On the best winter afternoons of all, I was left alone with the cases of bottles fresh from the liquor store, while my mother and father went somewhere. That's when I played out my delightful ritual. I extracted one small box from the case, more or less at random. That is, if you don't count things like *eenie-meenie-minie-moe*, or thinking that one box is speaking to you. No matter. I opened it carefully on the dining room table, covered with its protective pad.

I needed to take my time with this part so that I didn't compromise the precise cardboard tongue on the lid that fit so tightly into the slender gap at the top of the box. Then, I took out the precious contents: the bag. Inevitably it was made of thick velvet in a powerful colour, usually a stately purple rubbing against the spectral edges of a bold burgundy. It was expertly sewn together, with virtually invisible seams and a calligraphed monogram in fine gold thread on the front. At the upper edge, a gathering of folds held the bottle enclosed with a fine braided rope.

It never occurred to me to open the drawstring, take out the bottle, and drink. If I really wanted alcohol, and I didn't, I wouldn't have needed to go through that much trouble. Open bottles were inches away on the buffet, in the cupboards, and pretty much everywhere. I just wanted to touch the soft, perfect velvet inside. I only did this once each afternoon, not to every bottle. It took quite a long time, all that being careful with the fragile flap, making sure it fit back snugly and left no marks. I confess that if there's one point in my life where I see my repetition compulsion more clearly than anywhere else – my trying over and over again to work out, with a young mind, the acts against me – this is it.

UNE P'TITE CHANDELLE

The second thing my father's numerous contracts with the hospitals required was his silence, to which his sullenness predisposed him. For his anti-religious, anti-God sentiments were infamous, always returning to the summative view that only idiots believe in God. My mother, the good wife, held fast to her values, snuck off to church, and lit a few candles for him on the sly. If he was in an overly watchful mood, she'd delegate one of her sisters to do it over the phone because it was, and still is, commonly accepted that this is just as effective.

«Vas-donc allumer une p'tite chandelle, oké? T'sais, c't'un temps dur d'ces jours-ci.» [Go light a small candle for me, okay? You know, these are hard times.] No other explanations needed. Everyone knew my father, knew husbands, and knew the routine – which also involved checking in after you'd done it. Still does. You call up the requester, like confirming a mission, and state that you did light the candle, and tell the listener/requester what colour it was. But never the cost. Money has no place in these affairs. The cost invested is left to the conscience of the delegated lighter.

For the colour of the candle, you had only three choices, no matter where the church was in Quebec. Maybe it's like that in other Roman Catholic churches around the world, but I wouldn't know. For me, the limits of the province and the church overlap completely. Bright red, royal blue, white. I have no idea why yellow candles weren't there – or were, at least, extremely rare. And I certainly have no hope at all for purple, green, or orange – those questionable hybrids with no regard for purity. Those were questions – like the ones about the charges of various statues, or the eating of Jesus – that you didn't ask.

You picked a colour on instinct, on a feeling about which one best matched the theme of your request or your particular mood. Blue might be more likely when you needed a new job or house, white could be for mourning or inner strength, red for an emergency or a health matter. That's my own subjective interpretation. Another subscriber might well always go with red, say, except during holidays.

There was a selection of sizes – small, medium and large. The suggested offering was at the lighter's discretion, but of course a person felt compelled to give more to light a bigger candle. It was easily self-policed because you'd essentially be damning yourself to play it cheap, give only a quarter to light a big one. Besides, contributors had the clear idea that at some level the saint in question was watching. If you didn't believe that, why would you bother in the first place?

The colour was (is) so meaningful, in fact, that if someone requested that you light one for them and a candle wasn't available in that colour, you felt upset for that person – as if the request now had only the slightest chance of success. And how might a candle colour become unavailable? Two ways. First, every candle in that colour might already be lit. It's a popular practice, after all. And because of the association of shade and significance, at a particularly challenging time in society – the illness of a loved regional leader, for example – the white ones might be burning en masse when you got there.

Second, again because of popularity, the few unlit ones in your colour might actually be burned right down to the charred end of the wick. It happened easily enough then – and even more so these days, with cutbacks to church staffing and budgets, that sort of thing. You needed to come back another day if you were really stuck on a colour. Or (a riskier option), you could light an alternate colour. Better yet, you'd meander or drive a few blocks to another church and try to find the right one there. That was the decision the most determined lighters would make, without question.

Personally, I preferred the blue ones because when you lit them, the glow through the glass looked like neon – a modern look back then, clean, bright and bold. It also seemed more hopeful. Not like the white ones. The glow through that glass seemed ordinary, pedestrian, like it hardly had any sacred mileage. A hopeless sort of candle. As for red, it was eerie. It glowed like bright blood, a cheap bar lamp, or the light on top of an ambulance or police car. I didn't care for it. So blue it was, and only the size varied with the cause for me – a treasured habit I kept for decades.

LES MÈRES SUPÉRIEURES

The third and final thing these backroom deals between my father and the hospitals took was high-level intervention by my grand-maman with the «Mères Supérieures» [Mothers Superior] and the priests under their near-military command, a thick network in the thousands. In fact, anyone who was anyone in Quebec – even or especially anglophones – couldn't be successful in commerce, however good the patent or plan, without financially supporting the French clergy.

Gifts were discreetly put in envelopes in the collection tray with a glance to the brother holding the long brass arm. There wasn't enough «eau bénite» [holy water] in the whole world to wash away this sorry mess. Meanwhile, religious officials sang the praises of their benefactors from the pulpit every Sunday, reading lists that became embarrassingly long in parishes where ownership needed to be renegotiated to allow new buildings to encroach on prime land set aside for religious orders by previous governments.

I remember my mother walking out a few times just after communion, when the long list of thank-you's to «Monsieur Tel-et-tel» [Mr Such-and-Such] would be weakly woven into some public notices – a thin cover for what everyone recognized as payoff doubling as pious erasure. After all those centuries, we still weren't far removed from the days of "indulgences" after all, sinners paying for absolution, with the most prolific sinners still being the best money generators. «Ah, c't'assez long ça» [that's long enough], my mother said on more than one occasion, as we stood up from the back pews to make our way out the front door into the rain outside, our cleansing.

Yet business in Quebec couldn't have been imagined without the French Roman Catholic Church, where language, culture, and power wound around each other tightly, constraining all that was inside from all that was outside, and providing both the context and the limits of identity for all of us. Everyone knew it. Yet everyone kept playing their role, at least for now. After all, it was reasonably easy. All you had to do was sit close to the back of the church.

And finding a spot back wasn't difficult. It was locating a spot at the front that would have been rough. Seats there were reserved using tiny brass chains, sometimes even name plaques, for «Mr le Ministre» and his extended family, «Mr le Gérant de Banque» [bank manager] and his extended family, and so on. You couldn't miss their practised posturing – the best clothing, the most pious looks, and the slow walk back to their seats after communion, tough to do when they were so close to the front. But they managed it well, casting an indulgent glance to this or that duly appreciative parishioner in the seats right behind.

Families could actually buy the front seats, too, or permission to sit there. Sometimes the right to a bench was passed on hereditarily. I read in a history of medieval France that people had been killed over fights about whose right it was to sit in one front pew or another. But I didn't know that then. I just sat safely near the back.

What I did know then, and I extend this as a piece of friendly advice, is that if you ever need to put down the huge long piece of padded wood «pour s'agenouiller» [to kneel down], you'd better be slow and strong. That thing is extremely heavy in a Catholic Church, normally running the entire length of a long seat, easily six to eight feet. If you drop it even slightly from barely an inch above the pristine church floor, it will issue a bang loud enough to make the first families turn their heads, and the officiating priest give you an extremely critical look.

At that point, I might suggest, the best tactic is to get on your knees and look down as if you're praying earnestly. You will appear genuinely contrite while you hide your embarrassment. Quickly enough, folks will turn back towards the front and things will return to normal. No one will notice if a small tear trickles down your face. If they do, they'll assume that you are even more profoundly sorry and sincere. Your shame and sadness will remain, as they always do in this place, private.

Pronoun

My mother tongue,
French,
is, in a word,
gracious.
It's the language
of the pronoun «on.»

«On» can mean "you."
As in, «réaliser qu'on a un problème.»
Meaning, "to realize you have a problem."
«On» can mean "we."
As in, «On va règler le problème demain.»
Meaning, "We'll solve the problem tomorrow."
«On» can mean "a nameless person."
As in, «On m'a relié le problème.»
Meaning, "Someone (inconsequential) related the problem."
«On» can mean "an omnipresent everyone."
As in, «On oublie ce genre de problème facilement.»
Meaning, "This kind of problem is easily forgotten by all."
«On» can even mean "no one."
As in, «On ne m'a pas bien expliqué tout ça.»
Meaning, "No one really explained it to me."

The pronoun, «on.»
A word that hides identities.
A word that sustains opacities.
A word that allows multiplicities.
A word that obscures responsibilities.

My mother tongue is,
in a word,
perfect.

7

INSIDERS AND OUTSIDERS

LES GENRES DE MONDE

And so it was that religion remained the pointer, the identifier that could be spoken of, the recognized "glue" between groups, the sameness everyone accepted as a given. Of course, looking back on what was brewing in Quebec in the 1950s and '60s, I realize now that attributes of individuals and groups that were publicly associated with religion were a thin cover for those that were actually considered to stem from language. In this way, the whole world (read "local geography," or the only place that mattered) could be dichotomized as French Roman Catholic (read "French"), and *not* French Roman Catholic (read "English").

Of course, the real world included all kinds of other takes on Catholicism, and all kinds of other faiths. But not this world. Not the core place from which we drew our meaning and sustenance – our water. Those who weren't Judeo-Christians weren't even inscribed on the public record. Seems they had a curious world no one cared to take seriously or learn about, theirs being an error that rendered them people of minor importance, non-existent.

The system of tidy graphic organizers worked out well, allowing everyone to talk openly about incompatibilities between people based on religion (completely understandable and historically witnessed, as was said) whereas the incompatibilities being experienced were actually assignable to language as a deep and ancient problem for the population of Quebec, these French transplants and their descendants. The real issue wouldn't be spoken aloud – wouldn't have the right of speech, in fact – until 1976. That's when it finally became commonplace to look at language as a boundary between the people of Quebec, which it had always been, in fact.

The nuns tore off their veils in the wake of Vatican II* – «Pourquoi? Y'a rien à voir» [Why bother? There's nothing worth seeing], my father quipped at the time. Common folks started going to mass in their sports clothes, then stopped going altogether. The illusion of religion as a marker faded within half a generation, revealing beneath it the thick cloth of a linguistic identity that was seen and lived as difference. So it was that in the last days of cloak-and-dagger talk of religion-as-language, I was taught some elementary distinctions between «les genres de monde» [the kinds of people in the world]. It was my own indoctrination into what most certainly qualifies as an ethnocentric mindset. And yet the features attributed to each culture, according to the French Canadian worldview in which I was a raised, the snippets of knowledge from which I wove my earliest beliefs about myself and "others," seemed remarkably innocuous.

I wish I could say that I learned each story on a particular day, as part of some emotionally poignant moment. Or that I have one of those mythically perfect recalls of sitting on an elder's knee while I heard the intricate points of classic family lore that I'd later tell my own children. But what I most remember learning from an elder's knee isn't the sort of thing anyone would enjoy telling children. And there wasn't a day, or even an instant, when glorious tales of valour spun their generous mysteries by an enormous pot of simmering soup. As it turned out, my relationship with romance in my mother tongue culture was something entirely other than an embrace of legends.

So what I have in my head in place of such theoretical, confabulated wonders is an organized sets of boxes stripped of potency and sensory overload – Rubbermaid bins full of details, sufficiently neutralized and removed from the cobwebs that link them to what still lies beneath – dark, dirty, and repressed. That's how I can stack a few memories, move

---

* The Second Vatican Council of the Roman Catholic Church, from 1962 to 1965 (generally known as "Vatican II"), which allowed this choice.

them around, and even open them from time to time, when I'm rested enough or on an upswing.

As for the actual moments of learning these things I'm about to share, they're revelations about culture and society told almost in transference, between what was actually being said and done – tales that require at least as much inferencing as they do listening. They're subtle narratives, sometimes textured stealthily, and sometimes wedged sharply, within minor comments about setting the table, taking out the trash, or changing shirts.

These foundational understandings didn't get told as stories, didn't ever pass as stories. Rather, they infused the most typical dramas of daily life. As a result, they fled through the psyche like a shooting star. Did you feel that? What? Admittedly, then, they lacked the mystique of the allegories of glory that have fortified humankind for millennia, and they never felt the troubadour's deft hands or mouth. They were, instead, everyday talk by everyday people. But these folktales gained something in their transition to ordinariness. They became incontestable truth.

C'PAS CATHOLIQUE

In those parables of civilization that defined us and the Other, the divisions went like this. Catholics (read "French Canadians") could build fires when camping or at a cottage, and they could start up a wood stove easily. Non-Catholics (read "English Canadians") had trouble getting a fire started, and they needed perfectly dry wood (a rarity in the woods on any given day). And their fires (even with dry wood) would be smoky. This one was so firmly ingrained that I still recognize the ability to handle a fire as the ultimate test of masculinity, so much so that I fell in love with a Turk in late adulthood in no small part because he was outstanding in the woods. Survivorman. Strip away new knowledge, and only the ancient truths remain. A real man is a fire-starter. For the same reason, French boys didn't join boy scouts but the English ones did. French boys didn't need badges to live off the land. They could do it innately. Or so the story went.

I also learned in those years that Catholics (read "French Canadians") could handle their alcohol, while non-Catholics (read "English

Canadians") couldn't. The training for this happened young, so that a twelve-year-old was invited to watery wine to strengthen the system. It had the importance of passing on a life skill, like a profession or the language itself. There wasn't any choice about what you tasted that first time – in fact, it didn't seem to matter. It's not like there was some great coming-of-age moment when everyone cheered you on as you sipped from a special bottle or a favourite recipe. Instead, there was a moment, unannounced, usually at a party, where a couple of folks who had too much to drink themselves said to the host, just prior to a toast, «Bin comment ça qu'y a pas d'verre lui-là?» [Hey, how come he doesn't have a drink, this one?]

The youth in question would blush (or maybe not) and take the glass and whatever was in it – champagne or red wine, normally, but it could be anything at all. The elders drank from their own glasses quickly, and one or two among the dozen or more gathered would notice the youth as he or she traversed into adulthood – «T'in, vois-tu? C'est tout,» one would say. [There. See? That's it.] The moment passed without fanfare, and the youth might well be offered a refill later. Once broken, like virginity, it seemed that quantities became irrelevant. The line had been crossed.

My father was somewhat more ceremonious, I suppose, pouring me a glass of red wine one weekday at dinner, when no company was over and I can't recall what we were eating. I was eleven when he got up, fetched another glass from the cupboard behind his head, and poured three instead of two that night. «T'in. C'est l'temps q't'apprennes.» [There. It's time you learned.] My mother said nothing and served the meal. There was neither a smile nor a reproach from wife to husband. Initiation was, as it turns out, a non-event. A rite of passage as, well, just a passage, an ordinary walk. Then again, my own virginity was already long gone, so maybe it's symbolic that there was even less of a threshold, no celebratory context. Or am I just reading too much into everything, as usual? What did either of them know about my "troubles" back then?

At any rate, Catholics (aka the French) could also fix anything, from small engines to worn clothing. Non-Catholics (aka the English) had to «appeler quelqu'un» [call someone] to handle their equipment breakdowns. Catholic women (aka the French) got right to work doing dishes after meals, taking their wine with them; they washed their floors properly, on their hands and knees, applying wax by hand too; and they sewed, which was necessary to the production and maintenance of clothing. In harsh weather, to make thicker cloth, they became skilled with a loom. That's why my mother and her sisters attended a boarding school for domestic arts, in Ancienne Lorette (on Huron land), to learn to weave carpets, bedspreads, winter skirts, and curtains, to cook French food inexpensively, and to remove stubborn stains.

I still have one of their projects, beautiful blue floor-length curtains with huge peacocks. They've moved from closet to closet across the country as I've moved – too heavy and precious for actual use. At least I've managed to hang on to them. As for my mother, she plays cards to this day with her former classmates – gin rummy, apparently – though the games are a witness to the passage of time, like everything else, with members facing the usual challenges of old age. «Ça, ces des vraies bonnes amies» [now those are really good friends], my mother says, and I'm sure she's right.

But the truth is, I have no idea what she's talking about. Keeping friends for seventy years? Seriously? That's the comfort of roots set deep, I guess. All but one still resides in her own home too. They're widows of eighty plus, sturdy and immovable, who, like my mother, hold every still-living love of their lives in their thinning hands. Me, I only outlive men in my own home by ejecting them, and I can barely hang on to the slim contents of a linen shelf.

Maybe I'm more like the others, after all. Non-Catholic women (aka the English) shamefully let their dishes pile up while they drank tea with their guests after meals. They washed their floors with a mop, and they engaged in the pretentious arts of knitting and crocheting, making fragile garments of no long-term value, or ornaments for their furniture, doilies and runners, of which there were far too many in an English household. These were rarer in a Catholic household, and even then could be found only in the «salon» [the front sitting room], received as gifts from «les bonnes sœurs.» In the absence of husbands and children, the sisters at least could be forgiven for spending their evenings with handfuls of needles. I confess that I do usually have a craft project going on the side – but I can't crochet or knit to save my soul. I sit with guests after a meal, but I wash my floors on my hands and knees. Do I even fit in here? Am I in or out?

So common were these comparisons between insiders and outsiders based on religion that there arose a frequent idiom for describing anything that was substandard in some way or considered blamable or undesirable. As Jews use the expression "It isn't kosher," and Brits say "It's not cricket," Quebecers have a parallel idiom to convey the idea of something that's unfair, or unjust, or just not good enough: «C'pas catholique» [It isn't Catholic]. And that says it all.

ONE WORD, TWO WORLDS

It's remarkable what language can pack into a short phrase – or even into one word. Take «c'est différent.» On the surface, it's a self-explanatory acknowledgment. But underneath, it's a judgment. And beneath that, it becomes an imperative.

First case in point: a widowed cousin's new boyfriend. «Pis, comment tu'l trouves?» [So, what do you think of him?] It's the usual debriefing in the car as we drive home from a family gathering and run through the list of who's gained or lost weight, who's looking better or worse, who bothered to come and who didn't show up, and so on. «Y est correct,» I answer back, or maybe just «J'sais pas.» [I don't know, or, whatever.] I'm weary of engaging this particular line of questioning because I can already see that it's going where it always goes, and I'm tired of whipping round a short-curved U-turn.

«Y est différent, en tout cas,» my mother replies. [He's different, in any case.] In short, he's somehow unlike the rest of the clan, and she easily finds a co-passenger who'll concur. The issue is that he has a peculiar French dialect, not the local Quebec one. He's from Montreal – with those rolled r's, with the /oir/ at the end of words like «voir» and «pouvoir» that sounds more like /oère/ instead of our "normal" /ouar/ sound; and liaisons and ellipses where one doesn't quite expect them. On top of it all, he doesn't talk much. Irony? No matter, he's done. That one word has sealed his fate in the extended family.

He is, by all appearances, a kind and decent man simply presenting a variant attribute of speech – both more and less of it – in our heritage language. Yet because of that uniqueness, he's deemed less than satisfactory. What's implied, then, is that my cousin would be better off without him, so she'd be wise to break it off pretty soon. The confirmation? The very next sentence: «J'sais pas si ça va durer bin longtemps, ça.» [I don't know if that relationship's going to last too long.] In fact, it's been going strong for about seven years now, and my cousin seems happier than ever.

Second case in point: pita bread. At seventeen, I brought some with me on a visit home from university, my staple food back then. I prepared to serve my mother a piece, just so she could try it, anxious for her valued opinion. Like the near-expert that she is about food and homemade bread, she observed the packaging and the shape pensively, holding back her judgment deliberately. «Bin, c'est différent,» she slowly said. I knew then and there that she'd never buy pita bread for her own consumption, and likely never eat it again. It didn't really matter what she'd end up thinking of the taste: the decision had been made. That was more than thirty years ago, and it still holds. No pita.

Third case in point: vegetarian chili. At twenty, I returned from Montreal on another weekend, and for some reason I can't remember, found myself alone with my father at meal time – unusual indeed. Of course, my mother had left something for him, fully prepared and labelled, with instructions on the refrigerator about how I was to heat it up and serve it to him. I was in my one of my two-year vegetarian phases, so there wasn't a labelled plate for me, which was perfectly fine. A meal without meat was hardly worth cooking, in her books, so she understandably hadn't bothered.

I set about making some homemade chili and cornbread, quick and easy. As the minutes reached towards supper, I noticed my father passing by the stove more than a few times. He'd read the instructions left about his own supper, but what was that I was cooking? In a rare and precious moment of real dialogue with him, I explained the meal and he made a quick choice. "I'll have some of that instead. Looks like something different." He pointed to the bubbling pot. It was a temporary burst of light into our relationship. A seventy-year comet.

I served him as he preferred, in front of the television on a fold-out TV table. He ate a first helping and a hearty second. Then, in a moment that hung in the timeless space from which that comet had descended, he gave me the only compliment I can ever remember getting from him: "This is really good, you know. I wish I could eat like this every night. It's not at all like your mother's cooking. All those heavy sauces. All that fried butter. All that meat. She's killing me, you know. Killing me." And then a long pause. "Oh well, that's okay. I've got to die somehow." He seemed so terribly serious.

For the record, he survived another decade of my mother's expert French cooking – and in the end, her meals didn't kill him, as he died of something entirely unrelated to diet. In fact, she probably extended his life for years by dedicating herself to his every need and mood, making it her first priority as a wonderful wife of her era to accommodate a husband who would be eulogized, in the opening line, as «un homme difficile.» Yet there it was, the definite difference about *different*. For one parent, "different" represented a worthy exploration of the unknown – a wide road leading to possibilities that might be delightful. For another, «différent» symbolized the routine confirmation of the known – an uninteresting passage to a closed door that was hardly worth opening. Two views of being, and not being, within the boundaries of sameness – and two disparate consequences, too. The word sounded almost exactly the same in both of my languages, yet meant something so entirely *different* in both of my cultures.

A MANAGEABLE RELATION WITH DIFFERENCE

So it was, then, that the incomplex frame of what was and was not "catholique," in every sense of the word, became the means by which my mother and her family enjoyed a manageable balance of religion and culture, and how her insular family was able to get along with everything beyond its immediate sphere, with «c'qui est différent» [what is different]. A black couple from Chicago came for dinner once, Phyllis and Eddy, I believe. It was around 1967, when Sidney Poitier released the movie *Guess Who's Coming to Dinner*, and it had the same flourish.

It's unclear to me even now whether our family was just reflective of the changing times the movie was attempting to portray, the blurring of social boundaries, or whether my parents had seen the movie and deliberately sought what they saw as a hallmark experience of their era.

I never understood how my parents knew these individuals, given their life circle then or later. My father seldom socialized outside work and home, and my mother even less so. Perhaps Phyllis and Eddy had come through my grand-maman's boarding house at some point – after all, she rented rooms to tourists in the summers when the students were away. Or were they connected to an uncle and his wife, an American, living in Chicago at the time?

The fact that I never knew how they came to be there and never saw them again made the whole event that much more exotic in my mind, wee white girl that I was in my wee white world. For other than these new black faces, I'd only seen people of colour in photographs in the halls of nunneries, where the missions of «les sœurs d'l'Afrique» were displayed here and there. It would be decades before, placing linguistic considerations above all other immigration criteria, Quebec would open its doors to Haitians, Moroccans, Algerians, and others who would begin to give depth and complexity to the uniform sea of light-coloured faces.

Conceivably, hosting a black couple in the '60s was a bit like my parents' experiment growing marijuana on the dining room buffet «pour essayer ça comme y faut» [to experience life the right way], or hosting folk-music nights with another uncle and his American wife. Three guitars offered their tributes to Joan Baez as my mother fetched wine and hors d'oeuvres. In any event, having a black family in our home and in the city was «un très gros événement» [a huge event] marked by a thoughtful menu and an equally considered conversation about American politics. It was a subject that my father actually despised (hating Americans more than any other group of humans) and my mother usually ignored, knowing few people of relevance, in her eyes, from «les États.»

In fact, «les États» in the French-Canadian worldview was a common idiom for Never-Never Land, a place where one was considered functionally lost to friend and country, so that to say «y est parti aux États» [he's left for the United States] meant that someone was gone for good and we could just forget about him.

I still remember my mother's English that day around the dining room table, perfectly set, as I worked in the kitchen to ready the plates and assist, complete with a matching apron, uninvited to the adults' table but indulged by our polite company into a conversation about my studies. My mother smiled with exaggerated civility, a cigarette in her mouth for added effect (she wasn't a smoker) – «Ej trouve qu'ça donne un certain air à'ne femme, ça' l'air sophistiqué, non?» [I think it gives a woman a certain air, it looks sophisticated, no?]

Excessive niceties were extended as, for the one and only time in my life until I married «un homme brun» [a brown man] myself decades later, a person of colour sat at our table, shared our meal. My own «immigrant,» as my mother puts it, would be a man with an unpronounceable name who'd continue to be considered «un étranger» [a stranger, even more "a man from afar" in common usage] after seven years of marriage. Colour, then, was another thing like religion that formed a potent barrier between us and others. It wasn't viewed at all like French and English, which were, as they always had been, the warp and weft of society.

Daisies

I played with daisies
when I was small.
It was almost an obsession.

I grabbed them all.
Stripped them
of their tiny petals.
I wanted to know:
He loves me?
He loves me not?

But the daisies
never gave me
an answer I could use.

They hung limp
like empty heads
on a dying stalk.
They could not solve
the riddles of those men,
their empty words.

So I gave up
on the question:
was it love or not love?

Now I let the daisies
grow in peace.

8

RELIGION: THE LANGUAGE OF THE BEDROOM

AN ENGLISH-BUT-NOT-IRISH MAN

That perfect dichotomy of the world into Catholics and non-Catholics – where what we all really meant was French Canadians and English Canadians – would have worked out perfectly symmetrically, perfectly tidily, if it weren't for one group that straddled the border, spiritually "of us" and yet externally couched in «la langue anglaise» [the English tongue]: the Irish. For reasons no one could explain or understand, the Irish felt like the soulmates of French Canadians, despite and completely beyond the language barrier. Marriages abounded between both peoples, and 80 per cent or more of the bilingual families I knew were an Irish–French Canadian mix.

They agreed on an adherence to the Virgin Mary over Jesus. He was honoured as «p'tit» in French and "baby" for the Irish, compassionate and benevolent but somehow holding a kind of subordinate role to his blessed mother, «Notre Dame». They gave the highest standing to the same saints, mostly Saint-Joseph, Saint-François d'Assise, Saint-Antoine, and Saint-Jean le Baptiste – along with a local favourite, Saint-Thérèse de l'Enfant-Jésus. And they shared some old threads that none could deny or explain. When their music was played, Celtic and French Canadian reels came together through time, tying them to another life, another place. It was the same after a death, a French-Canadian get-together after a «funérailles» much resembling an Irish wake – «Y aura' voulu ça, plein d'joie.» [He'd have wanted it this way, full of joy.] In life and death, French and Irish echoed each other somehow.

I deeply loved an Irish man myself once, for almost three years. Almost lived out, willingly, at least one hereditary expectation. Almost. He was a wonderful human being. Warm, loving, intelligent, kind, funny, diligent, generous, and drop-dead gorgeous. Check every box. And he was bilingual just like me, with a francophone mum and an anglophone dad. As I was in my twenties by then, my parents were hopeful that this would be it, and they were almost more attached to him than I was. For my part, I loved his family too, especially his Irish father and his aunt – his father's twin sister who'd stepped in after his mother's premature death to hold everyone together. She's one of the finest persons I've ever known, a woman-saint higher up the Catholic echelons than my own grand-maman. In her eighties now, she still has a rotation of people in need she visits daily, ignoring her own pains and problems.

Through my many relationship issues after those times, I always visualized my Irish man in my rescue fantasies. He'd show up on my doorstep way out West, ring my doorbell, save me, bring me back, and take care of me. Or I'd bump into him on the street, just like that, and we'd rekindle everything previous and precious. In my hardest stretches, so many men looked like him. I felt, and dreamt, that I saw him everywhere. I told him, some twenty years later, how the years had played out like this. "Why didn't you just call me?" he asked. Why, indeed.

For his part, he'd travelled the world working for the CBC and never married. "I always wondered," he reflected one summer afternoon, "why you ended it so suddenly that day. Why you just decided it was over, and you never explained it." We were both about forty by then, and by some miracle in town on the same day. We spent a couple of hours at a «café terrasse» in Place Royale, time sliding by softly like a wide, thin water spill, then evaporating. Pleasant but tense, he looked at his beer and waited. I felt my breathing constricting, my head spinning lightly. A familiar feeling. Behind me, the cliffs that jut out sharply against the narrow, strangled streets loomed – dark, jagged, immovable. Before me, the Traversier de Lévis loaded its joyous passengers, about to take them from this shore, onto the open blue, away.

That afternoon, I couldn't explain what it would take me a dozen more years to figure out. That a voice inside crevasses of self had said one word – *Run!* – and I'd spent a lifetime learning to listen. That I took refuge in libraries all over Montreal – *Hide!* – reassuming my anorexia like a super-hero disguise, reading and ignoring him until he knew I was serious about ending it. I couldn't tell him then how his career in photography was a cataclysmic challenge I couldn't quite name, only sense. His was a family business in its third generation, housing countless images of old Quebec and giving him access to secret church vaults (for insurance photos). With the best intentions, he once gave my mother an aerial view of L'Église Saint-Sacrement and its parish in poignant sepia. It still hangs in her basement stairway. As our relationship grew, his family moved to Holland Avenue, a two-minute walk from my first home, my "ground zero." It's cruel whiplash, this business of repressed triggers, a switch you can't reach or see. But it was all too much for me – the cameras and flashes, the religious mysteries, his familiarity with the parish, and his house being so unfortunately located. My deepest fears awoke and wouldn't be still. So it ended.

At any rate, with this ever-present affinity for the Irish among the French – despite general resentment for «'es angla'» – one might wonder why my mother married an English-but-not-Irish man. They met one winter night on La Terasse Dufferin, beside the Château Frontenac where, in winter, a huge ice slide provided (and still does) a playground in the heart of the city. In those days, music played and young people slid and danced along the edge of the cliff under the watchful gaze of countless statues, a handful of miles from the Plains of Abraham where their ancestors had fought old battles in a new land, French against English, two hundred years before.

It was here one night, in the reverie of ice, snow, folk dancing, songs, and soft lights, that my mother and father caught each other's eye. It was love at first sight. And the rest, as they say, is history – a marriage lasting some forty years, through thick and thin.

UN MAUDIT BLOKE

But in those early years, its longevity was anything but assured. There was apparently considerable resistance from some on my mother's side to a marriage with a «maudit bloke» [damned blockhead], in the words of my mother's eldest sister. My bilingual father was fluent in French and had an equally fluent bilingual father with a family name that could easily trump my aunt's in a quick flash of elite French credentials – but no matter. My father's mother, my granny, was English. Thus, the language of his home, his mother tongue, was English. The French linguistic stock was contaminated somehow, impure. Seems that a single marriage to an Englishwoman was enough to mess up everything, negate hundreds of years of "pure ancestry."

Worse still, many in my mother's entourage feared this man who'd just survived the most devastating disease of the age, tuberculosis. Was he still contagious? Should she even be allowed to speak to him, let alone date him? Was it safe for her – or for the chaperones? But the reality that he'd barely completed Grade 8 wasn't an issue, it seems. In this worldview a man provided for his family, and it was assumed that he'd manage somehow.

The fact that he spoke French and had a French-Canadian father surely helped settle the matter with my maternal grandparents in the end. After all, my mother's four siblings had all married francophones by then who spoke not a word of English beyond the ability to give sparse directions on the street to lone English passersby in their ubiquitously francophone communities. Yet here was their youngest, the last left at home – a bright, pretty girl who'd unfortunately become half-blind in a childhood accident. And here was a reasonably good-looking suitor, «un jeune blond,» half-French. Quite likely, from her parents' perspective, it was more than could be reasonably expected.

Exploring my mother's sociolinguistic universe for a minute, I reflect on her only other marriage prospect, as she once shared it with me: the butcher's son. He was apparently a decent young man – «un bon gars,» my mother remembers – «mais erien d'spécial» [but nothing special]. Claude, I'll call him here, was her age, and they'd grown up playing together behind my grandparents' home – between the house and the old shed where my grand-papa stored his car, tools, unwanted furniture, vats of varnishes and tar paint, and a few other things. Claude and his siblings shared this play area with my mother and her siblings, running past the dentist and some shops, to the corner and back.

They played «cachette» [hide and seek], «aux billes» [marbles] and «à corde» [jump rope] on dusty gravel spread out unevenly under clotheslines that criss-crossed one another in all directions, an impassable net that was still there when I visited as a child. Sheets and underwear flapped wildly, barely keeping their edges clear of the worn corrugated tin sheets that covered iron staircases and back doors. Shields against the snow in season, each metal «cabanon» [small rustic house, hideout] gave its home a sense of closure and insularity, a thin degree of separation in that thick mesh of life beneath the string-and-sock cobwebs.

As she grew, my mother went indoors more often to learn baking, set the table, or starch the linens: to learn her gendered trade, become a homemaker-in-training, and be a girl with a predictable future. For his part, Claude took his youthful self into the meat shop that adjoined the boarding house, walls supporting one another: to acquire his gendered trade, become a butcher's apprentice, and be a boy with a promising future. But somewhere between all that familiarity, the girl-and-boy-next-door phenomenon, they lost interest in one another. After domestic arts college, my mother headed off to university to be further educated – in health and nutrition, of course. Perhaps it was seen as a clue to sure trouble at his end, a sign of the times, an omen of the changing cultural script my grandparents were editing slightly, here and there, as they went along. Claude stayed firmly put.

And that's how my mother ended up marrying a man who would, instead, start a television business in the very house she'd grown up in, on the inside edges of that adjoining wall – a man, my father, for whom she'd «faire les comptes» [do the accounts]. As for Claude, he accepted the challenge of continuity, took over the meat business, and married a local girl who would «faire les comptes» for him. Similar endings? Not at all. Difference lies in the possibility for change. And my mother, at least, embraced it for a while, in a way. Did her best.

On the other side of the arrangement, my father's family was mute. A son assumed for two years to have been on his deathbed, completely uneducated, had somehow found an attractive wife with proper domestic training and a friendly personality. It was more than anyone had ever expected of someone who wasn't supposed to live past thirty, according to expert opinions in that hospital room back in the late 1940s. (He lived past sixty, in fact, putting two packs of cigarettes a day through the remaining lung and working sixteen to eighteen hours a day.) There was little to lose, in other words, in agreeing to this bilingual, bicultural marriage.

Exploring my father's sociolinguistic universe for a minute, I reflect in turn on his only other marriage prospect, as my mother once explained it: the daughter of an esteemed family friend. I have a photograph of my granny's in my possession dated "Spring 1922, Washington, DC." Granny annotates it with the names of the five people standing on a CN platform, waiting for the train, on what was clearly a meaningful day and trip. The group includes herself and her husband (my grandfather), another couple, and the father of a girl whom I shall call Claire here.

Claire's family was close to my father's for so many reasons. Her extended family had been the first to befriend my granny in English when she first arrived in Canada. Her father was a colleague of my grandfather's at work, a man of Irish extraction. And her mother was a French-Canadian girl who'd been raised in Hadlow, which was then considered to be an English community on the "south shore" of Quebec and what is currently a cove within the larger region of Lévis. Claire's grandmother and my father's grandmother, both French Canadians themselves, had been best friends all their lives. And even as my grandparents moved to the suburbs, so did this family, relocating only three streets away.

It seems clear in retrospect that Claire was deeply in love with my father, though, as my mother tells it, he wasn't as keen on her. Claire was the only person who visited him in the hospital when he suffered for so many months with tuberculosis and was deemed terminally ill. She was unafraid of the curse of the age, or else bravely willing to take the risk each and every day, coming despite her own family's strict prohibition against it, for safety's sake. Meanwhile, their mothers surely plotted to set them up with one another if he ever recovered – assumed, even, that thoroughly bilingual Paul and Claire, respectably culturally English despite the French-Canadian threads that ran through their respective genetic fabrics, would eventually marry.

So what happened? Why didn't my father run into Claire's arms when he was finally well enough? She'd certainly hoped he would. That remained abundantly clear even in the decades that followed, so that I noticed it as a child myself when her family and ours, going on the fourth generation between the clans now, continued to intertwine. Who knows? Maybe it was hard for him to feel a romantic commitment with a woman who'd seen him through countless days of bedpans and fears. Maybe, like me, he was hoping for a relationship that wasn't a constant reminder of his trauma. Or maybe, like my mother – whom he understandably would have found dazzlingly refreshing – he wanted to explore the fresh terrain of possibility. Wanted to dare to hope for something different from the future than what the past so confidently offered.

LA MAUDITE RELIGION PROTESTANTE

That belief explains much about why my mother was so delighted when the three anglo women who married into the clan of five bilingual anglophone brothers (my father and his siblings) – as per my Granny's expectations – all ended up acting «un peu folle» [slightly crazy] around religion, in her opinion. Meanwhile the two francophone women who married into the clan (of which my mother considered herself the better catch – read: sexier – of the pair) were apparently «simplement des bonnes femmes d'famille» [simply good homemakers]. Or so the story went.

As a case in point, one of the English aunts was offered up as evidence. She was American and «tellement gentille» [really so nice], especially because she made some effort to conduct small talk in her broken French. But what could you do with a woman who was «complètement tombée dans' religion» [completely fallen into religion]? There were magnets and stickers all over the refrigerator saying "Jesus loves you," and she did «les comptes» [the accounts] for «son Église» [her church], some sort of Anglican or United congregation – we weren't sure which one. Besides, they were, according to the theory, «la même maudite chose» [the same damned thing].

This business of the fridge magnets actually became woven into the folklore of "us" and "them" – my child's ethnographic portrait of Self versus Other – added to the list of defining attributes of kinds among humankind. French Canadians didn't decorate refrigerators. English Canadians put everything there: baby pictures, children's drawings, reminders to go the doctor, grocery lists, favourite greeting cards, and on and on. In our home, the refrigerator was an appliance of modernity – even more, the valued repository of the most necessary tools of that critically vital trade: cooking. But in my beloved auntie's home, the refrigerator was a narrative all to itself, a wonder to read.

Funny thing, too, the pattern seemed to hold in every home I visited, as refrigerator decorations became the telltale sign of the mother's tongue. Even now my mother isn't entirely comfortable in her postmodern, post-homemaker days. She's conceded to buying two quite expensive fridge magnets, jewelled bees. One sits there with nothing to do all day; the other, on a rare occasion, holds a reminder about critical errands, no more than two or three, in a manicured hand on adorable notepaper. Cultural and temporal scripts borrowed, appropriated slowly, resisted mostly.

Going to church every day when it was empty to hold communion with God under the watchful eye of the Virgin Mary was deemed «complètement normal.» But working for the church, so that the wives of religious men became your friends and you went to their homes and cottages, well, that was beyond understanding. And what was the confirmation of that madness? A woman who'd seek a divorce just because a man drank – «Y a des pires choses dans 'vie, t'sais!» [There are worse things in life, you know!] And, in the ultimate rejection of normalcy, she refused to drink herself – «Ah bin, j'ai mon voyage!» [That's just the most ridiculous thing ever!]

Final support for French holding religion within reason and the English being unable to do so was another English aunt. A British nurse with impeccable diction and a relatively meagre command of French, she came to Quebec via New Brunswick as a war bride after World War II and raised her daughters as three proper ladies, the cousins ahead of me at the Catholic school we attended, in whose footsteps I tried to follow. They were the brightest, most gorgeous girls there, and although I rarely saw them – high school students on this side of the building with lighter tartan, and elementary students on the other side with darker tartan – their presence in the building and my aunt's commanding agency in the school community gave me imaginary psychological leverage. I belonged, I believed. On occasion, when girls across the ages intersected in tidy lines on the way to the chapel and back, I felt them signalling about me proudly to their friends, with a smile and a quick nod. Well, as much signalling as girls can do in an atmosphere where skirt lengths are measured each day and a whisper leads to hundreds of lines of punishment – a place of complete predictability that I loved with all my heart.

Yet all of this wasn't sufficient, in my mother's eyes, to salvage the image of a woman who was far too stern. The proof? High-cut shirts, almost no drinking, and her husband calling her "dear" all the time – or "battle-axe" under his too-loud breath, after a few drinks at our house had worked their predictable magic. Did we need any other proof of their stilted English marriage than this? Had we ever seen them kiss in public, or even touch each other? If anyone needed more evidence, here was the ultimate sign that the English language itself wasn't the real problem at all, but «la maudite religion protestante» [the damned Protestant religion] surely was.

A beautiful war bride married a hopeful bilingual Canadian. But as years went by, «toute la famille est anglaise» [the whole family is English], the husband and children speaking only English. Next thing you know, there's a husband «qui perd son français» [who loses/is losing his French]. And even though these girls were in a Catholic convent day school, they attended United Church services on the weekend – «Imagine-toi donc?» [Can you imagine?] It was nearly treasonous. It was all right *not* to go to Catholic church – that was a choice. But to go to a Protestant church instead? That was quite another matter.

To top it all off, they had dinner parties without even one bottle of wine, as if that were even possible, let alone humane. Of course, it was unenjoyable. In such marriages, the argument went, the woman takes control of the man; public fondling ceases; Protestant pastors become personal friends who lead a typical family life, whose children visit the congregation's children, and other strange things of that nature. Such events were so unlike that around «el bon frère» [the good brother] or «el bon père» [the good father] – aka the average priest – whose visits to a French Catholic home were layered dramaturgy involving absolutely no interaction with family, but only pomp and circumstance implicating a solitary adult in perceived need of moral uplifting, and some mute female serving tea and «des p'tits biscuits» [cookies].

STRANGE ALLIANCES

And so it was that my parents came to form a partnership, a franco-phone and bilingual anglophone alliance, a merging of self-appropriating Catholicism-of-convenience with Protestantism-disguised-as-converted-Catholicism. They formed a union on a micro scale of the two major social and political agencies in Quebec in the second half of the twentieth century. Marriage as an alliance: there was nothing much new about that in the annals of human history.

I did seek more than a few times to give the idea of an alliance my own particular twist, though. Tried my best, anyhow. Went looking for what lay on the other side of the fence, as they say, and how I could work with it – or it with me. My pattern of relationships as alliances was founded on an adherence to a straightforward, practical schedule: every couple of years, sometime between September and November, I'd rotate lovers with the goal of sampling other ways of *being*. I started in 1976, the first year I left home.

Subject number one was Aboriginal. It wasn't a serious relationship, more a hanging out together in groups, but it left us as friends and was a good start for my explorations. In 1978, I fell in love with an American Jew studying at university in Montreal. It was an intense romance full of promise that was sadly broken by an overdose of passion and immaturity. In 1980, I moved in with my Protestant boyfriend. But from being great study-buddies at university, we eventually dissolved into fighting. Maybe that's why I went back to Catholicism in 1981, and my beloved photographer, the chance I blew that forever became the path not taken. In 1984, I had a brief stint, fun despite its constricting gender roles, in Orthodox Christianity. This was replaced in 1985 by a Scientologist whose curious intellectual game I thoroughly enjoyed for a time, and who is the biological father of my three children. In 1993, I was infatuated with a Buddhist who, perhaps predictably, wouldn't commit. In 1994, I partnered with a neo-Pagan, an albeit supportive union that seemed to turn in circles. Then, in 1999, I became interested in a loose practitioner of Confucianism, a kind heart under a harsh exterior, though distances took their toll. And in 2000, I fell deeply in love inside moderate Islam with a diligent and brilliant soul much my junior – a man who spoke a language I didn't understand and who came from a country I'd never visited (and still haven't) – and I finally felt something for the first time ever with a man: safe.

I'll end the record there. It surely makes the point. Of course, there was the odd one-night stand or two-week summer fling thrown in between one or the other, completely unconnected to the schema. But all the most significant men in my romantic life can be accounted for by it. And while my plan wasn't explicitly formulated, it was absolutely impossible for me to deny the force of its implicit imperative.

Most women my age chose their partners by face, race, cash, promises, things like that. But every two to five autumns – my breeding cycle? – I chose by faith first. I let men hold me just so I could get close enough to hold their values, live by their beliefs, install their paradigms, acts by their rules, reinvent myself. Of course, I was condemned by my family as changeable, too easily influenced. No one, including me, noticed that I was stuck in endless mimicry of patterns bred in the bone. A child seduced by pedophiles whose identities issue from their theology becomes an adult convinced that sex and religion are inseparable.

Ironically, I was personally quite pleased with myself through these relationship journeys. I thought I was unethnocentric, multiculturally inclined, religiously open-minded, all-embracing, genuinely interested in learning from the Other – a real Renaissance Woman, in the modern sense of the word anyhow. Perhaps. But what if, instead, I was only performing my own spoiled identity, my body bound in replays of faint, familiar echoes along a predictable arc – an inadvertent Repetition Woman? No matter. It was the adventure of a lifetime, and I wouldn't have missed it (even if I could have) for the world. And that's why I don't put much stock in apologies at this point – or in apologetics.

My parents' own union, however, began with considerable more planning and organization. They imposed on themselves methodical precautions and delays that prevented the sort of impetuousness driven by instinct that was the hallmark of my own existence. They were engaged for two years, just to be extra safe about who knows what – as if the inherent risks, despite the obvious benefits, remained palpable. Marriage followed, and a life that would cast my brother and me into the dual role, the dual life between languages and cultures that is experienced by so many children around the globe.

Purple

In this house,
this childhood,
I am allowed one colour
for my own: pink.
Not even yellow or green.
«El rose, ça c't'une bonne couleur
pour une p'tite fille.»*

I dream of blue things.
Blue – the colour of the sky,
the sea, the whales, me.
I have a dream some day,
to make blue my own –
wear a blue skirt or sweater,
or maybe even a blue coat.

But then a small boy
is born, Bébé,
and blue is given to him
by inheritance:
«Bin voyons-donc.
Lui, c't'un p'tit garçon,
pis l'bleu c'est pour les gars.»†

*   Colloquialism for "Pink, now that's a proper colour for a little girl."
†   Colloquialism for "Come on now, he's a little boy, and blue is for boys/men."

It will take me thirteen years
to secure my dreams.
Wearing blue jeans as an
act of defiance that gets me
grounded for three weeks.
Blue tie-dyes, my new uniform.
Hippie girl.

From blue to gray,
to black and only black,
moving forward: twenty, thirty, forty, fifty.
I was in mourning.
Seems my choice of colours
was a momentous clue
I did not read.

Then out popped purple
as the colour of recovery
health, remembrance –
the work of therapy.
A holy colour of Catholicism?
A compromise of blue and pink?
Not at all.

A best friend's mother
from South Africa
taught us how to play
"Purple People Eaters"
one summer day –
dressed up, chased us,
made gobbling sounds.

She showed us how to run
from insipid monsters
that changed shape
and ate small children.
It was "Hide and Seek"
with a really twisted edge –
incredibly instructive.

It did not matter
logically, grammatically,
if the predators were purple
(I knew they were),
or the prey were purple
(blue-pink children) –
because both were true.

Like "Ring around the Rosies,"
it was laughter chasing death.
I took her as my prophet,
took purple as my emblem.
Not sweet pastels, but bold,
brave colour that dominates,
devours its components.

9

MY BROTHER: MY FLIP SIDE

BECOMING DIFFERENT

Only two years my junior, my brother has brown eyes whereas mine are blue, and brown hair in adulthood whereas mine is muted blond. He has light brown skin where mine has always been freckly white. By his teens, he was already tall and gaunt, taking after my grand-maman and maternal aunts, many over six feet tall, while I was a child of average height, with the slight plumpness of the females of the anglo clan. My brother was and is «un vrai bon gars» [a really good guy] who settled only a few miles from my parents, attended Laval, partnered with a French girl, and lives in French. He spent his youth hunting, fishing, dancing, drinking, and basically performing all of the expectations of our mother tongue culture to perfection. Even as children, we were different by our choices, he and I, and we became only more different because of them.

Most of his out-of-school friends around the neighbourhood were monolingual francophones, including his best friend, a boy whose family were militant «péquistes.» Meanwhile, mine were mostly bilingual anglophones, including my best friend, a boy whose dad was Scottish and whose mum was Aboriginal. As my brother became older, his girlfriends and lovers were virtually all local French girls, while mine were anglophones from a range of subcultures and cities.

My brother has, like my mother, kept the same friends all of his life, maintaining them like a precious garden, still calling people he met in Grade 4 to have a beer or congratulate them on a new baby. I have a crash-and-burn approach to friends, the love-them-and-leave-them pragmatics of a born traveller, leaving behind in far-off cities people whom I loved and miss but feel distant from now. And it's the same with homes. He's spent the last decade renovating a two-hundred-year-old home, windowsill by windowsill, careful to attend to the most minute details of the period. I've lived in rental property after rental property, a few times purchasing a home just to flip it for profit a couple of years later, finding the newest ones I can, with the least mold and dust, the least history.

He learned to make my mother's favourite Christmas sugar cookies and her famous cornflake pie, because they're the taste of home. I learned how to make spanikopita so that it's not too greasy, and to cook with spices and recipe books from places far from home. I performed in ballet recitals for a decade while he learned how to make a dovetail joint and use a soldering iron. He was sent to survival camps in New Brunswick to hunt, fish, and swim, while I was sent to religious camps on l'Île d'Orleans to learn small May Day marches and how to glue pretty patterned tiles onto clay plates. As we grew older, he listened to French music, mostly rock and disco in French nightclubs, while I listened to English music, mostly folk and blues in pubs. He formed his political opinions from the *Soleil*, *La Presse*, and *Le Devoir*, but mine came through the *Montreal Gazette*, the *Globe and Mail*, and the *Toronto Star*.

He mastered the best way to cut through provincial bureaucracy to get a permit to build a porch or an addition – quite a feat in Quebec – while I learned how to say hello in languages he's never heard, and how to time a trip across Canada to avoid traffic and boredom. He became an expert on which wines go with each kind of food, a topic I can't understand. And I learned to love mango shakes and bubble tea, drinks he's never tried. He's been settled for thirty years with a woman who speaks almost no English, and I've been unsettled forever, marrying men who spoke little or no French. Dinners over the holidays still can't be managed without a whole lot of gestures. A sense of humour is essential to make the talk go round when there's such a wide expanse to be covered.

EL LIÈV' PIS L'ARGILE

We've become, my brother and I, the flip sides of a bilingual coin. We both speak both languages, but in writing, his French is stronger than his English, while the reverse is true for me. We both started at the same English Catholic elementary school and attended it for a similar length of time. He transferred after Grade 3 when they stopped accepting boys, and I transferred after Grade 6 when the sisters went bankrupt and headed back to «les États,» never to be heard from again. From there we both went to the same English public school, the same English high school, and the same English CÉGEP (a two-year college prior to university).

My father showed my brother, in English, how to shoot a gun and clean an engine; and my mother showed me, in French, how to bake bread and sculpt «l'argile» [clay]. My father showed me, in English, how to collect stamps and clean a fish; my mother showed my brother, in French, how to skin «un lièv'» [a hare] and make «des crêpes» [very thin, traditional pancakes]. Same parents, same metal. Same educational system, same furnace in which to temper the substance of our selves. Same one-parent, one-language philosophy working on us both. And yet, such contrasting constructions of the self emerged.

My brother is «un francophone» both culturally and functionally – while I am functionally and culturally an anglophone. What else but agency – however motivated, engendered, or achieved – can explain the difference? For my brother absolutely draws from his francophone roots more than his English roots, in his choice of foods, entertainment, and friends, while I draw far more from my anglophone roots. And in a strange juxtaposition of identities, he works full-time appraising homes and part-time as a teacher, while I work full-time as a teacher and part-time unofficially appraising homes, relocating twenty-seven times since I left my mother's house.

We also have a distribution of traits in opposite proportions. He has a very French look to my rather English look. But he has an inherently anglo-scientific, rational approach to life and business, compared to my inherently franco-spiritual, holistic views. Add to that the fact that my French-dominant brother has an English uncle for «son parrain» [his godfather], but English-dominant me had my French grand-maman for «ma marraine» [my godmother]. We're a mash-up of genres, but a balanced mix as a whole. Neither language, neither culture winning or losing between us – if we're taken together rather than alone.

Trouble is, we're rarely taken together. We've lived in separate cities since 1976, and I can count on a single hand the times we've had real conversations – not those impersonal greetings over enormous dinners on visits home. Both over fifty now, we only recently shared a few secrets about our lives. They were precious moments on a front porch when a lightning storm stopped the flow of an ordinary day, and we both took refuge for an unforgettable hour. Our fleeting symbiosis was stolen from divergent agendas that grew more incompatible with every mile and year of distance. The devastating blame, worn unevenly: mine alone.

For while he stood still, within a stone's throw of where I last left him, I became a moving target across the Canadian landscape. This isn't my narcissistic distortion about controlling family outcomes through my intentions, or some grandiose delusion about being the vortex of responsibility. I didn't leave home, or him, as part of a master plan to accomplish magnificent things. I left home as part of a haphazard series of coincidences, part of a non-plan to attempt only one thing: to survive.

It was the pattern of escape I'd dreamt about back in those dark days when predators were choosy about their prey, and also why my younger brother – merely tagged as «Bébé» in my buried memories – is remembered as always being out of sight, out of range, unavailable, absent. It's no small blessing that he was spared because pedophiles manifest preferences for particular bits of flesh. That in this case, we weren't taken together.

That's the only comfort I derive these days from the fact that my memories of his earliest childhood are so few. But it's no big wonder, either. Because for years, inner voices beckoned me to *run!* – when all I could really do was *hide!* (or, rather, at least imagine satisfying scenarios where I did). And when I got older, I just managed to listen better, to act out those directives concretely, at last: to flee to nowhere.

That's how my brother and I ended up on opposite sides of the wide gulf that characterizes our relationship and strains our efforts, to this day, to recover what we've lost: our potential, our possibilities, and our time as a pair of siblings in a difficult world. It's as if we stood on opposite shores of a small river when a set of earthquakes began and left us, each time, with a bit too far of a distance to undertake with our immature bodies. Until, years later, we found that we were standing on opposite shores of far-distant continents.

We aren't a tidy coin where two sides are held in balance by a perfect theory. Rather, we're an entirely unbalanced set of wings on the flip sides of a tired bird, strained symmetry that would shame an albatross. And so the challenge, the near impossibility, of crossing back.

TWO CAKES IN A BOX

Yet the difference between my own and my brother's life shows how the language divide can also be thin indeed. It's like one of those crazy scenes in a movie where a national border runs through a person's living room. For here we stand, well into our adult lives, barely two years apart at birth but with cosmic lifetimes between us. We actually just began an effort recently to try to email each other more often – and to remember, at least, each other's children's birthdays. We're like a couple of recovering amnesiacs getting to know each other for the first time after decades – "Really, you did that then? Seriously? I had no idea!" We inadvertently spent more than forty years forgetting each other, after all, and going completely separate ways. We barely recognize one another.

I believe the last joint undertaking he and I ever had was in 1966, when we were seven and nine. We'd convinced our parents that it wasn't fair to have Mother's Day and Father's Day, but no Children's Day. They responded with the usual counter-argument at first, saying that "every day is children's day." But we pushed the issue, I guess, and they conceded, for just one year, to designate a Sunday between the other two dates as just that.

«Ça loge din' poche» [it fits in a pocket], my father had announced one day after work, giving us a clue about our shared gift. I heard his statement in French and immediately passed it through my English translation filter. That's how, as the authoritative older sister, I spent the whole week steering my younger brother down the wrong road, as we both tried to think of a gift small enough to fit in a coat or pants pocket, and yet still suitable for us to share. When Sunday arrived, though, we found that it was a huge, green, canvas tent, army-style, in a long duffle bag about as tall as my brother. This kind of bag, it's true, is another use of the French word, «poche.»

«J'vous ai dit qu'c'ta' din' poche» [I told you it was in a pocket], my father quipped in patois, laughing at the wordplay he'd engaged. It was one of the rare times I ever saw my father relaxing, so I can't begrudge him that my brother and I were left feeling pretty silly about his bilingual "gotcha" game. Get us, it did.

Yet when I think back to that last sibling project of ours, and how it turned our linguistic mash-up – read "flexibility" – into a family joke, I admit that I end up on a mental tangent where I struggle to come to terms with the more negative, dissembled aspects of the so-called bilingual advantage. Sure, on paper, we've both reaped advantages. After all, my whole premise of self, and of this story, is that I've successfully undertaken a psychological reconstruction in the second language I was offered, English. And just because he's stayed home doesn't mean my brother hasn't played the "English card" to his advantage either, albeit in the fluctuating political and linguistic winds of Quebec. He and I have enjoyed innumerable material and social advantages – a wider range of friends, interests, and employment opportunities, for example – because of our ability to move fluidly inside two language communities.

There are absolutely "advantages" to be had in the state of bilingualism, in other words – in this type of dual being-ness – and both of us have appropriated them, though in substantially dissimilar ways. The advantages aren't at issue. What is at issue is the full phrase as it's found in public discourse: "*the* bilingual advantage." It seems singular, definite and neat, like «l'addition» on the restaurant bill. But it feels like there are a lot of places on that tidy slip of paper where things have, indeed, slipped. Like things have fallen out of our pockets while we were reaching for the money. Vital things. Is the real issue the article, the *the*? As if it were assuredly and necessarily worthwhile to split a family into distinct language pathways? The jury's out. It often feels, in some intangible and unspeakable way, as if one of those elusive objects that fell out of our pockets was the best thing of all.

Don't get me wrong – I don't want to be like those detestable people who win the lottery and then whine about how it changed their lives too much. I'm thankful, so thankful, that I had a second language and culture to offer options unavailable in my first set. And my brother and I are grateful – if I can dare to speak for him here – that we can watch television on more channels, understand the lyrics of more of the popular music available, or read from more divergent sources. That we can tap into the pulse of the world through different conduits. Drink from variant cultural fountainheads. And so on.

Yet he and I live on either side of a thin wedge – one that was driven in by trauma, it's true, but fabricated from culture nonetheless. I don't know what my brother hates or loves the most, or what makes him happiest or most fearful, or which have been the best and worst days of his life. And I so much wish I did.

Long ago my mother took us on special occasions to buy delicious pastries from Kerhulu's downtown. There were two kinds we always bought: pink ones with a giant R (for rum), and white ones with a giant K (for kirsch). These cakes were my mother's perfect treat for both her children, Richard and Kathleen. Ever the gifted storyteller, my mother wove the most delightful tale on the bus journey back home with our precious white box of six cakes, three of each. She told us in complete earnestness how these tiny cakes, sold to thousands of people every day, were made just for us. I believed her to my deepest core so sincerely that I'd often wonder aloud why the pink ones weren't the K ones. «Ah ça, on'el sait pas» [Ah, that, we don't/can't know], she said, smiling mischievously. But it's been a long time since my brother and I were two cakes in a box.

CHEZ BIRKS

Funny what you learn from shopping when you're small, because the only other explanation I have for our conundrum comes from eye-level store data gleamed from my pint-sized view of the world. It's from Birks, a stunningly beautiful jewellery outlet on the best streets, and as one of the flagship businesses in the earliest and most splendid malls. I loved those magical words, the verbal string that summoned my call to higher ground: «Oké, on va chez Birks aujourd'hui. Y faut qu'ej trouve un cadeau pour …» [Okay, we're going to Birks today. I have to find a gift for …] It made wearing the crunchy clothes and putting up with the scratchy seams at the waist worth it, though it drove my poor brother into a classic tantrum. The rest of the utterance was completely irrelevant to me. The primary thing was that we were going, so we would *be* there.

First, Birks was perfect because it was so positively clean. No mold, no dust, impeccable. I don't even think anyone would have had the nerve to smoke in there, would have dared, though it was technically allowed in those years. The clerks looked matronly and proper, stern and efficient. I visualize them taking that cigarette butt right out of some cheap mouth, disdainful. They smiled, but not too much and not in a creepy way. And they spoke from behind a high counter, allowing a proper distance that precluded pinched cheeks and the other perils of childhood. All this made it homey for me from the start, intuitively safe.

Its second asset was its iconic colour: royal blue. What a colour! It was exactly the colour I dreamed of having as my own, but wasn't allowed. Girls wore pink, boys blue. Let's not even talk about yellow or green. And orange and purple? Not true colours, you know. So pink it was. Blue lived only in my dreams – and at Birks. Here were miles and miles of royal blue plush under my feet, deep carpet flawlessly vacuumed, caressing the soles of my crisp, black shopping shoes, like walking on water. And those royal blue boxes! Tiny, perfectly hinged wonders with their soft white satin linings. Miniature beds for jewel princesses! Snug velveteen cradles where a petite golden cross tucked its fragile chain, or a modest birthstone ring held its stone high while it sailed away in a perfectly blue Birks bag.

I forgave my baby brother for finding it hard to sit still on the expensive padded chairs with the rigid wooden arms while I cooled my cheeks on the glass cases along each side of the store – not the mouth or nose, it left a messy print – as I ogled their treasures. It was a place with limited possibilities for touch, or play, or even a bit of understandable silliness, but for me it was a palace – a kingdom in the sky, but on the street. I think they've changed the blue a bit over the years, made it lighter. Then again, perhaps it was always so. Maybe my memory of it is just hopelessly romantic, a reverie of a deep, rich, incomparable blue.

That celebration of beauty and inspired meaning began at the massive double glass doors with the huge blue B on the handles. The letter was properly oriented on the right-hand door, with the vertical downstroke to the left, but reversed on the left-hand door. When the doors were closed, they greeted their enchanted customers with these two stunning Bs with their backs to one another. It was an artistic monument to reversals, an inverted alphabetical masterpiece. You opened the shiny door with the right-facing B to get in, leaving the backwards B behind on the door you didn't need. Open the opposite door on your way out, and you were using the B that used to look backwards from the outside but now looked the right way because you were inside. And somewhere in that flip-flop, the view from outside and inside, I extracted significance that helped me handle a few reversals of my own in front of those other shiny objects, mirrors.

I saw you could do almost the same thing with a K and an R: put them back to back and have them look similar. That's when I understood that my brother and I simply had slightly different ways of seeing, doing, and being. It's just that his top circle was closed, and mine was open. In my preschooler's mind, I read it as some endopsychic symbol, another example of myth and meaning coming together in ordinary life. Common sense delivered in common things. When you have trouble figuring out what's going on in your world, I guess you grab your paradigms, and your hope, wherever you can. Philosophers call it primitive, but I call it sensible. For that's how, in a creatively deviant (deviantly creative?) way, I came to an early peace and considerable understanding about what was happening between my brother and me – our proximity versus our distance, our similarity versus our divergence.

It would be a full fifty years from those days before either one of us could interrogate how the various reversals in the characters of key people in our lives – including me – made any sense. But I extracted immeasurable calm and solace in those days from learning that the different linguistic orientations my brother and I were evolving were really nothing more than a mere inversion of signs, flipped Bs on a handle. And from learning that my funny sense of self was exactly like that double door – a plain matter of perspectives. With so much meaning to be had in a single letter, I dared to imagine what the entire alphabet – or even better, an entire language – had to offer.

Wings

My French self puts on my English self
like an oversized pair of wings,
every morning, in some archaic dawn.

No sense to try to think of day and time
when a small child was arrested,
quivered alone in a psychic rainstorm.

No matter how it happened – by what
means a body barely breathing
came upon such a pretty set of feathers.

They were recycled, just hanging there
in the closet of another culture –
faint images of white that became material.

Stretching tiny arms underneath the warmth,
I could move from where I stood
to find air among soft clouds of possibility.

10

ENGLISH ROOTS

SUNDAY DINNERS

For the proof of my success as a constructed anglophone, I have to
look no further than Granny St-Onge. In her tidy suits, complete with
matching pin – butterfly, pheasant, bird, dragonfly, or roses – her sensible shoes, her proper shirts closed to the neckline, and her hairdos
styled after her beloved Queen Mum, this avowed monarchist nomin-
ated me her "favourite granddaughter," a proper lady. It was the ultimate seal of approval that I could «passer pour une anglaise» [pass as an
English person].

Sundays at Granny St-Onge's had a uniquely English flavour compared to time spent at my grand-maman Dumont's boarding house.
The only commonality was the piano that both homes boasted in their
living rooms. My grand-maman Dumont had an ordinary upright, the
type that could be found in old movie houses playing along with the
picture shows. The sisters, or the priests, or some second- or third-
removed aunt would play a traditional air, and everyone would join in
to sing along, sometimes quite raunchy songs, as long as grand-maman
herself was in the kitchen out of earshot, as she inevitably was. Granny
St-Onge, on the other hand, had a baby grand, a Görs & Kallmann
brought by special crate from London, a family heirloom that still sits
in my mother's home. The piano was an instrument for playing, not for
sing-alongs, inviting only expert hands and closed on other occasions.

Dinners consisted of the same menu each week, the one she'd had Sundays back in England: roast beef, Yorkshire puddings (no one could compete with their puffiness), mashed potatoes (no lumps, absolutely no lumps), gravy, carrots, and horseradish. I don't remember desserts other than platefuls of Peek Frean cookies, or shortbread brought from England by a visitor or sent on to Canada as a care package. The table was impeccably set, everyone having their assigned seats, unchanging from week to week – and the most amazing thing of all, silverware that was really silver, lying like royalty on top of lacy napkins. The napkins, I learned early and well, were more for show than use, as any civilized person will tell you.

After dinner there was tea, sometimes in the "garden" – my granny's name for her yard, a tidy enclosure bounded by lilac trees and a wooden fence covered in ivy with huge, shiny leaves. In fact, it really was more like a garden, with peonies and pansies and my granny's favourite plant of all, lavender.

My English granny loved lavender, smelled like lavender, and crocheted hanger covers that smelled like lavender. If there was ever a gift to be bought for her, the choice was always easy: expensive chocolates from a real chocolatier, of which Quebec had many, or, the hands-down favourite, lavender-scented Yardley products. My granny worked to supervise in the kitchen more than to actually cook, and left the cleaning to others, as was proper. And while she drank her tea at the table after her meal (eaten slowly, of course), she asked about school, cared about awards, and inquired at times about specific subjects and ideas.

But what I liked best of all was that when someone came along to distract her from being a bit bookish, as they tended to do, by showing her a funny trick with some cards, or arm wrestling in front of her, Granny kept a stoic expression, and always the same comment would come: "Oh, my. Oh dear." And she'd return to our conversations, or let me sit as she chatted with an uncle about business or current events. I was a big girl then, a serious girl, and a "good girl." I dare say she may even have blurted out in a whisper, "not like those others" (meaning some of my cousins), on a few too many occasions.

She was in a cultural quandary, barely understanding her two francophone daughters-in-law and even less so the children of one, who were becoming "altogether too French" in her mind, attending French school and living their French lives above a «tabagie,» a tobacco store and barbershop in the heart of Saint-Sacrement that my grandfather had left as part of his legacy. Sadly, she turned her back on them early on, with the odd "Pity" muttered like a muted cough. Yet I had no time to feel sorry for them. I was too busy eating up my conversation about American politics, the Queen, the price of real estate, and the best tulip bulbs. It was delicious.

A MEMOIR

Just how it was that my granny reconciled this vision of herself with that of her husband's remains a closed mystery – not just to me but to all who knew her. It was beneath her station in life for a proper lady to discuss such matters. She was a well-educated woman born in 1897, beautiful in her time, the daughter of a teacher and homemaker who bought lavender, milk, and crumpets from travelling vendors on Kempe Road, in the Kensal Rise area of London. Granny was the granddaughter of Daniel Butt, the general postmaster of Hertfordshire County, and his wife, Jane Wilkins, who had married in 1875.

She'd spent her youth in an atmosphere of gardeners, cooks, and exclusive English schools (of course, not Catholic, oh my). She went first to Chamberlayne Wood Elementary School, then to Haberdashers Aske's Girls School, where she excelled as a scholarship student of great promise, commuting daily by train to a cottage home where French doors from the conservatory opened onto climbing roses and she could practise on the grand piano while dinner was prepared by the cook.

My favourite anecdote of hers is far more humble, though. The year is 1902, and she's five years old. She explains that her mother wanted her to get used to running errands around the community, so she was sent out to get "a pint of milk for her tea." She carried her glass jug as she walked about the streets looking for the horse-drawn milk cart, and listening for his tell-tale cry, "Milk-ho!" Soon enough, she found the milkman and watched him ladle the milk into her jug. But on her way home, she was stopped by "a couple of naughty boys" who wanted to drink her milk.

She ran as hard as she could, but she fell, broke the jug, and apparently grazed her knee badly. I suppose the boys ran away then, because she explains how she managed to get home, bruised and saddened, minus the pint of milk. When I think about this story, it seems incredibly salient. I see that day right before my eyes, the dirt road in front and behind her, the milkman and his ladle, and a diminutive blond curly-haired girl running for her life, falling and losing her precious charge – but at least incurring no further harm. And I can't help but wonder: simpler crimes for simpler times?

Of course, I wouldn't have known all of these details about her life – or remembered them, at least – were it not for the fact that she spent her final years writing a memoir that I inherited. She wanted to keep herself sane in those days, as she was "dying among those damned Irish," to quote her. As a girl in her prime, she had attended the London shows with well-to-do, upwardly mobile youth and summered on the coast with cousins of equal standing. She attended championship games at Wimbledon in chauffeur-driven cars. And later, she had worked in a secretarial capacity for jewellery firms in London, including the Goldsmiths and Silversmiths Company on Regent Street which, she often mentioned, engaged in business with the queen and descendants of Norman nobles.

Then came the First World War. London was bombed by German Zeppelins, and she could see the searchlights and gunfire from her bedroom window. One day she witnessed a dirigible come down in flames so bright that it lit up the dome of St Paul's Cathedral beside it. It was a direct hit, she explains, in which the entire crew was killed. On another day a large piece of shrapnel fell on their roof; they kept the twisted metal for many years as a reminder of the danger.

Within a year, the home next door to hers was split by a bomb, and she writes about the peculiar sight of pictures still hanging on the walls of houses otherwise reduced to rubble. And so it was, is, with danger. It approaches from a distance, stealthily. First we see it from what we think is a safe position, and then it moves in to occupy that space of safety, leaving us no other. And then, it arrives, excessive and arbitrary. It leaves us in its dust, random pictures still hanging in our memory.

Responding to the escalating crisis, allied Canadian soldiers arrived in considerable numbers to assist "the Forces." That was when my granny put to active use the ample French her elite education had provided her with and struck up a friendship with a young Canadian,

Joseph John Leo St-Onge, introduced to her by her cousin. He was soon deployed to the Second Battle of Ypres, where he barely survived, and then only because he bent down to pick up a religious scapula at the precise moment an explosion ripped his pack from his back. My granny kept that scapula all her life.

For various acts of bravery in that battle, the young man earned a military medal and admission to an officer's course at Cambridge – difficult for a French Canadian with only a sprinkling of English – earning his commission within six months. He became the very first French Canadian to earn entry into the 16th Rifle Brigade of the Imperial Regiment, "one of the oldest and most exclusive regiments of the British army," according to my granny. From here, he was promptly redeployed.

GRANDFATHER ST-ONGE

Like something of a Forrest Gump, then, my grandfather was a man-on-the-spot at some of the key flashpoints of modern history. Joseph Jean Léo St-Onge was born in Fraserville, in the county of Témiscouata, Quebec, on 21 September 1889. On 26 June 1906, then seventeen, he began working for Canadian National Railway as a transhipper, but he was readily promoted to "brakeman and yardman" within a year. In 1914, his attestation paper for the Canadian Overseas Expeditionary Force* records that he has already served five years in active duty. Unofficially, then, he'd been a soldier since 1909, apparently conscripted in some fashion for a purpose or mission that remains off the radar of formal government (or even family) registries. And that's how, just past the turn of the century, he found himself along the US-Mexico border as a member of Pancho Villa's revolutionary band, dressed in tattered khakis, sleeping in the open.

As to whether he went to Mexico really to work with Pancho Villa, or to track his movements for some authorities, or to use his position with Villa to report on other powers, there's an altogether different kind

---

* As noted in the Canadian Archives of the Soldiers of the First World War, Regimental Number 23053, folio 843, RG 150, accession 1992–93/166, box 8601-19.

of silence, an official stillness, a dead end. All that's certain is that my grandfather wasn't in Mexico on a young man's whim, the mere lure of adventure, for the national archive is clear. On the attestation paper, in answer to Question 9, "Do you now belong to the Active Militia?" the witness writes, "Yes." And in answer to Question 10, "Have you ever served in any Military Force? If so, state particulars of former service," the witness writes: "5 years [illegible] 10th Q.O.C.H."

The Queen's Own Cameron Highlanders (QOCH) was a volunteer British infantry regiment originally formed in 1793 during the French Revolutionary Wars. It was in action for a hundred years prior to my grandfather's joining, in regions as far afield as Belgium, China, Crete, Denmark, Egypt, India, Malta, Portugal, Russia, Spain, Sudan, the West Indies – and Canada. The regiment was apparently considered the "Queen's Own" from 1873 onward, and it was also associated with the "Territorial Force," a volunteer infantry service across the United Kingdom from 1908 to 1920 – my grandfather's window of participation.

Throughout the century from its formation to my grandfather's entry at nineteen or twenty, the QOCH had countless opportunities to fight against France and its interests, including in the famous Egyptian Campaign and the Napoleonic Wars. But by the time of the Crimean War, the QOCH was involved in what were now considered joint French-Anglo campaigns with allies such as the Ottoman Empire. I can't resist the speculation that this is, oddly enough, precisely what my third marriage was – a French-Anglo campaign with an Ottoman ally. Life imitating life, again and again. At any rate, here was Grandfather St-Onge – «un originaire de Saintonge» – doing who knows what from 1909 to 1914 for a British military organization formed precisely to combat the French.

My granny has written about half a page in her memoirs about the Pancho Villa episode, with the flourish of an aspiring novelist. She explains, "While there, he decided to join the Mexican revolutionaires under Pancho Villa, who was something of a Robin Hood, robbing to the rich to give to the poor. Leo learned to ride a horse and luckily was never captured … Leo did leave Mexico with a price on his head, like any revolutionary. Somewhere in my collection, I have a photo of him in the uniform of Villa's guerillas." Then, in the typical understatement that marked her speech, she adds, "This experience might have helped him to get his commission in the British Army."

A photo in the possession of an uncle now living in Connecticut (though I've never seen it myself, not that I can recall) apparently shows Grandfather St-Onge on horseback, dark-haired and blue-eyed, in the trademark revolutionary uniform. His modest French-Canadian frame, all five feet seven of him, disguises the considerable stature he'd soon acquire. There's also a trusted report that he escaped from Mexico by being smuggled out in the engine compartment of a train driven by a former buddy of his from his earliest work on the railroads.

TICKLER'S JAM

And that's how my grandfather ended up in a British uniform, having just survived Ypres purely by serendipity, smack on the front lines of the Battle of Passchendaele. He was badly gassed there, left to die on a wagon of corpses, pulled at the last minute when a private noticed him: "Gor' blimey, the bloke's alive, and he's sitting up." My grandfather survived, overcame temporary blindness, and lived to see the Armistice signed, marrying two weeks later.

On onion-skin paper, using a manual typewriter, my grandfather hammered out his report on the poison gas attack of 22 April 1915 that nearly ended our family right then and there. It's a one-page account that I also inherited and keep in the binder of my granny's memoirs: "Like some liquid, the heavy colored vapor poured relentlessly into the trenches. The sweet-smelling stuff merely tickled our nostrils, we failed to realise the danger ... It was in this last melee that I faced a six-foot Hun who succeeded, owing to my exhausted condition, in jerking my gun away from my hand. As he was lunging at me with his bayonet, I grasped his with my left hand and in doing so, slipped to my knees. The bayonet struck me above the knee-cap on the left leg, cutting to the bone."

Yet within weeks, he was recovering, then back in service. For his efforts in battle, he was once again promoted, this time to the rank of captain, and he received the Military Cross at the hands of King George V himself, in the throne room at Buckingham Palace, with my granny in attendance. The king apparently asked him where he was from, and when my grandfather told him that he was from Quebec, King George V answered, "Glad to have you here" – "though he seemed surprised to see a French Canadian in the uniform of an officer in the Imperial army," my granny reports.

There are few other artifacts of his in the faux-suede covered binder in which my granny placed her meticulous notes almost three decades ago. His medals have been scattered among family members, and what photographs of him there were have escaped my hands. So I can only try to know this man by reading a bit more of his account of the gas attack. My entire relationship seems to hang on this one day, this one page in his own hand. I read that just before the bombardment started – the moment where he'd defend "King and country" and almost give his life for it – he was having "a cup of tea, a slice of bread, cheese, and Tickler's jam," as it was 5 PM.

What in the world was Tickler's jam? It turns out that it was a typical First World War ration – Tickler's brand of jam made from apples and plums. The jam apparently even had its own wartime song, according to several postings on the Internet: "One pint pot, sent from Blighty, / in ten ton lots every night. / When I'm asleep, I am dreaming, / I am eating Tommy Tickler's jam."

There's something exceedingly powerful about that picture of my French-Canadian Grandfather St-Onge, in the trenches at the end of a day with his stalwart colleagues, likely wet, cold, and tired, perhaps even a bit ill, eating a modest English meal while singing an English jam song just before one of the key battles of that Great War. It brings his memory, and his reality, into my heart and wedges it there permanently. A grandparent I never met, yet I feel I know, in a sort of sensory fusion, a treasured soul. In my dreams, I dare to imagine his coming to my rescue during my troubles, had he been alive. I believe he would have. He was brave enough, and caring enough. It's my modest fantasy, my homemade legend. I love to tell it to myself.

The only other document in my possession that I consider to be his own is a copy of that attestation paper for the Canadian Overseas Expeditionary Force. He enlisted on 26 September 1914, less than two months after the declaration of war and five days after he turned twenty-five – and he's marked an "x" for Roman Catholic. The document is signed in Valcartier nineteen days prior to the formation of the 22nd Regiment, the famous "Van Doos." The numbers elude me – 19, 22, 25 – but my attention is drawn passionately to one thing. For whatever possessed him that day – be it nervousness, enthusiasm, or inattention – he's filled in his own name incorrectly as Joseph Henry Leo St-Onge. The witness's hand crosses out "Henry" neatly and writes in "Johnny" above it. It's a precious thought, my grandfather immortalizing his minor error in a public record like that. And changing his name back and forth like I've done too. For whether he was really Johnny Leo rather than Henry Leo, he'd apparently stopped being Jean Léo by then.

I worry too much myself about making mistakes on important paperwork. I've always assumed that my excessive stress about it, often bordering on compulsion, stems from my chronic anxiety. It's the enduring symptom – the victim stigma – that I struggle hardest to shake. But maybe it's not that at all. Maybe small slips of attention are a family trait. Maybe it's possible to be the sort of person who makes errors on the minor stuff, and still be courageous when it comes to what's really critical. So he becomes my hero here, again and again, my inspiration. A voice that's no less potent for being imagined, and that says what I need to hear more than anything: "You're doing fine."

LIFE IN THE MUD

My granny further notes the following in her memoirs, as a near-oversight: "Incidentally, before my marriage, I had become a Catholic, compulsory in those days if I wished to marry Leo." She adds, "Mixed marriages were taboo! I remember going to the pastor of our Anglican church to ask if he would marry us, but the answer was a flat, 'No!' I received the same answer from a Catholic priest in the neighbourhood, so the only thing to do was to convert to Catholicism … At our wedding ceremony, the little Catholic Church in Willesden was filled with family and friends, all Protestant … At the back of the church was the mother of the boy everyone thought I would marry. Such is destiny."

More so-called "incidental" changes stemmed from the typical choices offered to a military commander's family, such as locations for settlement. Offered a life in India, Afghanistan, or Canada, they chose

Canada. It wasn't because of any wonderful fantasy my granny had of life here, which she clearly didn't hold, but because the doctors prescribed cooler air for a gas attack survivor. And so it was that my granny gave up what she describes as follows: "I, as the wife of an officer and being European, would have had a very easy life there, probably in Rawal Pindi or some such place, with plenty of servants and social activities."

Instead, she found herself in Charny, Quebec, then in Edmonston, New Brunswick, for a few years, and back again deep in «la campagne» in Quebec. Her house in Charny was set off from the road by a field of mud, with a wood stove for limited heat – seriously threatening the wellness of the baby grand piano – and a backyard overlooking the cemetery where she'd bury an infant whose tiny grave she could see each time she washed her own dishes. Blaming the cold, the lack of qualified help – midwives, doctors – and low sanitation, she'd remain bitter as she raised five more children virtually as a single parent in this new land. In a rare betrayal of emotion, her memoirs state frankly: "For years, the phrase «Prends mari, prends pays» [Take a husband, take a country] was to remind me of the irreversible step I had taken."

She was surely an oddity in her tidy blazers and a spoken French suited to the social set of a London evening rather than the life of common folk in rural Quebec in the 1920s, '30s, and '40s. She admits that she struggled to communicate with her francophone mother-in-law, "with a little sign language and a word here and there, but my French conversation at the time was very limited." In another of her famous understatements, she adds, "I became quite a novelty among the people we met, as English war brides were not common in Quebec at the time."

Like so many war brides, in fact, she'd left home and family for a husband who was away more days than he was home. Laying down railway throughout Quebec, he laboured for forty-two years – interrupted only by his military service – until he'd risen to the position of Superintendent of Terminals by 1950. She tried a few risky journeys back to England by boat, but more than once a tiny uncle was nearly lost to disease at sea, so there developed in my grandfather a strong attitude against her undertaking such travels.

Stuck in Canada, she tried to cheer up by surrounding herself with proper young women, starting Girl Guide companies in New Brunswick and Quebec, the first ones there. Here were girls in uniforms with well-organized goals and hierarchies, her past dramatized in her present. So it was that her British world was transposed as well as it could be to this "backwards backwoods" place as she called it. And this obsession with systems, regularity, processes, and sameness would give her the only local interest she ever really had, the Dionne quintuplets,* the perfect daughters she'd always dreamt of. "The Quints" meant so much to her throughout her life that there's a newspaper clipping about them from the *Montreal Star*, dated 28 May 1979, tucked away safely inside the pages of her precious memoir.

For his part, my Grandfather St-Onge was apparently a courageous and passionate man. His obituary states that he had a "great interest in young people" and that in 1926 he founded the first-ever French Canadian Scouts (the 1st CNR Troop). To his dying day, he remained a member of the Army, Navy, and Air Force Veterans and of the Quebec reserves of the Royal Canadian Signal Corps. In the course of his life, he received not only the Military Cross but also the Military Medal and the Mons Star Medal – and he'd had commissions as a second lieutenant, then as a lieutenant, and then as a captain. He was buried in St Patrick's Cemetery in a tiny family plot that overlooks the river as it narrows, beside a tree that was just a sapling in 1953. Four decades earlier on 22 April 1915, exhausted from battle, he'd fallen asleep for a few hours on a stretcher, covering himself with "the blankets of the dead," until he felt a "padre" grasping his right arm and reading out his regimental number and name. But this time, he was really dead.

It must be obvious by now that I'm sad I never got to meet him. Other than his two documents in my possession, all I know of him is public record, hearsay. He first comes to notice in the press as a second lieutenant in the Rifle Brigade in the *London Gazette* of November 1917,

---

* Five French-Canadian girls born in Ontario in 1934 (around the time of Granny's five surviving sons), they were the first surviving quints in the world and were raised as public curiosities through government control over the family's life.

and by April 1918, he's already being cited for bravery: "For conspicuous gallantry and devotion to duty when in charge of a forward signaling party. He advanced with the leading waves and quickly established communication. As a result of his energy and complete disregard of danger, communication was maintained throughout the operations."

Lingering gossip among family members, though, reveals that my Grandfather St-Onge found his wife emotionally remote and that he spent his retirement on the borderlands of intolerable stress. By then my granny had constructed a near-perfect English life for herself in Quebec, in the respectable city home where a family of their standing was expected to live. And in her husband's constant absence, she had remade herself as entirely English, quite uncompromising to the provincial setting. She chose only English neighbours for tea (not Scottish or Irish, goodness no), and she brought much of her ancestral home with her to Canada in slow instalments, including her unmarried brother and widowed father.

Before long, there were paintings of the Thames in the living room, crocheted doilies on every surface, and dark wood panels rounding off dark tapestries and furniture. English was the language of the household and the language of «ses garçons» [his "boys"], from whom my grandfather apparently grew increasingly distant. Then, perhaps dreaming of the open road again – the hills of Mexico, the beaches of France, or the rail lines of the Saguenay – he slipped into sadder spaces where he became vulnerable to "a brief illness," as his obituary states, and succumbed on the operating table.

Granny dealt with it "remarkably well," as they say, stiff upper lip and all, looking relatively unaffected, by all accounts. And she summarily unconverted from Catholicism back to Protestantism. A basic flip-flop. It was a war of culture on a miniature scale, where the French identity of that home eventually surrendered to the English one over the course of almost forty years of marriage, even in the heart of a francophone city. And even though the defender was a military man with the highest honours and proven bravado, he was powerless to stop it. English had trumped French in that household, silencing alternate tongues and views slowly, and then finally.

Definitions

I am cut vertically:
right brain for symbols and early language;
left brain for complex language and writing.

I am cut horizontally:
top half links sensations to realizations;
bottom half mutes, subdues, attenuates.

I am cut psychologically:
an exteriorized self-sufficient intellectual self;
an interiorized emotional over-dependent self.

I am cut linguistically:
a mother tongue for the little girl I was;
another tongue for the woman I became.

I am cut socioculturally:
first two decades for the home soul of long ancestry;
next three decades for the nomadic, distant journeyer.

Theory is a sharp knife.
Read and learn enough,
and you will feel
like you are cut up
into minute pieces.

But the violence
is only apparent,
and a definition
is as good a place
to hide as any.

11

BATTLE LINES

S'ES PLAINES

On 13 September 1759, a pivotal battle in the Seven Years' War is fought on Abraham Martin's farm, in the heart of the new settlement, Quebec. British forces come stealthily up the river in the dark of night and dare to climb what is now Côte Gilmour – a rock face with a near-negative angle, an inconceivable feat. Local French forces are prepared for an attack, but not for tactical acrobatics from that foreboding place. The French general, Louis-Joseph, Marquis de Montcalm, awakens to the news, rushes to the front lines, and deploys cutting-edge manoeuvres. But the British general, James Wolfe, already has troops well into position by then, a horseshoe sweep of the entire plain. They fight.

Wolfe dies that very day, hit by three separate French musket balls – in the arm, shoulder, and chest. His last words are ostensibly, "What, do they run already? Then God be praised. I die contentedly." From that day he will be immortalized in countless English Enlightenment paintings that show him looking like Jesus in a classic lamentation scene. He will be depicted breathing his heroic last gasps on the battlefield, surrounded by various allies and officers, his doctor, and "noble savages" – elevated beyond the ranks of ordinary men. His body will be returned to England to be buried in the family vault at Greenwich. Its location will, within the next century, mark the new centre of "universal" space and time.

For his part, Montcalm is hit by a British musket ball in the stomach and dies at a field hospital by midnight of that very day. His last words were reported as «Tant mieux. Je ne verrai pas les anglais à Québec» [I am happy I shall not live to see the English in Quebec], but the phrase will come to be engraved in English-language historical resources as the far less defiant "I am happy I shall not live to see the surrender of Quebec." During his final hours, aware of his impending death and of the gravity of his defeat, he apparently asks to be buried unpretentiously – to be thrown into a cavity in the earth formed by one of the bombshells, folded into the land around him. But his lifeless body will be taken by the Ursulines to their small chapel, according to his death certificate, to be kept quietly for some 250 years and remembered as that of a solitary soul who fought with courage and faith. It will be the start of another millennia, 2001, before Montcalm is honoured ceremoniously, placed in a mausoleum at the cemetery of the Hôpital Général de Quebec. Here, his body will become the only memorial in the entire world to the Seven Years' War.

Ultimately, the (in)famous "Battle of the Plains of Abraham" – that decisive battle for Quebec in which French surrenders to English, changing the history of not only Canada but of France, England, and the United States – will last only fifteen minutes from start to finish. Fifteen minutes. In the time it takes to run the smallest errand, the battle will become one of the greatest military victories or losses in western history, depending on which political world one inhabits. It is a true story that, like my own, seems stranger than fiction. Trauma, as they say, makes as much as it breaks.

I won't venture further into ironic symbolism about how fifteen minutes can change a life. Or how the forced surrender of a linguistic identity can take so short a time, or even less, as tragedy freezes into psychic fields no one dares to climb. I know it all too well. But what happened there, on that day, actually can't be compared in the least to what happened to me – or to any individual trauma of any kind. It can't be compared to anything other than massive, communal traumas affecting entire traditions and their futures, battles in history where the fate of millions and millions of people hangs on an outcome that unfolds in the time it takes to have a shower or check email. Fortune can be harsh.

That's how this particular event – «la bataille s'es Plaines» – has been registered in the collective psyche, firm and immovable. And that's why even from a distance, ensconced in English Canada as I have been and still am, I seethe with personal rage – my own little impotent cauldron – when some new group in "English Canada" plans to re-enact that day as a tourist attraction. It's a nasty possibility that rears its horrible, hateful head every few years or so. That's when the electric current between my language selves completely reverses, a shift not unlike the bizarre physics of Magnetic Hill. Or is it metaphysics? For the battle is a profound wound to my core self, above and beyond my affinity for English.

Irreconcilable, you say? Incoherent? No, just messy. Not unlike any complicated personal identity, I'm an unsettled flux of loyalties. I embrace my English intellect, my escape. But I hold dearly to my French soul, too. And that everyday battle, just like that fateful struggle in 1759, haunts me. The grass itself, stretching from the Saint-Laurent to Grande Allée, and from the edge of town to its heart, holds meaning I can't even find adjectives for. As if its worth is experienced pre-language, unsayable. As if the winding roads that lead from La Côte Gilmour to Le Musée de Quebec and circle back towards La Citadelle comprised a self-contained world, a universe, a time capsule. To imagine it bathed in blood again (fake or otherwise), as the site of loss and injury, grates on me mercilessly – as it must on everyone who lives here, regardless of their position on the "separation" spectrum.* Then again, maybe I'm buried here too, folded into the earth. For here is a place where cultural birth meets cultural death.

That's why inside Quebec and also within French Canada – that diaspora from l'Acadie to Saint-Boniface – the plans for re-enacting that battle represent the complete disconnect that "the rest of Canada" has towards the province and the nation's «francophonie.» The aggressive coldness with which such plans, as sordid as they are foolish, are put forward demonstrates absent empathy brewed with callous insensitiv-

---

* A reference to the fact that the residents of the province of Quebec hold a variety of opinions about whether the province should separate politically from the rest of Canada.

ity – the typical aloofness of the conqueror. And that's precisely how it's read and heard symbolically. Those of us who originate in Quebec, who are directly implicated in its cultural and spiritual inheritance, infinitely picture «les Plaines» bathed in sunshine, fields beautifully trimmed, and iron lampposts polished, its timeless guardians left to whisper through the trees. It's a monument, a resplendent memorial to collective meaning, that enduring myth of life.

I capture special memories here in time-lapse photography. Countless groundskeepers go about their day, their chores changing with the seasons. New flower pots yield to shovels and snow-blowers, then back to lawnmowers again. In warm weather, families have picnics, play «pétanque» [a kind of croquet], have a quick ball game, or let their dogs run loose. In cold weather, cross-country skiers navigate its covered fields and impassable roads, break for wine and conversation. In daylight, tourists flock, snapping up moments (as if that were possible). In darkness, the wind blows up from the river, carries its faint but certain promise across the pregnant landscape. At special times, festival crowds gather over beer and music, mingling across lifespans of eighty years or more, sharing blankets with neighbours. At other times, its wide canvas waits.

And that's why I've gone «s'es Plaines» through every decade of my life. There was a day there I treasure among my favourites when, aged six or seven, I went with neighbours for a picnic of cucumber and fennel sandwiches on a broad blanket, just like storybook characters. There were evenings I made my way there with lovers, parking behind the Musée* for privacy, or sitting on the grass and looking out romantically at the Saint-Laurent. I went with groups for drinking parties at strategic locations where there was the least chance of being discovered. And I went alone, especially on visits home in adulthood, to compass my journey, take my own pulse. It was, and continues to be, the perfect instinct to spend time «s'es Plaines.»

Spring 1242: Flash further back as Sa Majesté Louis IX, Saint-Louis, sworn king of France since the age of twelve, takes on the invading king

---

* The Musée National des Beaux-Arts du Québec, located at the northwest end of the Plains of Abraham.

of England, Henry III, enthroned since the age of nine, who breaks the negotiated truce of 1238 to support his mother's new husband in France, Hugues de Lusignan. An unsuccessful exchange of letters, mere words, leaves a long-lasting feudal battle unresolved within the complicated context of the Albigensian crusades. Tens of thousands of soldiers on either side engage one another in two major encounters along the west-central coast of France.

The first phase takes place in April near the bridge over the Charentes at Taillebourg, pitting fifty thousand French troops loyal to Louis IX against thirty thousand English-French rebels led by Henry III and dissenting French nobles aligned to de Lusignan. It brings about the rapid retreat of the rebels. The second phase, in July, involves a siege just outside the walls of Saintes, the capital of the large stretch of land known as Saintonge, an expansive naval and agricultural centre comprising most of the modern region of La Charente-Maritime, including Brouage, from which Samuel de Champlain will originate and make his way to Quebec in 1608. Casualities over forty-eight hours – from 22 to 23 July 1242 – are relatively light as many of the rebels' French allies flee in the face of sure defeat, and Henry III retreats to Bordeaux.

The French loyalists easily take the victory, and Louis IX grants a quick peace agreement without further reprisals on 24 July 1242 – the day that ends La Guerre de Saintonge, the Saintonge War. How curious it is to see my family name like this, under the proud banner of the old French regime, its name synonymous with an ancient land that once comprised a province, and before that, a nation of its own – one rendered in historical records and folklore as «L'Ancienne province de la Saintonge» and «La Saintonge Romane.» A place that encompasses the geographic right alongside the mythical in its self-descriptions: «La Saintonge Maritime,» «La Saintonge du Nord,» «La Saintonge Centrale,» «La Saintonge Boisée,» «La Haute Saintonge,» and «La Saintonge Girondine.» It's especially strange to think that this is actually the half of the family I'd come to think of as my English side. There's that messiness one more time.

Then again, both Henry III and Louis IX were at least bilingual. Most likely, in fact, each was trilingual, or quadrilingual, or even more versatile linguistically. It seems that language was primarily an instrument of communication back then, not the main marker of identity as it is so often today. But how did that happen over the centuries, to such an extent that I'd lose track of my heritage inside a language not primarily its own? And then I'd suffer enough in one language to want to lose myself inside another? How curious this history of language, thought, and humankind.

COMME UN MAUDIT FOU

By the time I was a few years into my school career, I had heard my Granny St-Onge regularly deliver a patently lucid conclusion to our family's language history as she saw it: most of her grandchildren didn't sufficiently appreciate their English (British) heritage, settled as they were into the local surroundings. This primary realization was categorized detachedly along with so many other irritants in her life, like the mud around the home in Charny over which she'd first hauled her baby grand piano, the impossibility of getting a proper English suit or a good cup of tea in this town, and the overly informal tone of clerical and retail staff in their dealings with her. So she dug in her pumps even deeper, spending her time with the only daughter-in-law she could relate to, the British nurse who actually sent her children to visit "the relatives abroad," and taking the occasional trip to visit her cousin in Australia.

But for the greater part of each ordinary day, my granny stayed put in her upper middle-class home in a prestigious, older neighbourhood in Quebec. It was nestled on a tree-lined street only a ten minute walk away from «les Plaines,» and quite literally around the corner from where a huge sign now greets visitors with premature assurance, «Bienvenue à la Capitale Nationale.» Comfortably installed there, my granny spent her days chatting in an unblemished, undiminished British accent with neighbours across the lilac trees that bounded the southern edge of her home. They were an English couple who shared her critical views on the lack of refinement in this colonial environment and her great interest in following even the most minor events in the life of the British royal family. And so, she became perfectly atemporal and aspatial – detached and encompassed in a construction and performance of herself that to her last day remained entirely unconnected to her cultural surroundings.

Just like my home province, then, my family became the frothing edge of a linguistic tidal wave, the steady advance of a language that would become the single-stroke engine of the world, English, and its "one world" view so vehemently opposed to the eclectic pulse of local hearts. Meanwhile, I gained skill in that instrument of domination to secure my own survival, buying my way into new opportunities.

And so, as in that old English idiom, my world became a weaving of tangled webs. For quite unlike his own father's primary tongue (French), my father's primary tongue (English) was effaced over the years, as he worked in French each day «comme un maudit fou» [like a damned madman], as he said; he became a fan of Quebec folk music – loving, irreconcilably, Gilles Vigneault, an avowed separatist; and my mother's unrelenting vibrancy easily dominated his half-hearted participation in our home life.

Over the course of my childhood, then, our household became functionally francophone, so that even dinner conversations with my father, infrequent though they were, were held in French. But in my choosing English early on and hanging onto it for the long haul, when even my father had begun to abandon it, I'd eventually erode almost all that was French inside me except the actual words. It was a flip-flop «à la Granny St-Onge» executed one slow-motion step at a time over a period of twenty years. I became an untreatable virus that gnawed at the fabric of our family life from the inside, threatening the harmony that my mother's rule inspired and required.

And as I reflect on how the pulling and tugging of language and culture played out in the small environment of Granny's home, I can't help but connect what happened there to the precise fear that Québécois harboured on that day in 1976 when they were driven to try to change the tide of things by electing a government that put at the top of the agenda the preservation of the French language and its culture.

They were drawing a line in the sand. Not just on the land, but in the hearts and minds of the people. Blocking the steady advance of Global English that could be seen at every mall, on every store sign, and in a great many bilingual households just like my grandfather's, where the mother's tongue was English rather than French. Resisting the assumption that English would triumph here as it threatened to everywhere else, Québécois continued to perform their role as holdouts against imperialism, as they had for hundreds of years.

MOTHERS RULE

I believe the family battle over bilingualism was even more convoluted than that, though, because the parent attached to each language seemed to matter. My "evidence" – a fair-sized collection of family members, friends, and neighbours – showed that francophone mothers married to anglophone fathers generally tended to raise fluent bilinguals who were French dominant, linguistically and culturally. But if you reversed the gender, so that the mother was English and the father was French, the usual result was a child who wasn't as strong in French and wasn't as attached to Quebec – one who was ready to leave the region for the first job opportunity or lover.

It wasn't hard science or anything but a solidifying conviction that, in time, the father would become subjugated. Was it a testament to the matriarchy that underpins French-Canadian culture? Or was I just day-dreaming about women finding their power somehow, somewhere? Who knows. I'm becoming increasingly comfortable these days with how trauma scrambles reality and fantasy like that. Then again, maybe there is something to this pseudo-scientific logic. After all, my granny single-handedly gave the aristocratic French Saint-Onge lineage a decidedly English turn. That's a huge crank of the drawbridge – just like that. Working within a modest space between four walls, she managed to «anglifier» the next generations to such an extent that three of her five sons would eventually leave Quebec, and many of her grand-children now barely speak French. Maybe that's why it's considered a mother tongue, a mother's tongue. Mothers own it.

In this light, I'm forced to admit how much energy I put into resisting the typical outcomes in my cultural matrix, as I managed my psychological departure against this great social tide of matriarchy versus patriarchy that filled, and emptied, my known world. All other things being equal – the distribution of tongues between my parents, and the French of my perpetrators – maybe I wouldn't have felt as compelled to move out of province if my early life had played out in "English Canada" instead. Maybe the mother tongue culture and the self are so inseparable that you can't fracture one without risking the other.

Because the plain truth, likely obvious by now, is that I wasn't the only victim of the troubles. How could I have been? After all, it was engineered by a family elder and his confederates who, understandably, found many that fit their perfect body type among a genetically related group of small females. True, due to the placement of my father's store and my mother's work there for years, I was situated in the problem zone – one square city block – more than others. I suppose that's how habits grew so that things kept up even after I'd migrated to the suburbs. But other victims there most certainly were.

Of course, I have no right to break their silence, only my own. More than I'm able to describe, I respect the strength it takes for each one of them to craft her own version of survival. Yet a stark linguistic fact pierces my distress – dries my eyes and puts me back on the battle lines. Unilingual French survivors among us (two at least) have dossiers that use the difficult medical language of chronic severe depression, critical anorexia, and acute psychosis. Bilingual survivors (three at least, not counting myself) moved away from the Quebec City area in their early twenties, and English is in place of most of that medical language.

With French alone, it seems that there was nowhere to *run!* to in the mind, and nowhere to *hide!* – precious, formative instructions of the inner voice during crises. Every word, every cultural sign, served as a reminder of pain and betrayal, a confusion of what did and didn't occur, a brain scramble that wore on the soul like a slow drip of salt water. Mother tongue and self were left alone for too long, too often. The sexual trauma, in tragic irony, was played out in full in the metaphor.

With only that single paradigm of identity available, the technical discourse of illness – in another piercing irony – became an inadvertent, malicious second tongue. Bilingual, there was a doorway. Bilingual, there was a means to get away in thought and life. Respite and resilience. No more need to be reminded, confused, shamed, worn down with every word and sign. Our horizons of meaning were wide open.

Tragically, I think back to social gatherings where more than one of us girls of the clan were present, and how we shared (and yet did not share) our hideous truth – a common horror we kept unspoken, mutely trading an odd feeling of something sad, something missing, something wrong. Surely we each could have used a real friend to supplement our kindly imaginary ones. This is the single thought by which I'm brought to the limits of my ability to control my sorrow and my anger. And now to think – though we couldn't know it – that *semiotics* were the antidote, the cure.

But we hadn't discovered it then. We knew only what we knew, and we spoke only what we spoke – small, shy girls, charming for our silence and polite compliance. It's as if we mingled in French at those countless events without any hint that while we'd all been exposed to the same disease – acute sexual deviance – only some of us had been, quite accidentally, innoculated. Sent to English school by our ancestrally French mothers, divergently acculturated. And that the mere administration of an alternative language education would cast us in completely variant lives on either side of a deep, dark linguistic border. Monolinguals on one side, as psychologically more vulnerable, deeply encultured locals. And bilinguals on the other side, as psychologically more immune, sufficiently de-cultured exiles. As much as we were crafted "in the rough" by others then, it seems our fates were really in the hands of our tongues.

BODY COUNT

In a recent phone call, my mother shared her belief that while sexual abuse was my trauma, hers was English itself because of how she felt «d'm'êt' marié dans c't'a famille-là» [to have married into that family], and because it introduced such a schism between her and me. «On en a perdu bin des bouts» [We've lost many threads], as she puts it. There's irony in her analysis of which family was the most dangerous one to marry into. Then again, we're all too familiar with the idioms of hindsight.

The truth is, though, that language and trauma are often uttered in the same sentence these days when she and I talk: «C'pas moé qu'y a choisi d'aller à l'école en anglais, t'sais? C'est toé qui m'a mis là.» [I'm not the one who chose to go to English school, you know. You put me there.] I make myself sound innocent of the charge of cultural abandonment, and of my self-inflicted cultural attrition. But I did plenty to push myself along and away. I appropriated and used my agency to cut the hold of language through culture, and vice versa. And when I did, I predictably experienced the grief and disorientation that accompanies mother tongue losses: I became hooked on school, hid my successes in my new tongue, packed away memories bit by bit. I slowly shifted my values and worldviews, distanced myself progressively, and eventually acquired outsider status. I othered myself.

It's worth taking a minute to see how the body count in this linguistic battle played out over the years. Following my matrilineal line through three generations, there were five siblings (four females, one male), all of whom married francophones except for my mother, who married my bilingual father. Between them they had fourteen children. And while some of my cousins have moved around because of employment, all but two (myself and one other) speak French at home with their own families, wherever they live. On this side, I believe there are twenty-three living grandchildren at present: fifteen francophones, six bilinguals, and two anglophones. Following my patrilineal line through the same period, there were five siblings (five males), three of whom married anglophones, and two (my father and one other) who married francophones. Between them, they had thirteen children. Eight live out of province and speak English at home, while five have stayed and speak French with their own families. On this side, I believe there are twenty-two living grandchildren at present: four francophones, two bilinguals, and sixteen anglophones.

A total of forty-five young people have issued from the times I'm describing – the tossing winds of English and French in Quebec in the 1950s and 1960s – and the final numbers show them almost equally divided as a collective linguistic outcome, a linguistic estate: nineteen francophones to eighteen anglophones – with eight straddling the bilingual border, cultural emissaries within the family about what goes on here and there, with one or the other, translating not just messages but worldviews.

Of course, I can't tell you that my family is definitively representative. This is not a controlled experiment yielding valid, reliable, repeatable quantitative data. In fact, this life of ours has been a completely uncontrolled experiment. But I can't think of why we wouldn't be at least somewhat typical of the larger whole. The forces that pushed and pulled us, from within and without, in those decades of the triumphant merger of church, language, and society, affected the entire population of Quebec.

In other words, I don't think I'm special in the least, and my trauma is neither exceptional nor unique. It doesn't define or distinguish me in any disproportionate way. Furthermore, my extended family in itself has nothing to differentiate it socio-economically, politically, or intellectually from any other. We were (and are) an ordinary clan at an ordinary point in history, and what happened to the lot of us was, in fact, quite "normal" too. The human race is actually not racing at all. Rather, it's walking, meandering its way on a winding path between pathology and normalcy, crime and mercy, bad and good.

What I *am* stating is that this is how it turned out for us in the end. After all that cultural carnage, the tug of war between tongues and lifeways, the whirlwind of swords working their way into fragile bits of flesh, and the countless toxic secrets passed through the battle lines, this is how English and French ended up: dead even.

Thankful

If I understand the research correctly,
I should be thankful for the fact that
no one who laid a hand or body part
upon me was particularly sadistic:
the prognosis for that is far poorer.

I should also be indebted that another
language, English, offered its variant
spaces, faces, words, views and loves –
opened up schemas and attachments by
which there was respite and possibility.

And I should be thankful I can hold on
to a sense of self even when I am apart,
away, depersonalized – and that I grew up
among some spiritual women from whom
I learned a flexible perception of reality.

I am.

12

BECOMING OTHER

MY LITTLE PROJECT

Eerily, perhaps, I remember my first formal step on the linguistic battle-field, my first gesture in the process of "self-othering," as a deliberate and conscious act. One morning, almost fifty years ago, I woke up feeling a horribly familiar bodily and spiritual disorientation. I looked in the mirror and was conscious of saying to myself that day, "That's okay. I'll just learn this other language and be better at it than anyone." And from that day forward, at age five, I came home every night from my English Catholic school with a plan to which I adhered religiously, devotedly. I first changed out of my school uniform into a house dress, pants not allowed. Then, while my mother was busy cooking dinner, I snuck over to the linen closet to remove the precious object that my mother kept there, hidden between the towels. I had to be quick and quiet. My mother knew the sound of the closet, and she'd call me to help out in the kitchen if she heard it.

The treasure was an English dictionary, sort of flesh-coloured with two green-gold horizontal pin stripes on the cover – Gage, I think. I'd be in graduate school studying bilingualism before I'd understand the sheer symbolism of my mother, francophone to her core, hiding the English dictionary, resisting in small ways the anglicization of her children. Back then, I knew nothing of domestic, political, or linguistic incongruities, only of those weird mornings: the physical sensation, sore throats, nightmares, and fogginess of a morning-after feeling. It was something unnamed that propelled me into English. I knew only my own promise to myself to "learn five new words each day." That's how I inadvertently became the perfect example, for my own particular reasons, of the key role that personality, attitude, values, and motivation play in learning language. It makes all the difference in the world if you assign it a chance for a variant identity, one that taps into entirely new opportunities.

I began on page 1, and like a marathon runner determined to cross the country, I did not miss a day until I reached the end of the word list, some two years later, perhaps. I grabbed the book ever so quietly and went into my room, leaning gently against my door but not closing it completely – too noisy. Sometimes, I even took the book into the washroom. I read each word thoroughly, and I read the definitions carefully. I covered the words and ran the spelling through my head. I tried tricks to remember the order of the letters and made an effort to think of what other words I'd learned that each one reminded me of.

Then, as quietly as I'd brought it out, I returned it to the laundry closet, placing it perfectly between the towels. Alignment is everything if you don't want to be found out. I closed the door silently, waiting for a moment when pots and pans were clanging, cloaking my evil-doings. And as I stirred soup and set the table a few minutes later, I went over the words in my mind.

Of course, as we prepared supper together, my mother wanted to talk about my day and hers, like mothers and daughters around the world. But in her asking these questions, I felt pestered, hounded, invaded. I was straining so hard to remember the words, reviewing them over and over in my head, and she was interrupting the thinking process with her French «bavardage» [chatting]. I tried to lose her conversations, answered her abruptly, vaguely.

Our separateness grew, as did her sadness. But I didn't care much, my English mindset at the helm, because all I could think of was that there was no point in gaining five words and losing five. It was already a difficult job to master this language, and I had words to learn and places to go. She'd just have to be ignored for the "greater good," as I saw it. Thus I became fluent in English but increasingly absent in French.

I'm not a political person, or at least I don't think I am. But can someone ever be bilingual and bicultural without becoming a political being – composite, polarized, like this? And have I, in fact, lived a quite political life "incidentally," as my granny was so fond of saying?

A "REAL" QUEBECER

Almost fifty years forward from that project, I was thinking in French again for part of the day. For more than thirty of those years, I'd been hundreds or thousands of miles away, living in the shadows about my heritage. I passed myself off as being loosely from points east and didn't come out of the closet about my heritage for decades at a time. I hid being French.

I put up with distortions of my family name in virtually every community I lived in – seldom thought of it as anything at all, just took it for granted. I spent years being called Mrs Sponge or Mrs Stong, occasionally Mrs Sennon. I feel for immigrants who have trouble recognizing their own names in the mouths of others. With this much trouble with a French name, I can only imagine the distortions that would afflict beautiful names in Russian, Thai, Chinese, Korean, Urdu, and in the thousands of languages on the Canadian landscape today. How easy it is to stop being, or feeling, or sounding like the "real you" when you step away from your native soil.

I made a bold move a few years ago and decided to return to the ancestral spelling of my family name, Saint-Onge. To work against the tide of diminutives. To resist the alien's obligation to accommodate. The pronunciation improved with all of the letters present and accounted for. Maybe names in other languages would also have a better chance left as is. We'd get used to it eventually, especially here in Toronto, where there's more cultural diversity on a city block than in entire towns west or east of here.

My ability to teach French, and my identity in my mother tongue, have become a commodity in the current social and economic climate. French language instruction is becoming the favoured option of newcomers where I now live. It shouldn't surprise anyone: most children from overseas are already bilingual or trilingual, for there are few countries in the world with a monolithic tongue. So parents reach an uncomplicated conclusion. What's one more language? Better options for the future.

Immigrant families typically approach French without any of the political baggage around official bilingualism that prevails in the national discourse – only enthusiasm and determination. In turn, young allophones – who speak neither French nor English at home – become some of the most successful students. Why not? By the time they reach school age, they already have metalinguistic skills to rival the most dedicated adult learners, and not a speck of embarrassment about taking risks in the new tongue. It's dazzling to witness. And their zeal is precisely how French has become my "golden ticket" in Ontario, opening doors and opportunities by which I've been able to support my three children.

There's an interesting twist in that English was seen as an encroaching cultural threat on Quebec in the days I buried my head in that English dictionary, yet as I bury myself in the French dictionary these days, French is seen as a safe, profitable, denatured, economic asset. Multilingualism thrives right alongside multiculturalism in Ontario – and French just rides the wave. There isn't a great «rapprochement» or anything like that, beckoning people into sympathetic postures in regards to Quebec – and it certainly isn't a manifest embrace of French Canadian culture. It is, like most relations with French Canada outside of French Canada, a lucrative business proposition.

I enter the field as an exception – a "real" Quebecer, they say – typically through interviews where one of the few bilingual teachers already in position is able to vow for my fluency. I join a pool of largely anglophone bilinguals, graduates of provincial immersion programs, valiantly undertaking a teaching task with sometimes limited fluency. I love their courage, far greater than mine, and I really love that they can't catch my mistakes. Within these strange and blurry surroundings, where everything from morning announcements to staff meetings is conducted in English and children respond more often than not in English as well, I'm able to be comfortable in my tongue and to use it – whereas I'd never be able to teach French at a fully French school here, in Quebec, or anywhere else.

QUOI DIRE?

I confess that I did consider it once. I suppose I'd been living in Victoria for so long that I'd forgotten some of my insecurities. I heard that one of the local francophone schools might have an opening soon, and I put together my resume, not such an easy thing to do with three babies. I didn't have an appointment, because it seemed awkward to call ahead and ask for one, so this visit was intended as a kind of recon mission.

I remember being so nervous, rushing around to get breakfast for my kids before it was time to go. In the flurry, I went to reach for a cereal box in one of those self-assembled small pantries from Home Depot, and the entire works tipped over on me. It sent food flying all over the floor, smashing the pretty garage-sale vase on top, so that when the spilled chips, crackers, and Cheerios had settled, I found that a piece of glass had narrowly missed my small son's eye, landing on his shirt. An omen, I thought. My fear coming to find me.

Still, I'm a grownup. I try to listen to my instincts, but not let them rule me either. I improvised a quick change of clothing that wasn't covered in sugary dust and glass splinters, apologized to my sitter for the mess, and headed off to the school to try to meet the principal. It went downhill from there. «Elle n'est pas ici. Voulez-vous lui laisser un message?» [She isn't here. Do you want to leave her a message?] The dreaded question. I took a slip of paper. And that's precisely where I got stuck.

There was my usual worry over the grammar or spelling – a mistake would have been unforgiveable. But even worse was the problem of register, for it's an infinitely more complex matter in French than in English, where an inadvertent pronoun error – «tu» or «vous»? – can reveal unseemly judgments of your relative positionality, your lack of confidence, or your arrogance. What tone was I supposed to take for someone in a formal position, while I was using an informal medium (a "while you were out" slip)? I wanted to sound formal enough to be professional but needed to sound informal enough to be counted as an insider to give myself the hiring edge.

I blocked completely. Had no idea «quoi dire» [what to say]. So I said nothing, waited for the secretary to be overwhelmed with parents, and slipped out, discretely shoving the paper into my purse. I never went back – just got another ESL contract instead. I did something I was really good at that didn't remind me of what I was bad at.

My only other attempt at teaching *in* French was in Manitoba in 1984. Canadian Parents for French had just inaugurated a new program, and I was hired for it. This kindergarten job was certainly challenging for a first-year teacher: teach mornings in English, flip your head at lunch, and teach afternoons in French. There were more than fifty kids in all, with all materials bought, assembled, and prepared by me after individual trips to Saint-Boniface. It was a real labour of love where staff and parents couldn't have been nicer, but I couldn't last. And it was no one's fault.

I was a bit of a celebrity because of my new role and the relatively small size of the town at the time. So one fine fall afternoon, after the children had been dismissed, a board official showed up with a television crew to interview me live for the local news, for some understandable publicity. Lights, camera, action. Ancient triggers clicked alongside the over-sized shutter, reinstalled what I'd come hundreds of miles to forget. I quit. Left town. Tallied it as just another instalment in the lifelong silent management of stigma. Took embarrassment and inconvenience as the customary price to be paid.

DICTIONARIES AGAIN

Willing to give it another try after twenty-five years, I set out to prepare for my new roles in French immersion in 2010 by reading French curriculum materials from Alberta, New Brunswick, and Saskatchewan. I felt far more confident now than I did that first year of teaching. With decades of my beloved career already under my belt, most in language education, ESL, I knew I had plenty of transferable skills to draw from, and a well-seasoned classroom management style. Still, I had to learn how to say key words – like tundra, iceberg, feedback, rubric, graphic organizer, brainstorming – in French because I had no idea what they were. So for hours each day over the summer, and regularly throughout the school year – part of a self-study plan – I brushed up on my technical vocabulary, and still do.

It's a tricky thing, actually, trying to use French immersion materials from other provinces, but in this business you have to get creative about resources. Forget about finding anything you can use in Quebec, other than picture books from second-hand stores or activity books from the dollar stores. The reading that Grade 1s do in Quebec would be hard for our Grade 3s. When it's a second language, not the first, you need grammar and vocabulary pared down. Alberta and New Brunswick produce in-house French immersion materials, but they're expensive, considering the curriculum doesn't match. In Saskatchewan there's a good choice: *fransaskoise* materials for francophones, as well as decent, inexpensive immersion materials with considerable curricular overlap.

After a while, finding proper supplies starts to feel a bit like being inside the Goldilocks story. Curriculum that's too hard, too expensive, and (finally) just right. Yet it still leaves me worried about when those bears are coming back.

The problem – the bears – is my spelling of common words, especially verbs, with the proper gender and number agreement. The exceptions to the rules seem to come out of everywhere, leaving me insecure about knowing even words I think I know for sure. I keep looking over my shoulder, expecting growls and sharp teeth. That's why I'm into dictionaries again. I'm walking in the reverse order this time, though, trying to work my way into French rather than out of it, determinedly engaged in some kind of reappropriation, a re-territorialization.

The children in my French immersion classes are amused that someone who usually speaks French better than anyone else at school, a native of Quebec, runs to a dictionary and makes at least one mistake a day. They're delighted to catch any, as they should be. I give a lot of politically correct speeches about learning being continuous, referencing as a skill for living, and bilingualism inviting confusions. But in fact I'm too weak in written French for my own liking. And I'm reluctant to admit that I've never been to school in French, other than a three-week summer course in statistics before university in 1976, and a sixty-hour course in 1982 at L'École des guides historiques de Quebec, affiliated with Collège de Sainte-Foy, to certify as an elite, licensed tour guide.

The latter bit of additional training was in anticipation of the 1984 visit of «Les Grands voiliers» [tall ships] to Quebec, where the tour trade was expected to spike so that regular guides like me could expect even bigger opportunities for summer work. The interview for that prestigious job took place sometime in 1983. My spoken French was just fine, they said, but I didn't quite have the "look" they were hoping for. This feedback came courtesy of a friend of a friend who'd been offered one of the dozens of positions herself and whose father sat on the interview committee. I looked too English, they had apparently said behind closed doors, not «une vraie québécoise.»

No big surprise there. I was used to faking a French accent to get better tips during my walking and bus tours. Tourists didn't want a guide with such good English, after all. They wanted someone who could explain things and joke around with them, of course, but you had to have the French accent – the perceived authenticity – if you wanted good tips. It was easy enough to do. I'd turn it on at the beginning of the tour and shut it off when I was done. But this committee wasn't fooled. Caught me trying to pass myself off as French.

It seems that I'm still struggling to pass myself off as French. Recently I received an email from the obviously francophone supply teacher who'd replaced me the previous day. She had a French first name, Québécois, and an English last name. She came out exactly on the other side of the bilingual equation from me, I guess, even though on paper she and I would have looked the same in some scientific calculation of a "one-parent-one-language" system. Her email to me in French was far better than any I could have composed without the time to edit carefully. I wondered what she'd thought of my teaching space. Had she found errors in my French?

I looked around the next day, back in my classroom, and the first thing I found was a message I'd pasted onto a shelf of fancy project paper: «Ici, c'est le papier du prof, alors on y touche pas s.v.p.» [Here's the prof's paper, so don't touch it, please.] Of course, I saw it then. The mistake I'd ignored for four weeks, since I made the sign. I had, in patois, forgotten the «ne» particle, as usual. Even trying to be informal as I was, I should have written, «on n'y touche pas.»

I was deeply ashamed, as I am often, that I've never attended French school and never learned to communicate well in writing in my own language. The mistake wasn't huge, and it was easily fixed, but I felt those bears breathing down my neck. For the sorry truth is that I've been paid good money in my life to edit journals, theses, and books in English, but I need a proofreader in French just for a dozen words. Am I, then, a fraud in my mother tongue? A story character posing in this language I call my own, my first, my mother? Am I an interloper here, like Goldilocks?

UN TRÈS GRAND NOM

Beyond the drama around feeling French or not, I admit that I feel profoundly embarrassed as I hear some separatist shadow-figure berating me. It's not a persistent paranoia, just a horrible inner conviction that keeps semi-materializing as a cultural judge and jury. The source is a composite of everyone back home who detests people like me: folks who've abandoned the motherland and betrayed their hereditary trust.

«Ah, ça c'est un très grand nom» [Ah, that's a very big/significant name], a colleague once said to me. The year was 1982, and we had both been working at a poster store in Quebec for a couple of months. She spoke perfect standard French, pure and impeccable: «Tu devrais l'épeler correctement, Saint-Onge et non pas St-Onge. Il y a bien des personnes qui vont chez un avocat pour faire changer leurs noms maintenant. C'est une invention des anglais, la marque des vainqueurs, ce ‹St.› C'est une insulte, après tout. De plus, il n'y a jamais eu de ‹Onge› comme un Jean ou un Pierre. Tu vois?» [You should spell it correctly, as Saint-Onge and not St-Onge. There are many people securing lawyers nowadays to change (the spelling of) their names. It's an invention of the English, the brand of the conquerors, this "St." It's an insult, after all. On top of that, there was never an "Onge" like a Jean or a Pierre. You see?]

What she meant was that *Onge* was never a saint. It's not a proper first name in French, not like Saint-François, Saint-Joseph, Sainte-Cécile, or Sainte-Perpétue, so you can't use it like that. Her point was that it was surely bad enough that the English took away our hereditary way of writing our names – cutting us down from *Saint* to *St* for the sake of expediency in phone books and official records. But in my case, it was even more absurd because my name should have been written as *Saintonge* from the start. My family suffered an additional cleavage, lost its direct link to a grand narrative into which my colleague digressed briefly, subtext beneath subtext, painful digging while we walked into the stock room together.

That business of *Saint* instead of *St* wouldn't get fixed for another decade or so. I don't know the precise day or policy that made it happen. I was, as always, many miles away. But I do remember ordering a new copy of my «Certificat de naissance» for my teacher (re)certification when I moved to Ontario and receiving – to my surprise – from «Le directeur de l'état civil,» Jacques *Saint*-Laurent, on 15 March 2002, the official statement of my name as Kathleen Marie Cécile Saint-Onge. Even my father, long dead, had been retroactively renamed: Paul Saint-Onge.

We were a long way from my «Certificat de Baptême» issued by L'Église Très Saint-Sacrement de Québec on 17 November 1957, when only the church had been able to hang on to its *Saint*, and my father and I were both just St-Onge. From a few papers had come some powerful proofs of the move towards my colleague's predictions – and her politics. Reclaiming names from the conqueror, as she'd put it. I hadn't asked for it or expected it. It was just changed automatically on my behalf, executed as a simple correction of a 250-year-old error. By the new millennium, it seems the tables had turned in Quebec.

But unlike the case for human beings such as my father, it was apparently too late for dead streets. My childhood street, St-Cyrille, bypassed the revision entirely and went straight to René Levèsque Boulevard. Yet it wasn't too late to fix millions of maps and street signs, to rectify every name from the Fleuve Saint-Laurent to Sainte-Foy – and from Sainte-Brigitte-de-Laval to Saint-Gabriel-de-Valcartier.

To be honest, I don't mind so much about the split into *Saint* and *Onge*. Being canonized to honour a bureaucratic vision of tidy rows and columns, a Cartesian cross. I wouldn't expect the powers that prevailed because of «la conquête anglaise» to recognize my name's claim to ancestral land. It's par for the course for conquerors, after all – practical imperialism. What I find harder to grasp is that with the current retrofit of heritage, its reappropriation, the powers that prevail in modern Quebec didn't take my name right back to what it was supposed to be, grammatically and logically: *Saintonge*. Surely that would make sense to those who know well that there was never a personal name *Onge*. Why not change it all the way? Would I need «un avocat» for that? Or would that make it (me) too French – a name not sufficiently «québé-cois» – too «français»?

Because there isn't any question that this is another strong wind that blows through Quebec: the need to be francophone on its own terms – not on anyone else's. There's no desire to be reassimilated into a French identity. No sense of needing a mother again, if or when independence is achieved. And there's that strange quandary I'm in again: not French enough, and yet too French. It's tough being Goldilocks.

EL PATOIS

At any rate, this name business was the focus of my colleague's argument one afternoon, as we tidied up the displays on the floor and brought out the big ladder to dust and change the highest prints hanging on the back wall. («Ah, non. Moi, je ne mets pas un seul pied sur cette échelle. Ce n'est pas du tout mon obligation. De plus, c'est toi qui est la gérante. En fait, on devrait former une union ici.» [Ah, no. I am not putting a single foot on that ladder. It is not at all a job requirement. Besides, you're the store manager. In fact, we should all form a union here.]) I climbed up slowly, fuming as I went but saying nothing back.

The truth was that I'd been abbreviating my name all of my life, as all of my (English) family had been doing for generations. Inadvertently, we'd accepted without protest the loss of a few letters, the too-quick hyphen, the heritage interrupted. Turned out, there was no need for me to change anything at all if I wanted to reclaim my "unbranded" name, except for the minor matter of my choice to think, live, breathe, and just *be* in English. «Pourquoi ton chum est un anglais?» [Why is your boyfriend an Englishman?] And so on. I can't say those were my favourite shifts at the mall that summer.

So I give my imaginary linguistic accuser – my separatist shadow-figure – *her* voice. But am I really the «personne sans éducation» she accuses me of being, despite several university degrees (with honours), including one in linguistics and a post-graduate degree in education? Am I really what she calls me, a traitor to my heritage? A loser of language? One who's gone over to the English side? It's true that I find myself checking dictionaries, unsure if something is French or not. But I realize, as I explore the idioms and expressions etched in my mind, that not just my outlook but even my French is all wrong by current Quebec standards. Her French diction is textbook perfect, of course, a testament to the best language programs and policies. Yet it's not authentic to the ancient history of Quebec, which embraced for centuries a far more modest "brand" of French – the patois that represents French for me. I wonder, then, who's the real traitor in this skirmish of roots and stock?

In patois, the French I grew up with it, it's normal to feminize what is supposed to be masculine according to modern standard French, saying «une autobus,» «une avion» [plane], and «une pétale»; and, as a speaker of patois, I refuse the feminine on what is supposed to be feminine, according to linguistic authorities, insisting on «un introduction,» «un espèce» [species], and «un entrevue» [interview]. I never ever use the particle «ne» in negative constructions unless I force myself to self-correct. Its absence actually seems to be a sort of rule-based marker of patois. As a result, I naturally say «t'en as pas» [you don't have any] instead of «tu n'en as pas» and «a'est pas fatiguée» [she's not tired] instead of «elle n'est pas fatiguée,» and so on.

I invert the article «le» [the, masculin] to «el», saying «el moteur» and «el chien.» That's apparently a legacy of Spanish influences on the medieval French of a migrant population that became cut off linguistically from the original homeland, western France. I also open all of my vowel sounds more than the standard, smoothing out their differences, so that when I say «va» and «vais» (conjugations of «aller,» the verb "to go"), they sound exactly the same. And, for the same reason, I say «mial» instead of «miel» [honey], and so on. This is seemingly commonplace in rural regional dialects in parts of France even today.

I reverse the unstressed first syllable of every verb that begins with /re/ followed by a consonant – saying «ermarier» and «erjeter,» instead of «remarier» and «rejeter» [remarry, reject]. On the other hand, I add an /ré/ sound at the beginning of every verb that begins with /re/ followed by the vowel /e/ – saying «réempaqueter» instead of «rempaqueter» [to repack], or «réenforcer» instead of «renforcer» [to reinforce]. I almost always soften a /v/ to an /f/ sound, saying «ch'feux» and «ch'fal» instead of «cheveux» [hair] and «cheval» [horse]. Likewise, I soften /j/ to an unvoiced /ch/ in front of unvoiced consonants, so that I say, «ch'peux» and «ch'fais» instead of «je peux» [I can] and «je fais» [I make/do], and so on. I also overuse «on» – a someone/everyone pronoun – to such an extent that hardly any other is needed. It's not that there aren't rules – there are. It's only what I thought, and was taught, that French was as a child. Yet it's closet French now, spoken only «din rangs d'Saint-en-arrière» [in the back woods/agricultural lots of Saint-way-out-back, "from the sticks"] – a double swipe at language and faith.

Some of my favourite words from childhood are gone for good. Like s'abeaudir» [to makes yourself beautiful], «s'aboutonner» [to button yourself up], «amancher» [to fix or set up], «apitchoumer» [to sneeze], «décrocheter» [to unhook], «écrapoutiller» [to squish or flatten], «inventionner» [to invent], and «pigrasser» [to fiddle around] – plus the whole irreplaceable series of «s'abrier» [to cover yourself with a blanket], «désabrier» [to uncover by removing a blanket], and «rabrier». [to cover up with a blanket again]. And how many more? Seems like a lot of loss in less than fifty years, no? They're not even listed as «populaire» – slang or colloquial – anymore. Where did they go?

I realize, painfully, that I'm not teaching French from my own place of origin. I am, in fact, pretending to be a teacher while I'm actually a student of standard French. I can't help, then, but question my own legitimacy. Are these reflections in my pedagogy of the identity crises that frame my entire life? Am I a fraud? And even further within, my insecurity festers, for I have to wonder how is it that someone with this kind of heritage is unsure of what it even means to be French.

Party

My black ballet leotard and tights.
Bunny ears from the Kresge store.
A blob of cotton balls pinned to my butt.
A box you'd put a board game in
strapped right at my waist level.
The display is fully loaded – Player's,
Export A, du Maurier, Craven A,
a few cigars, some pipe tobacco.

I am eight years old – one of
three pretend Playboy bunnies.
My cousin, S., who's ten, has a box
of chocolate bars, peanuts, and candy.
My cousin, X, who's twelve, has a box
of spare ashtrays and a lighter.
I am the "cigarette girl" because
it's the lightest box, I'm told.

It's «une p'tite soirée, un p'tit
parté,» one among many.
My costume is my story
in a nutshell. My metaphor.

Olfactory triggers of my horror:
men, smoke, tobacco, nicotine.
Psychic death infects my nostrils,
imprints an indelible symbol
of interminable injury which is
at once my very own, and
at once a product of culture twisted:
«Bin, viens-t-en-donc. Y'a rien là.

C'est juste drôle, ça-là.
C'est juste pour faire un peu d'fun.»*
This from my mother's tongue –
my mother tongue.

Everyone is happy, having fun –
«Y sont dans leur élément.»†
But I am not elemental here.

I do not belong, do not enjoy
handing out pipe tobacco
and cigars to the Elder –
and family-friendly priests
pretending their embarrassment,
at taking what I am now
offering them in public.

A movie could not make up this shit
any better than I live it.
Forget the withering soul,
the faultering ego,
a man is snapping his fingers,
and my job is to «faire un beau
sourire pis servir les hommes.»‡

---

* Colloquialism for «Bien, voyons-donc. C'est drôle, c'est tout. C'est simplement pour le plaisir.» The meaning is, "Come on now, there's nothing to it. It's funny, that's all. It's only to have a bit of fun."
† Colloquialism for «Ils sont dans leur élément.» The meaning is literally, "They're in their element," which signifies that they feel at home, they're comfortable.
‡ "Make a pretty smile and please the men."

I am being socially constructed as a slut.
Compliant in my best smile,
I vomit only on the inside.

But in moments when
the men are «satisfaits,»
I lean up quietly against a corner,
flip the cardboard tops wide open,
move cigarettes into little lines,
smooth out tiny bits of foil neatly,
reorganize packages into tidy rows
and arrange cigars by label colours.

I want to keep my own display
as clean and sensible as I can.
My limited sphere of influence
hangs around my neck.

13

FRENCH ROOTS

LES GENS D'LA SOUCHE

My paternal great-grandfather, Joseph St-Onge – who was a "railroad man" just like my grandfather – had a home in Lévis with his wife, my paternal great-grandmother, Eugénie de Champlain. In her memoirs, my granny refers to Grand-grand-maman de Champlain, her new mother-in-law, as a "dear soul who did not speak one word of English." Further towards the mouth of the Fleuve Saint-Laurent along the south shore, in Mont Joli, lived my great-grandmother's sister, Odile de Champlain, who apparently also "couldn't speak English." It was at the home of «Arrière-arrière-tante Odile» that my grandparents lived for a month when Granny first crossed the Atlantic at twenty-one years of age, "very pregnant," to meet her new husband, and found herself terribly sick from the voyage. And it was in this very home that there was a framed geneological certificate issued by the government of Quebec attesting to my grandfather's descent, through his mother, from Sieur Pézard de la Touche de Champlain.

The certificate has been passed down through Odile's children and was last reported in Charny. According to Granny's subsequent research, her new husband's great-grandfather had been Pierre St-Onge, a widower, who arrived in 1798 from La Charente Inférieure in the Department of Saintonge in Gascony. He married again in Canada, in Sainte-Anne-de-la-Pocatière, producing two sons: Abraham Paillant dit St-Onge and Honoré Paillant dit St-Onge. I don't mean to question their status as «des bons catholiques» when I say that these sound suspiciously like Huguenot names. In any event, two of Abraham's sons married «de Champlain» girls, and one of his daughters married a «de Champlain» boy. So it was that «les de Champlains» and «les St-Onges» held each other's strands like a thick braid.

Sieur Pézard was apparently a close colleague of Samuel de Champlain de la Touche de Brouage de Saintonge, who was born in 1567. For his part, Champlain was an upstanding soldier of Henri IV, né Henri de Bourbon, considered Le Roi de Navarre and Le Roi de France – himself a former Huguenot chief converted to Catholicism. Champlain would become the founder of New France in 1608, according to the bronze sign that hangs below his world-famous statue next to the Château Frontenac. It was at the base of this statue, in fact, right on the stone steps there, that I often ate lunch those six summers I worked as a local tour guide in Quebec City. It was there, too, that my photographer and I had exchanged our first kiss one warm evening in our early twenties.

My ancestors are spread between Kamouraska and la Beauce, with the greatest concentration in the rural areas within a few hours of Quebec City and along la Rive-sud eastward towards the open ocean. My maternal «grand-grand-maman» was named Marie Émilie Blais née Brochu dit Raisin. Through the «dit» [said to be] name system, my grand-grand-maman is returned mythically or biologically – seems the family history rides a fine line here – to the relations of Marie Raisin, a literate sister and teacher with the Ursulines of Quebec. Arriving in 1659, she became the assistant mother superior in Montreal, second in command to Sœur Marguerite Bourgeoys – in her lifetime, the most respected woman here.

The great «sœur» was actually a lay woman born in 1620 in Troyes who arrived in 1653 to found a secular order in honour of Notre Dame. Her organization became an influential network for women that ran trade schools for girls to promote literacy and financial independence, and opened halfway homes for young, ill, poor, or elderly women throughout New France. For the settlers, this tireless woman inspired by the idea of «el bon secours» – the compassionate rescue – would always be «la mère d'la colonie.» It would take more than three hundred years for the Catholic Church to catch up with her and make her a saint.

It turns out that 95 per cent of the immigrant stock that was here prior to 1700 came directly from France, and from key areas in particular. That's why, according to recent research, the genes of 7,800 of what's now known as the QFP – the Quebec Founder Population – are detectable in 90 per cent of the inhabitants of every major region in Quebec, except in the east where it's only 76 per cent, due to greater Acadian and Loyalist ancestry.* Unsurprisingly, it's highest in Quebec City, at roughly 94 per cent. This homogeneity is why Quebec is a goldmine for "founder's effect" – the telltale trail of inherited diseases that marks my extended family and countless others. The population is a collective among which genetic traits and congenital illnesses are shared to virtually the same degree as values and worldviews.

So I'm among the «gens d'la souche» [the root people of Quebec] from both sides of my family. Research through my family tree (St-Onge, Dumont, Blais, Brochu, Paillant, de la Touche, de Champlain) and the naval records (all came by sea, and ships' logs are public)† show that I'm plausibly related through the road map of names and the sheer odds of the ancestral nets over Quebec City to a number of immigrants who were here by 1700. Among these are labourers, including Pierre Dumont, Louis Martineau dit Saintonge, Pierre Ménard dit Saint-Onge, Jacques Payan – and Marie Péré, a midwife to the growing population, who married Pierre Demont. My list also includes soldiers and officers, such as Jean Brochu dit Lafontaine, Vincent Boissoneau dit Saint-Onge, and Julien Dumont dit Lafleur; as well as seamen, such as François Saintonge, François Dumont, Yves Paillant, and Jean Payan.

---

* There's a bonanza of information about this subject online. For example, see "Admixed Ancestry and Stratification of Quebec Regional Populations," *American Journal of Physical Anthropology* (2011); "The Genetic Heritage of French Canadians," *Discover Magazine* (2011); and multiple scientific projects by the (recently closed) Quebec genomics firm Genizon Biosciences.

† At the time of writing, a number of Internet sites offer this information. The most user-friendly is http://naviresnouvellefrance.com.

It's impossible not to get carried away with the genealogical research around here. There's so much of it, crossing over, and over, and over.

Using the same rationale, I can also trace my family's links to Raymond Blaise, sieur of Bergères and of Rigauville, and his son, Nicolas Blaise des Bergères, both of whom arrived in 1685; Sieur Levy de Vantadour Destouches, Samuel de Champlain's ensign; and Pierre Dugua Sieur De Monts, a merchant who operated out of Acadia beginning in 1685. I also fasten back to Marie-Louise Morin (who married Jacques Payan). She was the daughter by second marriage of Hélène Hebert, widow of Guillaume Hébert, the son of Louis Hébert and Marie Rollet. There's no arrival date for her, though, because Marie-Louise was one of the first French children actually born here.

I stop and take stock. Seriously? Connected to Louis Hébert and Marie Rollet? The history books told me for years that this was the "first family" of New France – the first to winter over, make a permanent home, start a farm, raise children, and so on. They arrived in 1617 and never went back, so that Hébert is considered the first private individual to be given a land grant in the New World – quite the distinction. Of course, the local Aboriginal population had been managing it very well for centuries, millennia even. But when Europeans didn't die doing the same thing, seems it was worth writing a few books about. In fact, it's thanks to invaluable agricultural tips received from indigenous residents that Hébert and Rollet made it, though the history books certainly haven't been gracious enough about that fact. But I'm still proud of them both. Tough enough stock – folks «qu'y ont pris leu' courage à deux mains» [who grabbed their courage in both hands] and made meagre goods stretch and stretch. Kind of a loaves and fishes thing.

Then there was, of course, Étienne Pézard (Pézat), Sieur de la Touche de Champlain,* also known as Sieur Étienne de Champlain. He was «un Orléanais» who landed in 1661 and was entrusted with the Seigneurie de la Touche-Champlain, which encompassed a large chunk of what's now «La Mauricie,» including Trois Rivières. In 1681, he even

---

* The former commander of Fort Champlain, also known as Fort de la Touche (a critical defense post in the seventeenth century), who was entrusted this huge seigneurie by Samuel de Champlain himself.

became temporary governor of Montreal. He was married to Madeleine Mullois, part of the extended family of Louis Hébert through her mother, Sébastienne Hébert – cross-currents again. In turn, his daughter, Marie Madeleine Pézard de la Touche and her husband, Joseph de Jordy (Desjordy) de Cabarnac – who apparently had his own claim to nobility – would inherit the seigneurie and raise eleven children there. Meanwhile, de Jordy's nephew, François, would command the territory from Fort Frontenac, present-day Kingston (formerly Cataracouï) all the way to Montreal. No doubt about it, this was a dominant family.

In fact, Sieur Pézard was one of the highest-placed aristocrats in New France during his lifetime. And here he was, attested as being my great-great-great-grand-papa, etc., some 350 years back. To be honest, I'm not very impressed by these aristocratic connections. I've tumbled around too low at various points in my life, at rock bottom, to have any patience for pretension or grandiose delusions. But I'll admit that ever since I found out about him, I visit Kingston differently. I ask myself, *Did they walk here? Is this what they saw when they looked out on the river? What would they all be doing on a Saturday afternoon?* That sort of thing. I can't seem to help it.

LES FILLES DU ROI

More than any of these big-name immigrants, though, I'm touched by «les filles du roi» (the daughters of the king) – just over seven hundred young women in their late teens and twenties who arrrived between 1663 and 1673 as spouses for the French settlers. About three-quarters of them ended up on farms around Quebec City. The way these girls were chosen for their good morals and funded by «l'Ancien Régime» is widely documented. They came unaccompanied by family – many were orphans – and they all had to make the best of it because their lives depended on it. Having ten children or more was common – in fact, there were yearly payments to families raising more than that. And their lives hinged on learning to turn the page, too, when fortune took first and, sometimes, second husbands.

It took courage for this group of largely illiterate «town» girls who «ne savait pas signer» [could not sign their names] – as the official registers put it – to «bûcher» [work at back-breaking labour] on the land as hard as the men. These were females who successfully protested their marriages, annulled them, and even separated from husbands to take better ones. Brave women of power and an inextinguishable spirit. They would be helped in making their marriage choices and contracts – and housed comfortably, indefinitely, until they did – by none other than Sœur Marguerite Bourgeoys. That's how the line of descent in Quebec adheres so symmetrically to culture that it closes in on itself, forms a full circle, just like the whooping climax «d'une danse carrée.» «Pis el câlleur» [and the square-dance caller] is nowhere to be seen. It's only heard and felt. Intuited.

Funnily enough, even back then, the «patoisant et patoisantes» [male and female patois speakers] were apparently being distinguished from the «franciscant et franciscantes» [male and female standard French speakers] in the public registries – with the minority of women in the first category, and the minority of men in the second. So it was that urban girls with "central French" married rural boys steeped in regional patois; officials thought it noteworthy enough to record it as readily as they did the new babies. Seems that right from the start of the province, linguistic baggage was considered a factor in marriage and life. It certainly carried more weight than the tiny trunk each immigrant bride received as an official «trousseau»: one wig, one shoe ribbon, one spool of white thread, one pair of socks, one pair of gloves, one bonnet, one taffeta handkerchief, one comb, one pair of scissors, two knives, two *livres* of silver, four laces, 100 needles, and a million pins. Even in my most frugal days – nine months when, postpartum and newly single, I lived on welfare with three small children until I found work again – I'm sure I couldn't have made it on the modern equivalent of so little. I'm in awe of them all, patois or no patois.

There are fifteen «filles du roi» whose roots quite likely germinate mine, either through the sheer texture of their names and marriages or the tight knit of our shared genetic fabric: Élisabeth Blais, Marguerite Blaise, Barbe Boyer, Anne Colin, Marguerite Deshayes, Anne-Julien Dumont, Barbe Dumont, Marguerite Latouche, Marie Mullois, Marie-Marthe Payan, Marguerite Raisin, Nicole Saulnier, and Anne Talbot. I'm sure I've left out many for whom the record is elusive. But finding these women inside history matters a lot to me. I let myself imagine their lives, their homes, their chores. Their goodness, their concerns, their care. I picture them keeping a watchful, loving eye over their children, and their husbands. Biography is a great playground for fantasy.

My personal favourite among them all is Anne Talbot, the illiterate daughter of a master brewer from Rouen, Isaac Delalande, and his wife, Marie. Anne was born on 1 August 1651 and arrived in Quebec in the summer of 1670, aged nineteen, bringing with her the usual dowry of 50 livres from the king and personal belongings estimated at 300 livres. On 13 September 1670, she annulled her first marriage contract to Jean Barolleau, and less than two months later, on 2 November, married Jean Gareau dit Saint-Onge. Together, they raised fifteen children in Boucherville. By 1729, less than sixty years after she got here, she had an astounding 133 direct descendants. It's an incredible bit of math – producing more than two permanent offshoots per year, for more than half a century. And despite the obvious hardships of climate, geography, and resource shortages, she lived to a ripe old age, passing away on 4 August 1740, a few days after celebrating her eighty-ninth birthday. No wonder the population expanded.

In fact, it grew so fast that there were eventually eighty typonyms for Saint-Onge – names intended to be the same but written differently from one region to another, perhaps because of spelling errors. The sheer mass of all these people gives me a feeling of safety, starts to give me my own membership back. And that, in a nutshell, is how the population of «La Nouvelle France» turned into an island of French language and culture in the New World, seamed together by el Fleuve Saint-Laurent, curved like the backbone «d'une vra' bonne vieille» [of a dear old woman].

MAUDITCHRISTDECOTTERPIN

So it turned out that I was an island girl after all, quite outside my wildest dreams of living in a perpetually warm climate. I saw the St Lawrence River to the south, east and west, enclosing the rock-faced peninsula that is Quebec City and winding past my house, just a ten-minute walk below our street. I saw the thundering bridge that brought people here (at the time there was only one, not two like today), and

I remember clearly thinking that Lévis, on the south shore, was the United States.

That's how easy it was to be separate – you just needed a bridge and a river. I don't know that I ever thought about what lay to the north, past the great wall of forests we saw on fishing trips. I rarely ever left the city. Of course, there were a handful of trips for a week to a rented cottage here and there, a house away from the house; a few day drives to the country to visit an old aunt or uncle; and a few weekends spent on the other end of logging roads, watching adults measure trout lengths. But for seventeen years of my life, Quebec City was, quite literally, my island (until I moved to that other island, Montreal). And my home town was absolutely a French island.

The start of school complicated my geography only concentrically – fixed an English island inside my French one, like an inner fortress inside thick stone walls. Instead of rivers, my private English Catholic School, Marymount, had the woods to separate it from the rest. And while we did have French teachers, two female lay teachers brought in from France, the French they taught didn't connect with my life in the least. In retrospect, it was telling of what these American nuns thought of their provincial setting that they wouldn't hire locals for this task. But these two Parisians spoke a dialect that I hated, despised even. They could pass effortlessly as legitimate French teachers in the eyes of my classmates, who were mostly a random group of well-to-do anglo children of the powerful business owners in Quebec, the folks who'd later relocate to Toronto after the election of the PQ. But I thought there was something terribly, terribly strange about them.

Of course, I knew nothing of the fragility and volatility of Quebec in the Sixties, and I had no sense of my larger social context – of the turbulence spinning around language. At six, one's world is small. For example, I thought «Duplessis» was a swear word rather than a name.* That's how my father used it, liberally mixing it with English, demonstrating his bilingualism remarkably well when he was angry, which was often. So there was a lot of that "goddamduplessis" and "jesusfuck-

---

* Maurice Duplessis (1890–1959) was a powerful conservative premier in Quebec from 1936 to 1939 and 1944 to 1959.

ingchristduplessis" in our home, as he glanced at the paper after work, or when he repaired appliances and furniture around the house.

It took me years to figure out, for example, that "cotter pin" could be said without the prefix, «mauditchristdecotterpin» [damn Christ of a cotter pin]. My French teachers, transplanted Parisian souls in an English American Catholic school in the heart of this French Roman Catholic province, couldn't hold a candle to my father's brand of bilingualism – far more interesting and frightening. I immediately forgot everything they taught me, words and proper diction falling out of my head as if through a sieve. For me, French was our patois. And it was private, inaccessible to these foreigners' tongue and its pretentious ways.

UNE BONNE FILLE

It should be obvious by now that most of my French acculturation can be attributed to one person: my mother. She's a wonderful chef and a born caterer who dazzles everyone with her «p'tites soirées» [little fancy evenings], complete with themed food, costumes, and decor. Many of these events were planned for our birthdays, my brother's and mine, and there are plenty of pictures to prove I was there, in handmade costumes, though I can't remember a thing about most of these. That's a source of great sadness for my mother, those beautiful moments lost in my efforts to erase the bad, I suppose. But more than anything, she took great delight, throughout my youth, in greeting my father at the door with a cocktail for him in one hand, in sexy clothing and high-heeled shoes, with soft music strategically playing and children sent to their rooms or outside. It was something she'd read about and trained for, with pride and determination.

Theirs was a passionate union lasting four decades. I, on the other hand, could barely get around to cooking for my three husbands, let alone serving them. I insisted that shoes be off inside the house, and I picked the first (my children's father) and third (my impractical desire) because they didn't drink alcohol – while I left the second (my next-door neighbour) because he did. I didn't dress up for them, nor did I read anything in search of becoming a better spouse. But when I review my married life – nearly twenty years, in three instalments – my mother makes a convincing argument for why I failed where she succeeded. A French woman pleases her man. An English-Canadian wife is almost as bad as an American wife, someone who just doesn't look after herself. Someone who, «Mon Dieu!», goes to the mall in curlers – something my mother once witnessed and that marked her as much as a crime.

One can hardly blame a husband for his wandering lust in such cases, the logic goes. My French mind regrets that I couldn't have been a bit more compliant – but only for a moment, and only because my mother is so remarkably capable of making her case. Then my English mind takes over, won't give the French «bonne fille» [good girl] a chance. Thinks that, yes, in fact, one can blame a husband for that. And that if a man is so superficial as to enjoy such trivialities, he isn't worth having. My mother looks at me despairingly. For in addition to losing my language, I've clearly lost my good sense.

To her chagrin, as I got older, I gained the power to articulate my preferences even more strongly and developed a firm resolution to resist her lifelong efforts to feminize me in a manner appropriate to my social position and culture: short skirts, sexy tops, and «des beaux souliers féminins» aka sexy shoes that show a feminine calf. Instead, I was a perpetual hippy, invisible out West, but incongruously completely foreign-looking back home. And so it is that, even today, I often don't feel like a "real woman" in Quebec. I always wear the wrong shoes, shirts, or pants. Not feminine enough. Not French enough. The imprint has stuck.

I was only six, for instance, when my father placed a quarter between my thighs. Of course, the quarter dropped. (Truth be told, it still would.) He repeated the gesture with my mother, where it stuck, and stated triumphantly, "You see? Those are the legs of a real woman." And he kissed her passionately. Starting at age twelve, when Marymount closed, I wore jeans, plain tops, and sandals as he bemoaned that I was "his second son, not his daughter," predicting that I "would never meet a husband looking like that." And everyone worried about my utter lack of cleavage: «Y a des exercices qu'tu peux faire pour ça, t'sais.» [There are exercises you can do for that, you know.]

It was that very year, on a sunny fall afternoon in 1969 or 1970, when I heard myself say "fuck!" out loud for the first time. A cathartic word from the very start, it was a sharp mark on my record, a noticeable change in the life of «une bonne fille.» I screamed it at a French neighbour across her driveway, enjoying the sheer power of using my burgeoning English on our very French street. I remember the English friend I was with saying, "Wow, Kath!" Little did I know then that "fuck it" would end up becoming my mantra for the next twenty years, whenever I fell headlong into my own cobwebs. My love for the language grew and grew.

PATCHOULI

But even looking like a boy, according to my father, I managed to date, from the age of twelve. For the next five years I went from one young male to another in a continuous chain. I was careful not to overlap them, but just as attentive to line them up like small soldiers every few weeks or months, so that the next would take the relief as soon as one was summarily dumped. The sorry pattern of repetitions was beginning. And every one of my soldiers had to be English, never French.

Or, almost never. There was one once who came close to being part of my line-up. Réjean, we'll call him, and we were fourteen or fifteen. My parents had bought their fishing camp by then, a lodge in the woods where we went every weekend, rain or shine. It was without electricity, phones, toilets, or running water. To my teenage mind, it was hell on earth. I fought against going with every fibre of my being, and I was occasionally successful. Most of the time, though, I was sentenced to accompanying them, and rarely allowed to take along a friend because my parents liked so few of them – these English girls from schools, or "little sluts," as my father referred to them in perfect diction. The adjective here, "little," didn't seem intended as a softener in the least. Rather, it seemed to be a pejorative levelled at their low rank in the sexual kingdom of adults, their being mere amateurs.

Réjean and I had been good friends for two or three summers because his family had a camp on the same property, along with a dozen other families. He was one of the few people I knew with more parental problems than me, and that in itself was reason enough for me to love him. He was handsome, too, in a rugged way, with a savage kind of look. And he could make it in the woods on his own, my automatic hero. Of that, there was ample proof because his parents, who got along poorly even with each other, left him alone there for weeks at a time with no food, sometimes returning when they promised and sometimes not.

That's how he took to drinking a lot, ingesting a few too many barbiturates, and staying up there into September, even once school had started, barely caring about what he was missing. He was bright and funny in the sarcastic way I love, but his lack of educational ambition was a worry. After all, that's what I lived for. Yet it was his addictions that I found unforgiveable. They were so dangerous in my world, for such complicated reasons.

One weekend I arrived with my parents and brother and found him delirious, his left hand swollen with pus. Diving off a low dock, he had cut it badly on a broken 7-Up bottle. For the better part of the week, in the absence of a first aid kit, he'd been pouring beer on it. It was a smelly, disgusting sight, the wound running from the top of his index finger almost to his wrist, the skin turning colours I'd never seen skin be before. He was crying slightly, one drop slipping out of the corners of his eyes at a time. And he was almost immobile and spoke slowly, drifting away. I quickly fetched supplies from our camp while my family fished in the middle of the lake, and I stayed with him for hours, doing indescribable things to his hand that took me to my nausea threshold and back several times.

There's no other grown male I've ever done this for: mended a real wound. For Réjean, I played doctor willingly, though that game was scarier for me than his drinking. He did get better, thankfully, but the relationship was never the same. When I tried to kiss him, it felt all wrong, as if we were violating an incest taboo. Had it been the doctoring, the re-enactment of a game infected with problematic triggers? Or had it been seeing him so exposed – the pus, the tears, the weakness? I'm not sure, but it was over from then on. My almost-something relationship with the only French male I ever loved was reduced to casual conversations. He did leave me with a treasured memory, though – patchouli. I don't know how he managed it, but his skin exuded it from every pore, and his hair, even dirty, did too. To my female heart, it was the smell of heaven, and still is.

UN CAS PERDU

In one of the summers that followed, I decided to listen to my parents' ideas about love and men and set out quite deliberately to engage in a three-month trial of being a proper French girl. Honestly, I think it was just out of boredom. Then again, maybe I was trying to bring home some of what I'd been learning at McGill, the scientific procedure that was the hallmark of modernism, a minor experiment on cultural and personal boundaries. In hindsight, some thirty years later, I also admit a growing urge to explore the edges of my trauma, a curiosity about dreams and inner convictions for which the evidence in the here and now was entirely lacking. So just how easy was it to be sexual bait?

I was working selling tours in a downtown location. I wore sexy skirts, tight pant suits, high heels every day, makeup, and hair down my back instead of my usual, tied back or up. In stilettos, I navigated a tricky path to work at the corner of Rue du Trésor from where I parked near Les Ursulines, as my heels threatened to catch in the cobblestones. But my mother was happier that summer than years later, when I announced my pregnancies, or when I graduated, multiple times. And my father looked genuinely proud and relieved as though, finally, I'd stop embarrassing him.

I received two marriage proposals in the course of the experiment, quite serious ones. One was from an American marine and another from a Montreal businessman. And I grabbed the sudden interest of two older males I'd known since high school who'd virtually ignored me until then. I apparently even made the cover of a Japanese tourism magazine. Easy game, being chicken on a bone – a French girl smiling in her pink jumpsuit with the deep-cut back and slender sandals, in the heart of the Old City.

But the English girl inside was thinking, *Stupid men. Is this all there is to it? A dog is harder to trick than this.* And I married no one, dumped them all, four men on a puppet string cut down all at once. The experiment ended. I donated the clothes and the shoes and went back to being me. The usual funk returned to my parents' household. «C't'un cas perdu» [It's/she's a lost case], they declared unanimously.

From my perspective, these comments were experienced as another invasion of the sexuality I was trying so desperately to mute, for reasons that weren't clear to me. I was protecting myself from what I-didn't-know-and-couldn't-quite-remember, as I looked for young men whose mothers thought that I was a nice girl sensibly dressed, and thought that it was my mother who was far too flamboyant for her own good. It was, and is, a clash of cultures, a painful one, this battle over what makes a proper woman.

I was instinctively determined not to be «une belle poupée» [a pretty doll] on display for all to see – to be more sexually conservative, to try not to tempt men. So I resisted the French-Canadian vision of the feminine without understanding why, except for the vaguest notion that in dressing me up and promoting my sexuality, my mother was setting me up. And my father, for reasons I attribute to a combination of parental apathy and physical self-interest, was evidently willing to buy into French sexuality for the mere joy of living in a city where women make themselves look sexy to run out for milk at the corner store.

Yet in each of my languages, I'm embodied in a particular view of the feminine. And these different perceptions of my gendered self – my variant possibilities as a woman in each culture – have distinctively affected my linguistic undertaking. In choosing a language and its world, I effectively select a particular version of myself as a woman. This is a huge idea for anyone to consider. But for a victim of sexual trauma in one particular language, the potential for rebranding in another language is dramatic – an invitation that can't be refused.

Angry Bird

There's a part inside of me that used to be an angry bird.
Diving at things with its beak: gouging, clawing at their eyes,
grabbing bodies in its talons and dropping them into quick rivers,
flying recklessly from one sky to the other, feeding off dark winds.
Well, at least that's how it felt and seemed within my own head.
In my face, I really don't know what it looked like. I didn't see it.
But I understand from all the reports of my childhood that I was
extremely docile and compliant, never angry or impatient,
a calm child you could take anywhere: flexible, malleable.

I only know that the angry bird existed because its beak kept
tapping inside my skull like a raging woodpecker from time to time,
and once I let its reckless wings fly into a plaster wall. I know that's true
because I saw the knuckles of my sixteen-year-old body scraped and bleeding.
That's the last time that I felt the angry bird, the last time it appeared.
And uncoincidentally, I think, this was first time I got mononucleosis.
After that, whenever I felt oppressed, engulfed, caged – by now,
eleven times in all – out came a much more pleasant sleeping bird,
a calm adult you could take anywhere: flexible, malleable.

14

THE DOUBLE FRAME

FACES AND FEATURES

I often find myself staring at the double wood frame that sits on the shelf facing my bed. On the left-hand side of the frame, there's Joseph John Leo St-Onge and Gladys Louise Garland on their wedding day. My paternal grandfather is dressed in his full military uniform, half-sitting on the right arm of an expensive-looking wooden upholstered armchair. My paternal grandmother wears a modest string of pearls, a white hat with a medium-sized brim, and a luxurious stole – fox, I think. Her satin shoes with fancy bows rest on a bear skin, and her arms are crossed neatly in her lap. They each have a confident smile, as though their success is assured.

On the right-hand side of the frame, there's Gérard Policarpe Dumont and Cécile Marie Blais on their wedding day. My maternal grandmother wears a white shirt with three buttons below the simple neckline, highlighting a tiny chain with a cross. Around her head, there's a ribbon tied with a loose bow – in the Charleston style of the 1920s – and she wears a pair of plain round glasses. My paternal grandfather leans in towards her, but not too much. His hair is stylized and hatless. The look on their faces is serious, worried even.

These frozen moments in the lives of my grandparents on either side of a thin piece of wood, captured on their respective wedding days, perfectly render not just their present but their future along the socio-economic arc. The first couple spent life at the top of the middle class, while the second spent life in the middle of the lower class. The first took trips around the country, to the United States and occasionally back to England, as time and busy lives allowed. And while my grandfather worked away from home much of the time, my granny performed her role as an educated homemaker dedicated to raising children and a proper garden, occasionally travelling by bus to the city to the best shops or an occasional restaurant.

The second couple took infrequent day-trips within a two-hundred-mile radius, to aging family members in need of urgent care, or to pick strawberries, apples, blueberries, or «les têtes de violon» [fiddlehead greens] in season. My grand-papa juggled odd jobs that eventually turned into a small business, as my grand-maman managed her home and everyone in it, including the boarders. She baked for local priests and nuns, purchased only a minimum of basic goods from the shops on her block, and considered a restaurant meal a scandalous waste.

Time would wear differently on each one, on each image, as photographs of them taken decades later, in colour, tell well the comparative stories of relative affluence versus manageable hardship. Yet even in the black and white of the original wedding photographs, the contrast couldn't be stronger between my French and English family in terms of money, standing, and promise. And by putting them side by side like this, my grandparents are reduced to their features – noses, eyes, smiles, shirts, hair, skin. I study their faces intently. Where am I? Whom do I most resemble? And how has time worn on my image?

I look at a few of my own frozen moments. They're pictures that mean enough to me to have been culled from the collection at my mother's house, put into recycled frames, and placed on my bookshelf in Toronto just last year. I lived through more than fifty years of denials around the sexual abuse, and all that time I displayed not a single picture of my youth, nor did I even bring any into my home. Erasure: just one of the ways I lost a sense of ownership over memory.

But now that I'm on the other side of that mountain, with truth in hand, it's time to work hard to reclaim my past, to embody it. To consolidate one part of my life and self with another. It's a tall order, but it's one that's helped (painfully so) by tangible reminders. The most powerful of these memorials are three black-and-white Kodak prints, each about three inches square, on the narrow bookshelf by my window. When I look at them now, I remember that this child that was wounded was me, and I affirm that she/I lived after all – that she/I survived.

SON APPAREIL

In the first picture, which I've named "Old World," I'm two, and the setting is Christmas in the primary neighbourhood of my childhood, the locus of "my troubles." I'm between two other children, an eight-year-old female cousin and a male cousin who's about six. We've clearly been posed. The piles of presents on our laps are far too heavy for our young bodies. A fake Santa lurks behind me, his right hand pointing at my pile. I'm looking right at the camera, eyes popped wide open. No smile at all. Not even a pout for having to wait to open all of those gifts. Rather, just an abject absence of expression. My female cousin isn't smiling either, appearing sad and distracted, refusing the pile entirely. But my male cousin, happily hoarding, has a broad grin.

We're being recorded inside every paradigm we have here. Small family females marked by trauma – males clean and clear. Aspirations of upward mobility made patent in the volume of gifts abundantly displayed. My mother has explained the background of that image, as she saw it, numerous times: «Nous aut, on ava' des oranges dans nos bas d'Noël. Pis si on ava' un seul cadeau, comme une p'tite poupée p'têt, ou bin un p'tit jouet, bin c'ta' beaucoup.» [Us, we had oranges in our Christmas stockings. And if we had a single gift, like one small doll maybe, or a small toy, it was already a lot (more than we could expect).]

The times are changing for the family during this race to the middle class, and yet not changing much. More money – but the same liabilities. At least the costumed Santa in this photo isn't the costumed Santa that infects my dreams, that to this day causes my confusion (curiosity and repugnance in equal measure) with a particular male body type: visible pores on hands with translucently white skin where tiny orange-red hairs erupt, a round and bulging shape of eyeball, a distinctive angle on the nose – a "red-white man," as I've named it. Here's another problematic confusion of reality and fantasy, joy and chaos, trauma and tricks: Santa as a ruse. But no matter. This time it's my cousin's father – I recognized him then as clearly as I do now – who's relatively harmless.

Unsurprisingly, then, the well-intentioned accumulation of material goods on my lap seems to mean nothing to me. «Bin voyons donc. Pourquoi tu fais pas un beau sourire? Vous êtes jus' gâtés, vous-aut', la nouvelle génération.» [Come on now. Why can't you make a good smile? You're just spoiled, you kids in the new generation.] Not strictly text from that day, though. My mind is entirely blank about the dialogue within that image. It records only the smells, the affect, the tiny cracks inside my skull, a persistent click, click, click, as if something serious and fragile is breaking.

It's the feeling that happened at the most difficult moments, after which my inner world became absolutely peaceful and my sense of time and space felt bathed in warm water, or released in open flight. The monologue here is admittedly a creative composite of what I heard hundreds of times as I was called to witness the benefit of the bargain – social gain for social silence. Women moving up in the world by accepting the price men charged for passage in that *zeitgeist*. Their trade with the devil.

In the second image, which I've named "Woods," I'm entirely alone, aged about four, on the grounds of what seems to be some sort of a petting zoo. My chubby arms hold the waist-high log railing of a small enclosure. Behind me, there's a lone log bench. The path I stand on is sandy, about six feet wide, and turns in an obvious circle around the enclosure. Behind the path and bench, along the outer edges, is a forest. My hair is fine and light-coloured, just reaching to my ears, and I'm squinting in the sun.

There's no smile, but my mouth is open, as if I were going to say something. My skirt barely reaches to the bottom of my butt. It's precisely as my mother would explain it in my baby book that same year: «Elle est la plus adorable des petites pitounes.» [She's the most adorable of all the little girls (alternately, «pitounes» means little dolls, little sluts).] Of course, my mother intends her comment well, but the connotative ambiguity speaks far more than I could ever say with my half-opened mouth.

Yet there I am, immortalized as a little girl/doll/slut, with the peace of the open woods behind me. It was a physical refuge I didn't enter that day, but a landscape that would become mine in treasured fantasies, when I let myself happily enter there, or was safely carried. "Dissociation" may be the technical term, but "living in the woods," which is how I remember it, was so much more beautiful than that clinical hook. So I choose the idea of the woods. I appropriate language, not just English or French, but the vocabulary of "hard science" too. Why shouldn't I?

I don't remember what I thought of the animals in their enclosure as I stood there with my hands on the walls of their pen. There was nothing much to think about, really. It was just the way of life for everything – fences, limits, entrapments, inevitabilities. But where were the crowds that day? Why does it seem as if there's no one but me in this place, on what was obviously a lovely summer day? There's not a single person walking in any direction, and no one at all in the background. It's as if I were a solitary soul on an empty terrain, a cutout pasted onto reality. Perhaps that's close to the truth.

In the third and final image, which I call "New World," I'm ten. My thin, pale hair is in the «chignon» that in my mother's books was the only allowed hairdo for a girl, aged four to twelve. I'm wearing a tank top – it's summer, after all – and I'm posing in our back yard in the suburbs. The photographer cuts my body at the waist, and since my arms are straight by my side, my hands are gone too. Artistic genius: a perfect correspondence to reality.

For in those days, I was long past my capacity to act on my surroundings, and the purely physical aspect of my troubles had stopped. But those events had left me with a profound disconnect between my head and the lower half of my body that would take a far longer discussion to explain. Yet in my face, the results are clear: I squint for the camera on what looks like a cloudy day, unable to open my eyes for flash photos, as always. My brow shows deep distress, almost pain, the weight of the world. The forced smile could hardly have satisfied anyone. If I ever had a student with this expression in one of my classes, I'd be terribly worried for her, for what might be wrong in her life.

This picture, for all of its ordinariness – the grass behind, the roofline of the neighbour's large brick house, the swing set, the lawn chairs – is more than any other able to provoke my rapid, seamless transit from conscious to unconscious. My waking dreams. One minute, I'm looking at her, wanting to hold her and tell her it's going to be okay. The next, I'm inside her forehead looking at that male photographer, and the roofline of my/her own house. The most powerful sensation in here is the quiet. It's so, so quiet in my/her head at that moment. Complete stillness.

The closest analogy I have is of an airport control tower where only one operator is working and the building is closed to public access. Look around and there are shiny floors, clean machinery, dials and knobs of all kinds, control panels and monitors. Look ahead and there's a giant window, wide and high, a full wall through which she/I view(s) the world, intellectually detached, functional, efficient. Clearly, the performance self on which I've relied through all of my adult life was comfortably at the helm by then.

I set the three photographs back on my shelf. Take a deep breath. Grab another coffee. Appreciate the grace of age and time. "Don't you wish you could be a kid again?" adults ask each other in typical conversations at work, in stores, everywhere. I never wish that. In fact, I remember clearly as a child wishing so hard to be an adult, to grow up.

I leave the last reflection to language here again – one thought – and it's the expression «son appareil.» That was the customary name for a camera in the patois of my childhood. Literally, the word means "his tool," or "his device." The noun was a witness to the Kodak camera being the instrument of choice for the most popular male trade in my culture. Here was my mother tongue, then, providing its own irrefutable evidence of exo-Darwinism – the human embodiment of mechanical extensions. Meanwhile, the blurred line between the two pursuits – kiddie porn and communal record – was dissembled, as always, inside language, in another single word, the masculine posessive adjective, «son.» Gendered for the masculine noun, «appareil,» it became accidentally, but most auspiciously, gendered for its primary user – men.

Women never took photographs in those days, in my world. When I recall the cameras of my childhood, a woman was never behind the lens. The women had their shiny black «cuirette» purses, the men their stiff leather «sacs à caméra.» And the finger on the trigger was always male. So it was that in Quebec, in the 1950s and '60s, world history and the dominance over females continued their mutual course, entwined like barbed wire. An enclosure of an entirely different kind.

UN GRAND POISSON

Somewhere in the life behind that sequence of three photographs, I transitioned through layers or phases of self, a bit like an arthropod. Not at all like a butterfly – the dramatic metamorphosis, huge changes everyone can see. Really more like a snail – same fragile being, slowly growing, finding shelter in progressively larger, sturdier outsides that looked much like the previous versions. And in that dangerous progression from infancy to adolescence, I guess I shed a few elements of identity along the way. That's the way it is with shells. I left a «Petite Fille» behind and replaced her with a "Little Girl" – so effectively that the latter would, in time, pretty much forget about her first shell and move on with her life.

Only seldom would memories of that early embodiment come to mind as curious interruptions in ordinary days that slipped backwards into no-space as easily as they arrived, caused no visible disruptions whatsoever in the new, perfectly managed exterior. I moved from one language to another as I moved from one state of existence to another. Kept and lost things along the way. Lived and died.

I realize that my psychological revisions – my self-editing, quite literally – greatly complicate the reason why I feel like I don't quite belong in either language. I misunderstand everything, or I understand everything only partially. As a case in point, my parents graciously registered me in a painting class at nights when I showed an interest. The French painting instructor's studio was a short walk away, and I was to be a part of a group of four, the rest francophones. On the first day of class, the instructor asked us to paint «un des grands poissons» [one of the big fish] and went off to do something, who knows what.

We were left to look at the tank of fish he'd placed in the centre between our easels. By the time he noticed me, I'd completely filled the canvas, about sixteen by twenty inches, with one gigantic fish. Nose to back fin, it reached perfectly across. It was a really big fish, splendid, I thought. And I'd gone ahead and taken some creative steps to paint him with orange, white, and black stripes. I was delighted with him – right up until I looked at the three monolingual francophones and what they'd done.

They'd filled their canvases with the tank and had represented a few of the fishes and plants, making one of the larger fish be a kind of star in their paintings. All of them had a large tank of many fish with one fish hero. I had one really huge fish swimming on white paper. How could I have misunderstood like this? What had I missed?

«Je t'ai demandé de peinturer un des gros poissons, et c'est ça que tu as fait?» [I asked you to paint one of the big fish and that's what you did?] The instructor was incredulous. I couldn't blame him. I asked myself the same question. But I see, some forty plus years later, my error. It was my understanding of the «partitif» [some]. He'd implied "one of the big fish here." I'd understood it without the sense of "among," without its context, without even water – just the big fish, alone.

And so it was that the painting went into my closet at home, and I guess my parents were told I was hopeless as a French realist because I can't remember going back. Just as well: I was missing Batman for these lessons, the original series. Pow! Blam! Zap! At age ten, my painting career as an «artiste» was over, but I could have cared less.

Besides, what did that instructor really know about art anyhow? How could he possibly understand more about it than *National Geographic*? For in November 1966, barely a few months prior to that painting lesson, my authority on absolutely everything featured a single giant fish spread across its front cover.* How I came to look to *National Geographic* for guidance about life is a whole other subject, as you'll see later. Suffice it to say at this point that there was nothing but the man's pretentious manner to challenge the magazine's unquestionable wisdom in my eyes. It's the most beautiful fish in the world, ample and bold against a non-descript background, just like mine. Nose to fin, it fills the paper from edge to edge, as mine did. There was no way for a minor has-been painter from around the corner to contest this eminent vehicle from the wider world.

EUCHARISTIC ART

I'd already heard these rumours about my lack of artistic talent – my English art teacher was of a similar opinion. A couple of years earlier, in 1965, I was given a book at school. Given a book! I couldn't have imagined a better day. It would add to my rather modest library, the dictionary in the linen closet and *The Cat in the Hat* in my brother's closet. (I could not, would not, count the textbooks borrowed from the encyclopedia friend year by year, that didn't smell right and with which

---

* Cover 850, *National Geographic* 130, no. 5.

I had to «faire attention» [be careful] so they could be passed along to her next two daughters.)

But here was the most beautiful book I'd ever seen. It was small, about four by three inches, with a dark blue jeans-type cover, a fabric imitation. It was *The Blue Jeans Bible*. I think we were getting ready for Confirmation, but I don't remember for certain why I got it. I remember flipping through the foreign contents. The Bible in English? What an absurd idea – the Bible was a French or Latin text, of course. But I didn't care at all about what was inside, only that it was a book, and it was mine.

I remember that it was spring the day we worked to paint paper covers for our new books. A rare thing, painting in a religious school: the sisters didn't tolerate messes easily. Even spots from our obligatory fountain pens needed to be blotted, explained, apologized for. But this day, I had plain newsprint on my desk for protection, a white box of eight watercolours in a row, with a tiny brush beside, and a small cup with a half-inch of water in it. I was in the last row at the back, near the window, my favourite spot. The sister tried to put the project in a meaningful context for us. She explained how the American bread company Wonderbread had a package with coloured circles. She said the artwork on that package represented hosts. Hosts of many colours. Eucharistic art. She had no package to show us; she assumed we'd all been to the United States where she was from, and that we'd all seen it. It would be more than a decade before I'd notice a real package of Wonderbread and figure out what she'd actually meant.

That day, we were left to concoct a religious juncture between ourselves, our new Bibles, and our paints – painting for itself clearly considered frivolous. I began by painting my whole paper yellow. There would be no second pieces of paper, we were told, so we needed to be careful. I was done quickly, being handy with crafts, and the paint dried well, given my seat near the window. While I don't remember how long the period was, the sister was happy – Bibles for the masses – and more indulgent and patient than usual. So I had more time, a tiny rupture in the predictable cut-and-dry, move-it-along pace of my schooling.

I looked for a long time at the box of colours that day, that perfect day on which the sun forced its way through the window, there were paints at school, and I was being given a book of my own. In my reverie, I couldn't imagine which colours from the box to exclude, which to leave out of the celebration. It was just too glorious a day for such sadness. So I decided to use them all, equally. I dipped my brush in water, then into one colour, being "careful not to dirty the paint box." Then flick, flick, flick, I snapped a finger softly against the brush and sent spots of colour in all directions onto the yellow. Flecks of blue. I rinsed the brush, and tried another colour. Flick, flick, flick. Purple, red, green, orange, yellow, white, even black. Tiny splashes of every colour in every direction went onto the yellow. It was an impressionistic masterpiece, I thought, and I was in love with it.

"Where did you learn to do that?" the sister asked when she finally made her way to the back of the room. It wasn't an obviously kind tone. I looked around to see that everyone else had actually drawn *something*: butterflies, flowers, suns, trees, things like that. Instead, my paper had splotches – pretty, pretty splotches.

That's when I received a look from her that I can't really describe. Then many looks, this time from classmates. But I could take it all, didn't let it worry me one bit, because I got to keep the pretty paper and the book, and that's all that mattered to me that day. I folded the paper neatly onto the Bible, apparently following instructions somewhat better now. And I covered the paper in the extra layer of plastic with which we covered all of our school books. Then, best of all, I took it home where it would live, stowed away in the place where I kept everything really valuable: my right-hand vanity drawer.

At age eight, my painting career as an American contemporary artist was apparently over, but I didn't care about that either. It was only another example of how I'd misunderstood something, somehow, again. It was a familiar feeling by now. Confused and alien in both my tongues, I held a vision of life that fit neither.

Crafts

I went from paint-by-number sets at three
or four, learning games with strict rules,
and few chances for getting out of line.
To carving handmade pipes from acorns
hollowed out, and toothpicks skewered
right through, when I was six or seven.
To making life-sized rag dolls from
discarded cloth, when I was nine or ten,
the kind you throw down on top of beds.
To binding scraps of recycled fur to
make rugs, when I was fourteen to eighteen, tying
worn flesh with a twisted leather rope.
To sewing quilts from cotton shreds,
fragments of disjointed colours, when
I was twenty, trying to make the patterns fit.
To stripping furniture by hand, when I
was twenty-five, scraping to get past the years of
paint to reach the real wood underneath.
To building fragile lamps from rice paper,
when I was thirty to thirty-five, so that even lit, each
form looked opaque and multi-layered.
To drawing animals nursing, at forty-five to fifty
– from bats to bears to pigs – for a kids'
book on motherhood I never published.

I swear I am not making up this list of
fifty years of products I have crafted.

My core was talking through my hands,
but my eyes were never really listening.

15

INHERITANCE

NO FRECKLES ALLOWED

Regardless of semi-professional opinions on my talent, or lack thereof, I liked to draw and to paint, just like a proper English girl, or so I was told by my Granny St-Onge. And I drew proper English subjects too, or so it was said: pastoral images, insects, flowers, trees – all settings, no people. «Ah, y'a jamais d'monde dans leu' peintures, c'est ça q'j'aime pas» [Ah, there's never any people in their paintings, that's what I don't like], my mother remarks in a sweeping criticism of the dozens of artworks now in her home by my granny and my granny's mother.

She's correct, actually. There are no people, not even animals or birds, no signs of life other than landscapes, homes, churches, and barns. I have several in my possession: one of the lobby of the National Gallery in London, another of the inside of my great-grandmother Garland's home in London, and countless scenes of village life where there is, somewhat oddly I suppose, no life, no people. Yet they're lovely, strangely so. They feel peaceful and open without people to clutter them up. Silence on canvas. I love them, hoard them.

This absence of people, it would turn out, wasn't without its symbolism. For I'd discover early on, in fact, that the world of my Granny St-Onge, and the world of my father, was founded on a paradigm that was more scientifically informative than spiritually fortifying. A kind of linearity based on predictable dichotomies of us and them. What was good, acceptable, normal versus what was not. Good old boys and their families, versus those who weren't. Simple systems. Things like that.

The realization came courtesy of my great-uncle George Garland, who was an illustrator of some fame (some would say notoriety) in the United States and who, unlike his sister, was quite fond of painting people, women especially, with or without clothing. Painting me at ten, he refused to add my freckles. He told my mother that they'd vanish, a comment I pondered for years. He'd clearly assumed that the origins of my freckles – the French-Canadian heritage by which my mother and her sisters have a ruddy, almost Spanish, complexion, and my mother's arms and face are covered in brown specks – would be cancelled out, inevitably, in the marriage to my father. He not only symbolized but articulated, then and there, the flagrant aspirations of Global English. The ease with which he presumed it, and the cold tone in which he delivered his prophecy to my mother that day, left us both speechless. My mother giggled sociably and laughed it off, but he wasn't laughing.

It was a good thing that he finished the painting when he did, though, because my "look" was about to take another turn. It was September 1966, the Sunday afternoon before the start of a new school year. I was polishing my school shoes for tomorrow, Grade 5 – a central part of the uniform that I was re-using from last year, same small feet. I had at my disposal the electric shoe polisher, that consummate symbol of modernity bought from the door-to-door Fuller Brush man. It was in my right hand, and one of my black leather oxfords was fitted loosely round my left. I turned on the power.

What was ten seconds felt like ten hours. My hair was breast-length by then. As I leaned forward to begin my polishing, a hanging strand caught the edge of that whirling carnivore. Faster than an ant-eater's tongue, my wisp of hair was drawn into the engine, wound around and around, closer and closer to the root of my hair, my scalp, until I finally had a gadget the size of a telephone receiver bouncing hard off the top of my head, ripping enough hair to hurt violently, yet leaving enough attached to hold on for dear life, smashing and burring.

My scream was loud enough to bring my father flying up the stairs from his workshop at the farthest end of the basement. He was a smart man, and he ventured a good guess that I was being electrocuted. He grabbed a wooden spoon from the kitchen counter and smashed it down on the electrical outlet – one sharp swing, hard, like a samurai sword. The cord popped right out. The noise, the banging, the whirring, the screaming stopped – but not my crying.

For hours that night, I sat in front of the television as my mother tried to save what hair she could from the motor my father had meticulously disassembled. As I sat watching *Walt Disney's Wonderful World of Colour*, with its great promises of technological advance in the age of full spectral glory, I humbly begged to differ. I had a growing sense that technology was conspiring and sinister – a feeling I struggle to shake even today. I think it might have been then when my neo-Luddism officially began – my anti-technology orientation. My history with modernity was already pretty uncomfortable. Whatever my series of unfortunate encounters might really have been, I was starting to think that «c't'a' pas jus' une maudite run de bad luck» [it wasn't just a damned run of bad luck]. Irons created the problematic smell when you pressed them against polyester armpits. Soldering irons spilled burning drops of ugly silver-black metal in all the wrong places until it caused a perfectionist father to reach his frustration threshold. Cameras were clearly beyond any hope of reconciliation. And now, the shoe polisher had become a tool I'd never touch again.

As for my scalp, it was too late. I had a lemon-sized bald spot on the top of my head for the entire year. It was, however, an anomaly that healed much faster than others in my life, only taking ten years or so to fully disappear. A haircut was apparently absolutely out of the question. That we couldn't do. It wasn't feminine to have short hair.

What we could do, though, was to manoeuvre the «chignon» creatively, so that hair from the other side could be brought over to cover the bald spot, and extra fabric flowers could be added to the daily arrangement pinned to its top to provide an additional distraction. In retrospect, I must have looked like a fusion between one of those balding men with long stringy comb-overs, and a deranged flower fairy.

MADONNA IN SORROW

My mother tells me that I'll inherit the freckle-less painting of myself when she passes on, but I don't want it. «Ça t'a jama' ersemblé» [It never looked like you], my mother confessed recently. «On ava' t'jours dit ça, même dans l'temps.» [We all said that, even at the time.] I don't remember those justified critiques at the time, though. What I do remember were the compliments lavished upon my artist-uncle, and the plastic look of a girl that never existed.

The painting I want to inherit instead is the one that hangs in the hallway right next to it. It's great-grandmother Garland's (Granny's mum's) copy of *Madonna in Sorrow* by Giovanni Battista Salvi da Sassoferrato, and it was brought from England by ship long before I was born. It's a canvas from a British museum sitting in the heart of modern Quebec, an Englishwoman's copy of an Italian master's version of a symbol at the core of the French understanding of Roman Catholicism. Eclectic in its very being, it's a mess of identities unto itself. It isn't a portrait per se, in that my great-grandmother Garland intended it as both a master's copy and a saint. But I love it far more than any other object in that house, my mother's house.

Its frame is a plain wooden one, dark and slightly golden on the edges, and it needs a good cleaning. But it's rich and full of light even through the dust. My great-grandmother Garland was one of the few painters of her time allowed into the National Gallery and the Tate Gallery in London – a "copyist" by special permit. There she sat for hours among the tourists to paint the masters, taking with her my tiny granny, her daughter, then a young girl. There's painful satire in my hanging right next to the world's most famous virgin like this, for I am no such thing at the time of painting. Ironically, the Madonna has a one-inch rip that's needed mending for years, ever since my mother tore down the hall to pick up a doctor's call. Her canvas is torn, but mine is intact. It should be the other way around.

In any event, my great-uncle George was wrong: I still had those freckles as an adult, fainter but etched in my face nonetheless, permanent. As a result, the painting truly has never looked like me – only a stilted, perfect me, "de-Frenched," blonder than I really was by then, for my hair had already begun to darken. I'm dressed primly and properly in pink and white against a sky-blue background like a stock photographer's shot. I was never as innocent as he made me look in that picture. In painting me like this, he inadvertently highlighted the part of me that was the victim more than I care to see. In fact, he's captured all of the adjectives that made me into such a prime target: feminine, blond, passive.

Am I really a collection of random adjectives, of features, like this? Only colours and lines in service of a brush? A composite rendered by what I and others make up as we all go along? An accident here and there, and a mere change of clothes, chignon flowers, and background? Is the image I present to the world only a layer, after all, an imposition, like my freckles? Is my face – reworked as it is by my family, culture, and setting – merely a mask that I can at any time remove, outgrow, ignore? And am I the subject or the object of this weird art that is my body, my life?

I can't be sure. But as a case in point, one summer in my infancy, according to the baby book again, my parents and I took a trip with my granny to the beaches of New England. It was long before the days of infant car seats or seat belts, so my granny and I loosely shared the back seat. When we arrived at our American destination, she was distracted getting out of the car, or else she thought I'd come out the other side, and accidentally slammed the car door on my leg.

It turned into the usual sort of hospital emergency, ten stitches across my left knee that left an inch-long scar that's still visible today. So I guess the cut was fairly deep. But my granny never mentioned it again, and my mother omitted the incident entirely from the record of that trip which she so meticulously kept. It simply reads: «Vacance à Hampton et York Beach pour 10 jours avec son daddy et grand-maman St-Onge et mamie, à 1 ½ ans, en juillet-aôut 1959.» [Holiday for ten days with her father, grandmother, and mother, etc.]

Forgetting about the incident was how my birthmark on the same knee – at least as large as an egg and hardly subtle – was scrubbed hard one night when I was about eight, as I protested insistently. «Bin voyons donc!» [Come on now (don't be ridiculous)], my mother exclaimed, as she kept on trying to remove it. For in forgetting about the scar, the birthmark was easily forgotten too.

At the time, it seemed a bit odd, almost funny, even. But in hindsight, it coughs up its moral philosophy onto the cold, tile floor. After all, in a culture that invests so much in silence – the cornerstone of forgetting – it was only natural that the unpleasant history of my knee would be erased from the public record. My mother wasn't negligent in forgetting such things. She was being quite deliberate. She had learned how. Most cultures pass on their stories from hand to mouth. What was being passed down here, from hand to mouth, was the culture of silence. And my mother, like a typical woman of her roots and generation, had been raised to think that hushing «el mauvais» [the bad] was the essence of good living.

So effective was the instruction, the indoctrination, of the women of her times that even after the death of perpetrators, secrets were kept by wild women across the landscape – every last living auntie and third cousin, and out through tortured filaments from there. It was as if the living were never given their voice, and only the dead could speak, repeating their monotonous incantations, «Dis pas un mot à personne» [Don't tell a word to anyone]. So family legends of piety, merit, and fidelity to «la patrie» were honoured with a reverence that increased with each passing year. It was only late in the history of families, at the onset of the old age of a few of its foundational characters, in the absent-mindedness of a humble quasi-dementia fuelled by champagne or «digestifs», that a few choice bits of information contrary to legend might be retrieved from the bottom of the memory pot. Then, they spoke – but only because they forgot to forget.

In sum, it was a legacy where the best «raconteuse» was the one who could keep the best stories to herself for the longest. As a result, generations of women were not divided so much by the particular opinions that might be spoken on any given day between mother and daughter, or aunt and niece, about shoes, men, or sauces. Instead, women were separated from one another by irreconcilable differences in their views of silence. For what passed as «normal» to their female forebearers no longer did for the new generation – it required action instead, intervention, no excuses. «Bin, y faut bin essayer d'comprend'» [Well, we really have to try to understand (the times)], it's often said. But those multi-generational silences underwriting the myths are tougher to grasp than the myths themselves.

Ironically, the provincial licence plate in Quebec states point blank, «Je me souviens» [I remember]. It's a beautiful thought, and I wish with all of my heart that it were true – not just for my entire family but for countless victims of the crimes of the times. But my experience in those decades was that precisely the opposite mantra grounded the local epistemology. That's why just reading the license plate turns me stone cold. "Bullshit, you don't remember at all," I often find myself accusing those anonymous rectangles at traffic lights and mall parking lots, in English. But there's no point in saying it. It's not like they'd ever answer back. They'd be silent, as usual.

MA PATRIE

I've received deliberate instructions about silence myself: «Dis pas un mot à personne!» It issues from a haunting male voice, a white ghost that infects me even as I try to write about this, as I finally dare to tell. But despite all of that silence in its varied registers – suggested, enforced, implicit, explicit – I heard plenty. Felt even more. Realized early on that these older women and I were similar deep in our souls.

Maybe it's because we were victims of the same type of oppression – they in their time, me in mine. Maybe it's because in that multi-generational quiet, we actually shared something tremendously powerful. It was something that inadvertently enriched rather than depleted our collective cohesion. Foiled the best-laid plans of these men. My amateur's conclusion is that one can't stop transference – hearing and saying far more than what's consciously intended. That unconscious language is out of everyone's overt control, beyond the grasp of those who consider themselves its most powerful. Through the unspoken language of warmth and empathy, the human connection, the women found ways of understanding and helping one another between the imperatives that were set out on the misogynistic agenda.

However it came to be, the women of my French clan communicated effectively «leur optique spirituelle» [their spiritual worldview] – literally, beautifully, "their spiritual light, or lens." But it was far more like osmosis than explicit lessons in catechism. Just like those divisions of the world into "us" and "others" that snuck or wedged their premises into daily life, faith became wisdom worked into ordinary moments: dishes being cleaned, seams getting stitched, or husbands "sleeping it (alcohol) off" before the long drive home. Sense and sensibility were passed along like hand-me-down coats, as faith went rogue in the kitchen. But the women were speaking now, completely ex cathedra.

Scrubbing pots and darning socks by hand, they cathected meaning deep into the gaping holes that the men and the church left behind.

Through this sharing underneath the surface of things, the women of my matrilineal world ignored the strain and inconvenience of their narrow grounds, and claimed their potency on those same grounds instead. That's how it comes to be that I have a core deep within me where their foundational beliefs dwell – where resides my faith, my mother's faith, in hidden goodness. It's the anchor of my enduring spirituality and can be summed up as follows: belief in the spiritual dimension of life is an indispensable idea. That anchor still means something, everything, to me – holds me even as I drift away from French toward English. It's a faith founded on the prevailing idea that benevolence reigns, come whatever. And it produces a philosophical orientation that is optimistic, premised on the fact that good can be found in everything, though not necessarily in everyone.

So when the house floods, for example, we consider ourselves blessed that we're unharmed. Or that in cleaning up after a flood, we find a precious document lost a long time ago that we wouldn't have found otherwise. And there's unofficial prayer everywhere. Not just over chickens, as my grand-maman uttered, but over car engines that don't start, husbands at the door, the phone ringing, letters being opened, and so on.

Such unofficial prayers keep their sure but silent peace with supersititions and convictions rooted so deeply in the French-Canadian soul that even to name them, to describe them, is to admit to some distance from their voices. A bird in the house augurs death. A dropped knife, fork, spoon means a visiting male, female, or child. Intuition is the most decisive of your six senses. Always go out the same door you came in. Angels permeate every place and time. Touch wood.

And the dead live around us, and with us. Not like a haunting or a channelling or anything New-Agey, but just as nature. I was reminded of this recently by one of my aunts who told me in solemn certainty that on a Christmas morning past, a fine snow fell around her cottage, covering everything in white. She was then already eighty, and surrounded by the three of her four daughters who still live, the other having been lost to cancer some years ago. She explains that they were all four women together in their pyjamas, watching the snow that quiet morning.

Suddenly, out of the edge of the woods, a beautiful buck emerged and nibbled on the grass right by their window. Unable to speak, they wept in silence – for the sheer beauty, for the blessing, and for time hanging so mercifully still that day. «Ergarde, c'est papa. Y vient nous dire Joyeux Noël» [Look, it's (our deceased) dad, and he's come to wish us Merry Christmas], the youngest, nearly fifty, whispered. And everyone believed her.

I can't relate this story without tears rolling down my own face. It's not about my believing that the dead uncle is a deer, which he isn't, of course. Nor do they believe that for a moment. Rather, it's about finding occasions for hope in nature, stillness, and the blessings of ordinary life. Such is the sense of the spiritual that I have inherited, and such is what I believe in to the core of my being.

"You can find hidden meaning in a stapler," my then twenty-year-old child once said to me cynically, insightfully. Such is the faith of «ma patrie» which the women of my French clan have infused in me. «La patrie»: a unique word with no exact correlate in English. It is faith, home, belief, and land – rolled into one.

UN P'TIT PARI

For good or bad, I was initiated into my «patrie» before I was born. I take a moment to return to my baby book, that trusted reference, one last time. I struggle with it – fight waves of nausea and dashes to the bathroom. Even its smell is a trigger – dry mold. A page titled «Précieux souvenirs à se rémorer» [Precious souvenirs to remember] features statements of wagers, «des paris.» There's a general belief that I'll be a boy: «Durant l'attente du petit poupon, tous était convaincu [sic] de la venue d'un petit homme. En voici la preuve.» [During the period of waiting for the infant, all were convinced of the coming of a small man. Here's the proof.] My mother's words are a testament to the reality that will soon be mine. For a child's actual identity – or problems – are irrelevant to the common consensus. If «tous sont convaincus» [all are convinced] of something – however wrong it is – it must be true.

And it becomes so. From here, there's a pseudo-scientific demonstration that I'll be male.

The first is the «pari du médecin Dr ...» He bet twenty-five cents «sur la venu d'un garçon» – that I'd be a boy. Seems he paid it to my mother as she left «la salle d'accouchement» [the birthing/operating room]. She evidently holds it with prestige because she adds that it is, in fact, «bel et bien celui payé par le médecin» [truthfully and correctly the one paid by the doctor]. The doctor was a family friend in the second generation of his relationship with my mother's family, a point that would end up having further relevance to my future.

His conviction is a simple matter of Cartesian logic: my mother was huge, so I would be huge. This was the verdict of the measuring tape. At birth, I was admittedly at the high end of the weight charts for a girl, nine pounds, «une p'tite pat-a-pouf» – a fatso, a baby Amazon. Yet I'd end up being an average-sized adult female on the thin side. Still, the register was solid about the cold facts that day for Bébé St-Onge in Lit No. 411, Salle No. 464. The numbers become weighty themselves. Clearly, an individual that strong in utero couldn't be a female. I can only imagine the waves of disbelief upon my arrival, and the multiple genital inspections which would have followed, all in good fun. An apt beginning, I suppose, an early omen. But if the doctor was really convinced he was correct, with the confidence typical of his profession and social rank, why not have wagered more?

It seems that the business of my gender wasn't serious for him at all, a paltry joke. If I came out male, he'd make a quarter – enough for a large Oh! Henry bar back then. If I came out female, he'd lose the prospect of that single candy bar. But in this culture (in every culture?), gender isn't a funny matter. It's terribly serious because it makes all the difference in the world. As an "ob-gyn," he'd have had plenty of evidence of why that was – in clinics and in emergency wards. But it's his cavalier approach to his work – hush-hushing sexual injuries in the service of family myths – that explains why he'd wager only the loose change in his pockets. For here was a doctor who'd leave me with the distinct impression, over encounters in later years, that I was worth little.

Nonetheless, the quarter lived snugly in the baby book in my mother's trust until the works were transferred to me in 1993. Years later, I noticed it was missing. After so many moves, I thought I lost it along the way. I couldn't find it for years, and I was actually sad about it. I imagined it dropping to the bottom of a box, pretty much anywhere from Victoria to Toronto. The tape had become brittle and had broken free from its page. I guessed I wasn't as careful as I should have been.

But that quarter's story is stranger still, a bit more disturbing. Turns out I hadn't lost it, though it is unstuck. It's paper-clipped to a different page in the baby book. I'm looking at it right now: 1952, a moose on one side and King George VI on the other, blackened and smelly. The scary thing is that sometimes when I look at my baby book, it's there. And sometimes, I *over*look it. Like everything else connected with my trauma, this quarter is elusive.

In fact, it's a common human experience to lose important things, search for them for days, and then suddenly find them when we're not even looking. Stress blinds. But as for this coin, depending on the position of the first "a" in *gratia*, it's now apparently worth up to either $3 or $5. So if I ever have a day when I can actually see it and I'm missing some change for Tim Hortons, I'll consider taking it to a numismatist. Just like I went to the philatelist in 1996 to dump off the entire stamp collection my father left me after his death. To wash my hands of it, once and for all. I have my own experts, too.

THE GENDER JOKE

The second bet was entered into by an employee of a television repair business my father worked at prior to owning his own. This man bet a whole dollar because, the record states, my mother's right foot (as opposed to her left) had swollen during the pregnancy: «car le pied droit avait été le premier à enfler. Voici la carte reçue lors du séjour à l'Hôpital» [because the right foot had been the first to become swollen. Here is the card received during the stay at the hospital]. My mother's scientific and non-scientific evidence are liberally mixing here. I don't know why she spoke about her swollen feet to this man. It's a curious subject, no?

But I do understand a bit about his character beyond his inclination towards what is supposed to be women's lore, his folk medicine. That's because he left a note on a white index card that's fallen off the page since then but which, at least, I've never lost and always see. On it he records in an elaborate, methodical cursive hand, in blue felt pen, his own version of the gender joke: «Je regrette, mais je ne peux pas rencontrer mes obligations envers toi cette semaine. Mais pour montrer ma bonne volonté je t'envoie une acct. Dû, $1.00; Acct, .10; Bal. .90. Mes félicitations …» [I regret that I cannot meet my obligations towards you this week. But to show my good faith, I am paying this amount on my account … My congratulations …] And he signs it with his full name.

I thought I was worth a bit more for this one, but clearly I was wrong. Only ten cents. I doubt this was a deep reflection of the value he gave to the female lore he appropriated. But if it was, it was a masterstroke of biting wit. More likely, I think he was, like the doctor, just partaking in some harmless comedy at my expense. Gender as a joke again. This from a man who, given his membership in my culture of origin, should have known better. Then again, maybe he did and his valuing me at ten cents is another bit of humour on his part. If so, he was a comic genius and I hardly dare criticize him at all.

The ten cents fell out, but that was lost on my mother's clock, not mine. Most likely, it ended up at the bottom of some filing cabinet, rusted to the back of a drawer. So without any of those funds, I'm left with just one question. The question isn't why my mother would bet – I know the answer to that. My mother enjoys having fun, likes a good game, has been known to go to the casino on occasion. My question is, with all that she knew about her own life and the life of the women around her, why wouldn't she hope, and bet, that I'd be a boy? Why wager on the other side?

Two answers present themselves. First, had she thought I'd really be a boy, she'd have found no one to bet against her. Which male in the professional world would think of putting up a quarter, or even a dime, on hopes for a girl? A complete absurdity. Besides, girls were cheap and easy to find in this view. Why bother wagering at all? Second, my mother honestly wanted a girl with all of her heart. She truly didn't think of female gender roles as hardship. By then, her silence was already woven tightly with her elaborate sense of «la patrie» – enough to make a cozy cloth that reached from head to foot. And she loved being a woman herself – embraced it fully, presented it boldly, and took on each day confidently. She wanted a girl, a friend, an apprentice, to pass along her wisdom to.

What a disappointment I would be. Seldom listening. Often rejecting. Barely respecting. Refusing my role. Embracing silence as a necessity – first through intimidation, and later through repression. But engaging my patrie absolutely insufficiently, at all times. Perhaps I should just have had a sense of humour about it? Taken the two bets against me and found the comedy in it, too? Considered, like everyone around me, gender as a joke?

But I couldn't, and I still can't. I've lost much of my sense of humour for cheap laughs along the hard road I've had to walk sometimes. What I think is funny now is darker, smarter. I don't care for simple nonsense, one-note jokes. I also have every reason to believe that gender in a patriarchal society is anything but funny. I don't see comedy in misogyny. For in either common male vista, modern or traditional, the odds were against a female. At best, womanhood was a gamble here from the start.

What remains of their wagers now is a half-dozen brown rectangles with ragged edges that look like stains from watery excrement. They're actually fifty-four-year-old glue marks from the absent adhesive tape. Now the page looks right at least, makes sense. Art imitating life.

Codes

One speaks in a learned and literate language.
One speaks in the mother tongue of culture.
One speaks in archaic myths and symbols.

All speak for *me*.
All are *me*: choices,
valences of the self,
fluctuating identity.

The whole of *me*
would be incomplete,
inarticulate, without
input from all three.

Language is a messy
flow of coded sense
within each of us –
an essential trinity.

To be human is
to be multilingual:
a semiotic hybrid,
constitutionally.

16

ON BEING NOT QUITE RIGHT

UN MOUTON NOIR

There have been many indicators along the way that I'm not quite right inside «ma patrie,» nor inside the English-Canadian culture that I also claim for my own. It starts with something as obvious as my name: Kathleen Saint-Onge. Either half of its cultural voices is virtually unpronounceable by the other. I'm an imperfect blend of traits, «un mouton noir» [a black sheep] as my mother tells it with a combination of flourish and authority.

I wondered more than once as a child if there had been an error at that hospital and I'd been assigned to the wrong mother. I saw her brown skin and brown eyes next to my fair skin and blue eyes. I saw her dance while I shied away, and laugh at tired old jokes while I buried myself in a book. I saw her look fancy in shiny bangles and scratchy synthetics glamourously cut high or low. But I insisted on cotton and plain things, an inner Quaker, and claimed an allergy to acrylic and polyester to buy myself that chance.

Often, she'd catch me just sitting between chapters in the corner of the den, looking ahead at empty space, thinking. «Bin voyons donc! T'es-tu là encore? Pourquoi tu fais pas un peu d'bricolage? Ou bin qu't'appeles pas une amie?» [Come on! Are you still there? Why don't you do some crafts? Or call a friend?] Too much thinking already. What good would it do? It was hard to believe these were my roots.

But then there were my freckles, the baby book, and my looking so similar to one of my maternal aunt's daughters. There was also the birthing day coincidence, of which much was made over the years. For I was born on a special Sunday in a cold November, on my mother's twenty-fifth birthday. We shared our birthday cakes every year. There was the further fact of my absolute resemblance to my father. Skin tone. Eyes. Intellect. Temperament, even, if I'm sincere – too serious, leaning towards an intensity that few people can match or tolerate. Despite my aspirations, then, I couldn't really believe that I was adopted. I was the child of this culturally francophone mother who appeared to be so unlike me, and this culturally anglophone father whom I so dangerously resembled.

Those early doubts about belonging would implant themselves permanently, though. I believe they played no small role in pulling me towards teaching English as a second language – in myself becoming «un étranger parmi'es étrangers» [a stranger among strangers]. It was the best employment in the world for someone like me, a perfect job for «un mouton noir.»

I spent fifteen years working in "language-intensive programs" on the West Coast, and another five instructing newcomers to Canada in Toronto. In either framework, that meant getting a new cohort about every three months. With an average of sixteen per class and two cohorts per term, a conservative estimate is that I had over 2,500 non-Canadian students over the years with whom I shared not just English grammar, comprehension, and pronunciation lessons, but authentic history, life, culture, and emotion. It was like travelling around the world without leaving my children behind. I was snugly entrenched among people who either couldn't see my differences, or who embraced them. I couldn't believe I got paid for it. Were it not for the obligation to rent and bills, I'd have gladly done it for free.

Of course, there were young adults trying to improve their economic futures in my classes. And fellow ESL teachers in a conundrum. They were considered "advanced" in English in their own home countries, where English was a minority language accessible to but a few. Yet their fluency was in doubt, considered "intermediate" here, where English is the majority language. Theirs was a classic case of relative bilingualism – where the tongue's dexterity doesn't change but one's respective power on the landscape absolutely does.

The greater share of students comprised a collage of complex lives that profoundly informed my own. There were doctors, lawyers, writers, and artists. Parents and grandparents. People who had walked for days just to escape. People who watched their entire families fall away through indelible hardships. Heroes better than any in a book: a quadri-lingual Japanese man, blind from childhood, who'd lived in a dozen countries; a seventy-two-year-old Japanese widow embarking on a lifelong dream to learn English; a teen from Kosovo who'd carried her grandfather to safety; a Chinese woman my age who worked three jobs to support her family of eight; an Eritrean human rights activist; a Polish custodian with a PhD in literature; a Mexican grandfather who came to class after shift work because he wanted to be able to help his Canadian grandchildren with their homework; a woman who'd been gang-raped back home; and a man who'd been incarcerated for more than a decade for his support of democracy. I could go on for hours.

In a curious manifestation of an embodied teaching practice, I ended up helping them to do exactly what I had done: use English for safe passage. Give up a bit of home for the sake of better odds, invest hope in change, a shift. The mood in academia these days supports this as a positive and progressive approach to teaching – this idea of pedagogy as autobiography, and vice versa. Yet I can't take any credit here for being clever or visionary, for I had no master plan to do anything even half as grand. I just went looking for the sort of job I could do well enough and thought I might like – then I got pretty good at it and loved it. The fact that my work repeated my life while my life repeated my work was accidental. And the fact that my work provided therapy as a result, well, that was more along the lines of a miracle.

When I reflect on those years in ESL, I realize that teaching produced – and fed off – another one of those transferential bonds that needed no language. After all, my students and I were all seen as black sheep at home just for wanting to learn so much about the Other. And we were also all sheep made black on arrival, experiencing our difference at our new location just for having our origins elsewhere.

KITCHEN TABLE PHILOSOPHY

As a result of my own shifting, it seems that I remain in the accounts of my family an odd blending, a weird mix. I'm like one of those children's books where the cardboard pages are cut across, and you can flip the head of a donkey onto the hind quarters of a lion. And here's the evidence, as my family observed it around the table quite recently – kitchen table philosophizing. We aren't talking linguistic relativity here, or anything approximating cultural theory or anthropology. It's about a mother's lore, a mother's instinct, and this is what it said after a drink or two.

First, there are still signs of my francophone heritage. I haven't lost my oral language one bit, at least, even after thirty-odd years «au loin» [far away]. And I have, after all, come most of the way home now that I've resettled from British Columbia to Toronto – and «p't-êt' Ottawa dans l'futur» [maybe Ottawa in the future], even closer someday? Furthermore, I'm working in French, teaching French immersion. Even better, I'm wearing heels sometimes, and «même un peu d'rouge à lèv' des fois, non?» [even a bit of lipstick once in a while, no?]. Well, muted shades. At least it's a start. Or so the story goes.

Then again, as the kitchen talk also notes, there are ample signs of my rejecting my francophone heritage. I have a stronger vocabulary in English because I read (too much) and love studying (too much) in it. My skirts are still (too) long and West-Coastish. And I still resist anything tight, low-cut or high-cut. My children don't speak French at all, except for the eldest, who's quite recently learned it for work, without any support from me. Or so the story goes.

And then, there are signs that I belong to no one, to no one familiar at any rate. I have an enduring penchant for East Indian clothing and a Chinese shirt collection, with clever frog buttons on hand-embroidered silk. There's also the fact that I'd gladly sell a pig (the French staple) or a cow (the English staple) for a handful of olives and some figs. I won't dance or sing, and I don't care for drinking. A nomad from neither here nor there – more often from there than here. That's their obvious conclusion. Then again, maybe being from neither here nor there is as good as it gets.

In Quebec, for example, the word «immigrant» is used differently than in standard French. In the standard, an «immigrant» is someone who arrived relatively recently, while an «immigré» arrived some time ago. But locally, the word «immigrant» captures both meanings. It's apparently a borrowing from English, which has only the one word, "immigrant." «Immigré» is edged out here, no longer used. Seems that when languages collide, concepts change.

We can imagine the two versions of the word meeting on a semantic field – maybe very near the Plains of Abraham. As the languages make contact, one happens to push harder than the other. Today, the English meaning wins the day. Part of the French contingent, our «immigré,» is lost, buried quietly, like other war casualties. But when it comes to «embarrassant,» French takes the victory, with two meanings (embarrassing or burdensome) to one (embarrassing).

It's an uneven and wavering battle, this duel between languages and their words, one that's repeated around the world wherever languages coexist. Some languages gain ground, others lose. Concepts are traded, stolen, and borrowed like spoils of battle. Others become dead words that disappear from memory. It's never an even match-up, word for word. There are always misalignments in the ranks.

At stake is far more than the names of things. Words affect our dialogues, how we speak about ideas to others. They alter how we refer to ideas in our minds, how we think. When two French speakers meet nowadays – let's say one from Bordeaux and one from Montreal – they won't agree on «un immigrant.» They share the same tongue, but their words don't mean exactly the same thing. And it's unclear if they'll ever understand each other perfectly, just because of their different language histories. Language contacts have complicated consequences.

AH, C'T'ASSEZ!

That's how I made matters worse at home, or so it seems, as I developed a philosophy and a set of values that bothered both of my parents and pleased neither. For example, when they returned from their bi-annual promotional trips sponsored by Admiral and Zenith – my father's television business was thriving by then – I was always struck by the colonialism of the enterprise, obvious to me from about age ten. Here they were, middle-class French Canadians spending a week in Hilton Hotels in Nice, Monaco, La République Dominicaine, and a dozen other sponsored locations. It was a lobby tour of the world. Insulated.

Artificial. Perfected for western consumption. And when they came back from la Côte d'Ivoire with a carved elephant tusk – «C'tu beau un peu, ça?» [Isn't it beautiful?] – I wept openly.

For my father, of course, the acquisition was a logical outcome of the anthropological education he'd received himself from his *National Geographic* magazines. For my mother, it was just a «p'tite aventure» [little adventure] of the sort she was so fond of. They'd apparently gone off to the distant edges of the hotel compound, to the farthest market stall, to buy something under the counter from a shady character: «J'ai voulu prend' sa photo, mais y voula' pas.» [I wanted to take his picture, but he wouldn't accept]. Dead elephants. Poacher economies. Living spirits turned into ornaments. «Ah, c't'assez!» [that's enough], they both exclaimed when I protested. And the tusk still sits on the fireplace mantle today, outlasting me in that house by three decades.

At home, we feasted on «tourtière» [pork pie], «cretons» [pork paté], «cipailles» [baked, layered wild game pie], «crépinettes de perdreaux» [partridge meatballs], «soupe au pois» [pea soup with ham], and «pudding aux atocats» [rustic cranberry pudding]. But I took great delight, as I got a bit older, in being invited to English neighbours' houses, tasting delicacies like cheesecake, roast potatoes, and lentil loaf. My poor mother, in her broken English, actually called a neighbour once to try to find out what it was that I'd eaten the night before that I'd loved so much. It was corned beef. Miracle food.

And even though I could eat a half-pound of bacon at the age of two, a matter of some pride in my French-Canadian culture, I insisted on it being really crispy, almost burnt. Worse, I ate the blackest part of the roast, apparently, «c'qui est dur comme un sabot» [what is as hard as a wooden clog], just like my English granny did. This was not the way meat was supposed to be eaten, in my mother's eyes – it should be fresh, bloody, barely cooked. «Prends juste une p'tite marche à côté du poêle» [Just take it for a little walk next to the stove], she'd say when asked whether she wanted her steak well done, medium, or rare.

What's the end result of this being neither here nor there? Is there an end result? Should there be? Linguists talk about bilinguals living in neat categories, as "subtractive" and "additive" bilinguals: those who lose part of a language when they gain a new one versus those who somehow manage to hold on to everything. But the truth is that you always win and lose when you become bilingual, because language is laden with cultural values. No one gains without losing – there's always a cost being felt somewhere. And no one loses without gaining – there's always a new opportunity or some kind of change to be had. The gains and losses of bilingualism always coexist. The winners and losers share the same soul.

One evening, aged about fourteen, I was helping my mother hang wet dishcloths on the wide log railing of the fishing camp at the edge of dusk. Suddenly the sky turned grey-white, then darker. There was a light wind and a flurry of movement, like a minor dust storm, as the lake directly in front began taking on an entirely new texture. It was marked with a few tiny prints at first, like raindrops. Then more and more clusters of imprints lit upon its surface. On our soaking cloths it was the same, as this curious material kept falling from the heavens in soft, thick drops, covering everything before our eyes. What in the world?

After about ten minutes it stopped, as seamlessly as it began. The normal haze of dusk returned to the sky. The lake stood perfectly still, covered in a strange grey shadow, irregular, vaguely fluffy. There was stillness for an instant, and then trout started jumping out of the water, attacking the material like starving sharks. Sixteen-inch fish, huge for that lake, worked their way from the deep where they eluded fishermen to pierce the water boundary, arching their muscular spines to grab what they could. Younger trout, their backs arching in between the larger ones, came up for the feeding too. It was like a Roman cathedral forming and unforming, arches large and small, interlacing then dissolving against a sliver of a moon. I could only gasp.

«Ah, c'est d'la manne, ça. Ça vient du Bon Dieu quand'es poissons ont faim. Ça descend comme ça pis ça'es nourrit toute. Pis apra' c'est fini.» [That's manna. It comes from God when the fish are hungry. It comes down like that and it feeds them all. And after, it's over.] I share this, like so much else, through captive breath. For I've never seen anything more inexplicable – disturbing and magnificent – and I never saw manna again. When I tried in later years to research it, it seemed that it was only a myth, partially biblical. But with absolute certainty, I saw those clouds of dead insects fall all around us that night. My whole family and neighbours spoke of it later too.

My mother still remembers that evening. And she considers «la manne» to be an accepted if unusual phenomenon, one with a frequency somewhere between «el grand verglas d'quatre-vingt-dix-huit» [the great ice storm of '98] and major winter blizzards. I recently asked a friend who as a youth spent time in the woods of Quebec if he'd seen manna. He had, he said, every few years, even in some cities. He recalled it being reported in the local paper in Lachine one year, as the short-lived insects spent their entire lives above ground, bloomed, and died, then fell in thick layers onto the streets in a near-cataclysmic onslaught.

The manna on that special day of my youth fell on the same lake I occasionally walked into for a dip to encounter dozens of leeches – slimy, thumb-sized, purple-red creatures, flacid yet firm, with pore-sized dots all over them. They clung to my inner thighs and swelled to a larger size when they sucked blood. I leave to the imagination how those leeches eroded the thin barrier between consciousness and unconsciousness, becoming devastating installations that were repressed for decades. But on that familiar body of water that opened onto an inner darkness for me, here was food falling from above, mercy for starving fish.

Blessings while you do the dishes. Grace as humble as a dead bug. Dusk as hope. Eternal nature as fleeting. Unconsciousness as consciousness. Archaic symbols as objects. Myth as reality. Existence in all its blurriness. There are no fixed definitions, no solved equations. The gains and losses of living always co-exist. The good and the bad share the same world.

A LINGUISTIC SEESAW

How is that linguistic balance held, even today, I ask myself? I confess that when I paint and draw, I do it in English: the names of colours, the techniques, the paper, everything. Cooking, I count measures only in French, even if the recipe is in English. And I only know my social insurance number in French. If I want to tell it in English, I have to recite it in French, write it down, and then read off what I've written.

I can explain the fine points of pedagogy far better in English, but I'm more supportive of colleagues in French. I scan the Internet in English, but my internal monologue when I'm driving is usually in French.

I watch television virtually always in English, but the songs that fill my head when I walk are French folk tunes – «À la claire fontaine, en m'allant promener …» In turn, my fables and legends are split down the middle. For instance, I remember «El p'tit chap'ron rouge» [Little Red Riding Hood] in French – a familiar panorama of wolves, woods and grandmothers. But Sleeping Beauty existed only in English for me – "Just get up already," I thought every time, "What's wrong with that girl anyhow, just lying there, waiting?" What's wrong, indeed.

I sew and I strip furniture in French, but I tend to my small garden in English. I'm an opinionated social commentator in English, but my only real hero is a fourteenth-century French feminist and critic, Christine de Pizan. I speak to dogs and cats in English, but I care for stranded bugs and snails in French. I'm more efficient in business in English, hammering out handouts, marking at lightning speed and processing reading quickly. But I'm more relaxed and informal in French, even with my students – «Eh, les amis, savez-vous que …?» [Hey friends, did you know that …?] instead of my customary English approach – "Yes, sir, how can I help you?" – even to a ten year old. I'm more easily angry in English, likely because this is where most of my adult life is situated. And I'm more easily tearful in French, probably because this is where my more innocent self resides.

My writing style varies too. In English, I hedge, producing sentences replete with "maybes" and "seems." In French, I'm more decisive, infusing my texts with «très» [very] and «vraiment» [really]. And my emphatic tone seems completely opposite. In English, I have a chronic problem with overusing the word, "important." In French, it's «petite» that's too frequent in my writing. It's as if I don't weigh things at all the same way in my two languages, so that things mean too much or too little. Goldilocks again.

I have no control over the language of my dreams or prayers. And strangely, my humour register differs in each language. In English, I use and receive only sarcasm, irony, dry wit, and a sharp tongue. Gone from my instruments and possibilities are the «p'tites blagues» [little jokes]; «des bonnes histoéres» [good stories]; the ability to «s'agacer parce qu'on s'aime» [to tease because we love each other]; and the nerve to join in games and «d'êt' d'la partie» [to be part of the fun].

There are other examples of this pivoting towards each side, this constant flux of personality, ability, and loyalty curiously called by theorists "balanced bilingualism." There is, in fact, nothing balanced about it – no equilibrium, no point where everything is just right. That isn't how bilingualism is lived. There is instead on an hourly, daily, and yearly basis – and on the personal, family, and social level – a constant churning, an ebb and flow that dwarfs the tides of the Bay of Fundy. So when I try to come up with a reasoned, detached political opinion on one side or the other, I can't.

I walk a thin line between belonging in each language and not belonging at all. I'm different in my languages, and not fully myself in either. But are my possibilities quantitatively or qualitatively changed from those of a person with only one language? In other words, do I merely have more words and ways to say the same thing? Or have I acquired the possibility of saying something substantially different? Does bilingualism completely change the relationship between thinking and being?

Fish

One fish – a salmon,
coloured silver, purple, yellow, pink –
sees herself swimming wildly upstream
fighting gnashing currents
to find her way home.

One fish – a river trout,
coloured silver, dotted red and gold –
sees herself moving up step-wise sensibly
in locks upon the seaway
to get somewhere else.

Two fish souls sensing
currents mix warm and cold together,
cast but one shadow from the surface view,
appearing as a single lifeform
in the oceanic feeling.

SHIFTING GRANDMOTHERS

A CLASH OF CIVILIZATIONS?

The closest I ever come to understanding the linguistic tension that
inhabits me is when I'm alone outdoors somewhere – listening to crickets, camping, or walking – even in the modest stretch of woods behind
my mother's home still today. That is, when I'm not talking to anyone
at all, in French or English. In silence only can I understand the language debate on the ground in this country, and in my head.

But silence has been hard to find since 1967, a curious year when the
sexual abuse seemingly stopped, crowds first rallied to the call «Vive
le Québec Libre!»* and fifty million «étrangers» invaded Quebec for a
world fair. My mother took my brother, me, and my granny by train
to Montreal in a serendipitous assembly of all of our family's symbols.
Granny travelled first class for free because of my grandfather's service
to CN. And my mother made matching frilly red tartan skirts for her
and me, poofy and knee-length, like a French Canadian line-dancing
costume.

We were going to «erprésenter el Québec,» she said, yet the only
thing I remember of this extraordinary day – other than the skirts and

* As said by Charles de Gaulle, the French president, on a visit to Expo 67, the
World Fair; it became one of the most charged political phrases in provincial
history, rallying separatist fervour then up to the present day.

how my brother became lost for moments at a time, over and over again – is that I stole, yes, stole, a smooth black stone shaped like an apricot pit from the Japanese pavillion. It's a sin I later confessed but didn't regret. I clenched it my hand all day, seeking meaning among the shouts of strangers. That was the year one tension stopped and another began in its place.

This constant tugging at identities, origins, and symbols embroiled everyone around me, so much so that what was tragic and outright funny was often one and the same thing. I have, for example, a clear recollection of my Granny St-Onge arriving, innocently, for one of my mother's famous dinner events in a light blue woollen skirt and jacket, one of her peacock pins on the left lapel, a shoe bag holding sensible black pumps. My mother, smiling ear to ear, informed her that no one could walk in before weighing themselves and paying a penny a pound for the party. My granny politely resisted, insisting on her 115 pounds, an underestimate to be sure.

But fortified with her own champagne, my mother wouldn't let up. And there they stood, for ten minutes at least, my granny caught in the vestibule, my mother blocking the inside door. Each refused to budge. The scale waited. Granny slowly became angry, incensed at the rudeness of asking someone of her age and social stature to be humiliated like this. But my mother slowly became angry too, at a woman who couldn't put away «ses airs» [her airs] for just one night and have a bit of fun. A clash of civilizations, family style.

I finally negotiated a truce, a devious compromise. «Vas-donc voir si l'pain brûle! Y m' semb' que'j'sens quequ'chose.» [Why don't you go and check if the (garlic) bread is burning. I think I smell something.] I said it to my mother with my customary seriousness, which she had no reason to doubt. And since my mother was famous for enjoying her parties and finding a forgotten ingredient in a cold oven the next day, she dashed off.

I winked at my granny and had her walk gingerly to the side of the scale while I put my own foot on it to mimic the scale's sound. I knew my mother's attention to detail, even at a time like this. Then my granny put some coins in the jar just as my mother returned. «Pis, combien?» [So, how much?], she asked me with a giggle. «Cent vingt»

[120], I answered steadily, trying to make it believable by upping my granny's estimate the tiniest bit. Just then a carful showed up and lined up for the scale, true to the party ethic they held, taking my mother's attention off my granny completely.

Yet this confusion in the vestibule remains a vivid portrait of cultural contrasts. Among French Canadians, you called ahead before visiting even close relatives, but on arrival everyone got kissed. And when asking how things were, you injected hope and empathy: «C'pas grave. Qu'est-ce'tu veux? Ça'rrive.» [That's all right. What can you do? It happens.] English Canadians, on the other hand, popped in unannounced, but they could make it to the kitchen and back without even a hug. And when inquiring about things, you demonstrated intellectual engagement: "That's really interesting. I heard that too … Have you tried …" In Quebec in those years, you were always crossing worlds when crossing doorways.

UNE BONNE MÉMOÉRE

The same tandem operated on those many occasions when my parents went out of town. My Grand-maman Raisin, my francophone great-grandmother (my mother's grandmother), was left in charge for years. She was a whisper of a woman at eighty years and as many pounds, who dabbed herself behind the ears with vanilla extract and pinched her cheeks for colour. She routinely lifted her skirt to stand on a chair in our home to reach a pot of jam, a fresh jar of peanut butter, or a new packet of «p'tits biscuits,» her worn socks rolled down. In all the years I knew her, I remember seeing those coarse, brown stockings bunched at her ankles far more than pulled up where they were supposed to be. She was too busy for such a fuss, didn't care.

The snapshot of her that endures in my mind is nothing at all like the few photographs the family has of her, taken on some wedding day or other special event, where she wears a dark, modest suit and a small hat. This look doesn't capture her essence at all. Rather, it's this: a plain cotton dress, patterned on a white background – she's sewn it herself, of course. There's a round collar and a few buttons, usually at the back, and the sleeves are short. In sum, it's a practical dress. The skirt is plain, falling just past the knee, its front protected by an apron, mostly white and never perfectly clean, which she's made out of a similar dress that wore out over time. It was good fabric to recycle, so I had nighties she made for me made from her old nighties. When they wore down too, I kept small squares of the soft cloth as my comfort treasures. In my memory shot, she's elbow-deep in bread dough. When visitors come in, she erupts in smiles, throws her hands under the tap furiously, and wipes them on the edge of her apron before coming to grab a face, pinch a cheek, and offer everyone a warm hug.

She always wanted to give us something special for a late-night snack, «juste pour une p'tite folie, une p'tite traite» [just for a little fun/joke, a little treat], she'd say, giggling, a timeless squint in her eyes. She was a bright, young soul inside a misfitting shell. It wouldn't have been a visit with her without a teensy treat. She sneaked fancy cookies from the secret reserves she knew my mother kept for «la compagnie,» and dug Glosettes for us stealthily out of her purse as if they were illegal contraband.

She gambled with us for sultanas, tiny hills of them by our left sides, glasses of juice on our right, the pairs of jacks and sevens laid out in between. When she got tired, she started eating her own pile of raisins, a few at a time. She couldn't help it, she said, just hungry, as she let us win our way to a bedtime that was at least on the decent side of mid-night. A child who was also a grownup when she needed to be. My first favourite human being in the entire universe.

She held her cards with hands worn raw, a real worker's hands. I loved those hands of hers – long, straight, muscular fingers, unfinished at their tips. Natural. No rings, no jewels of any kind. Only a few minor scars, perhaps a recent scrape or cut. She often cheated at cards, and everybody knew it, but she did it with deliberate panache, inviting us to catch her. It was just an excuse for another laugh, training us to stay sharp, and she was delighted when we were on to her. The hours passed without any definition except for the full current of joy. But when it came time, I couldn't sleep. I worried she'd fall climbing on another chair. So I became her caretaker, straining to hear her move-ments. When she was done the dishes, she scrubbed the frying pans. More chair sounds. Then not stopping for a second, she took on a corner of the linoleum that wasn't perfectly clean. And this, well past midnight.

Sadly, she became too ill to care for us at one point, then too ill to come to see us, then too ill even to be seen by us. «C'est mieux qu'tu' gardes une bonne mémoére que d'la voir comme al'est là» [Better to keep a good memory of her than to see her as she is now], my mother said in sorry tones. Leaping from one Sunday to no Sundays, I never got to say goodbye.

AN IMPECCABLE GUEST

So the next time my parents were out of town, we had a new grand-mother and atmosphere. Granny St-Onge brought her tidy suitcase and accepted reluctantly to sit with us for a few days. Admittedly, it wasn't quite what she envisaged herself doing as a comfortably retired railway and military widow. By then, she had a beautiful four-bedroom home to take care of, and even though her five sons were grown, there were clear standards to uphold, not easily achieved without help. Yet she maintained her home, garden, and self impeccably.

That's why the pictures I have of her, of which there are a sizable amount, all look precisely like her. She had no house dress that was any different from her Sunday best, as far as I could tell. It was as if she had a uniform, unchanging for the circumstances: expensive suits from England or Holt Renfrew, skirts exactly to the knee, matching blazers, themed decorative pins on the left lapel, tidy white shirts underneath, and plain pumps. In summer she wore linen suits in pastel colours, with tan or white shoes. In winter, she wore wool suits in dark shades, with black or navy shoes.

My favourite part was the lapel pin from Birks, surrounded by faux-diamonds and silver filigree – treasures to look at but not quite touch. Surely she wore other things to do her daily chores, but I never saw her engaged in anything other than putting the finishing touches on a meal. At those moments, she would still be in her immaculate Granny uniform, only without the blazer. And she would have added a crisp, smart apron in a soft floral print on white, perfectly starched, that cov-ered not just her skirt but went up over her chest, often with ruffled edges along its sides. Given her slight roundness, the overall effect was like a fancy version of Mrs Tiggy-Winkle in the Beatrix Potter books I adored.

When she watched us, that uniformity enveloped our time together, became its strength and its weakness. Gone were the games, the laughs, the midnight jam. I don't remember her ever coming into the kitchen. It isn't that she couldn't have cooked for us – for she was an excellent homemaker – or that she was unwilling to. It was a simple case of her respecting social norms to the letter. You didn't enter another woman's kitchen, upset her cupboards, inspect her ingredients. You didn't presuppose that there would be the right sort of spice or meat for what you'd have liked to cook, or eat. Rather, you let the matter unfold as it had been planned, according to the detailed list left on the refrigerator by the woman of the house. And in the matter of reheating, a young girl should easily be able to manage, and was certainly of age to develop useful skills.

So instead of taking those moments together to teach us how to make crumpets or cook a better steak, well done, my grandmother acted like the respectable guest that she was in our home, performing her role as she herself had grown to understand it in the high-class days of her own youth. She retreated to the den where she remained, gracious and steady, smelling of soap, expensive perfume, and foundation makeup, a garden of a woman. There she knitted for Protestant church bazaars with plump, manicured hands adorned with diamonds, pearls, and sapphires as she watched Ed Sullivan on TV – but not those horrible Beatles, oh my, certainly not. She napped between rows of green and yellow, a footstool propping a calf with deep blue veins that showed through her silk nylons. And she made small requests of the kitchen help (aka me) as I became her servant, responding as best I could to her legalistic sort of interest in our comings and goings. There was no passion, but there was safety. I went to bed early.

LIFE IN THE VESTIBULE

In those years it never occurred to me that those shifting grandmothers were such a salient demonstration of my bilingual personas. There was the strong-willed woman full of intensity – exuberant, dynamic, passionate to the point of danger. She was my freedom, my love, my joy. And there was the upstanding lady full of sensibility – logical, steadfast, intellectual to the point of dryness. She was my compass, my stability, my calm. The balance between grandmothers, between selves, always threatened to tip, like a shallow boat in a November river. But somehow, it never did. Instead, I rowed upon the different emotional currents of my languages, on one side, then another, moving in the unpredictable flow of human life. Language became a membrane, more porous than tight, letting reality in and out, diluting my languages inside a single self, becoming the mess of alternative linguistic identities that I think are "me," and that I make be "me."

Book junkie that I am, I began to notice writers along the way talking about their own multilingual messes. I found kindred souls meshed, churned, embodied, exiled, inhaled and exhaled in one, two, even more languages. Memoirs of bilingual lives started to populate my room. And the idea of bilingualism being primarily an emotional phenomenon began to consume me. After a while, I was reading rather than eating – not an unfamiliar pattern by now – hungry to surround myself with people who were hanging between worlds, perpetually liminal, like me.

Of course this liminality is shared not just between me and a few bilingual memoirists but by billions of people around the world. It's because multilingualism is the rule rather than the exception around the globe. My handful of linguistic capital, counting only two tongues, looks meagre indeed compared to the gold reserves of those who function routinely in three or four languages or more. Even so, little is actually understood about bilingual beings. Of course, there's research on where language is located in the brain, most of it based on aphasics, individuals who've lost functions or fluency after an injury or illness. But this work is really the study of language pathology – language damaged rather than language lived. Besides, does anyone really believe that physiology is enough to explain language?

Are there any bilingual individuals in the world who do not realize that language is a powerful social instrument? For example, that employing (deploying?) a dominant language can get them ahead in business? Or that they tend to choose their mother tongue for baby talk or romantic endearments? Or that swear words come out more easily in one language than the other – sometimes the mother tongue (because it's emotional), and sometimes the new tongue (because it's neutral)? Or that hiding their knowledge of a language can actually help in some sensitive situations? Or that favourite movies, songs, and memories are more poignant in one language than another?

Language encompasses all of that, and more. Of course, language choice includes finding the best word for an object – knowing which language to use, when, where, why, and all of that. Even more important, language represents choice for the user – options about lifeways, worldviews, and tools for thought. It offers communicative systems that are more attractive or less so depending on one's needs, and that are sometimes hard to decide between. That's because bilingualism is complicated and multi-faceted, and can't be reduced to simple frameworks.

Like shifting grandmothers coming over to stay for a while, each language comes with its own baggage, history, and possibilities. That's why the relationship between a person's languages is always ambivalent. The bilingual can exist or not exist on either side, or in between. Bilingual language worlds are separated, but connected too. Language lets the bilingual flow thoughts from one field to another, but language also can arrest the soul and heart to provide grounding. The bilingual is a complicated hyphen. In French, «un trait d'union»: a connection, a line between.

MOP AND NECKLACE

So how does it feel to be a complicated hyphen? The year was 1965, a catechism lesson. We each had our books on our desks, literature in the fullest spirit of modernity so that it perfectly aligned not only with our reading level but also with the designated themes of our English-style Catholicism. The discrepancy with my own brand, staunchly French, would soon become apparent.

In hindsight, the story seemed to be a deliberate derivative of de Maupassant's *The Diamond Necklace*. There were two brothers and their poor mother, a "washerwoman," and her birthday was near. Each boy thought about what to buy her, given his limited funds. One brother spent an outrageous amount of money to buy the mother a diamond necklace so that she'd feel glamorous and beautiful. The other brother spent a more modest amount to buy her a shiny new pail and mop. Which was the better gift? There was a teacher-led class discussion on the question for a few moments. For those unfamiliar with Catholic schools in those years, I can assure you that the idea of a class discussion is being liberally applied here. In reality, Sister asked rhetorical questions, made eye contact with a few who could be trusted to nod "yes." And then she opened her gift to us: *the* answer.

Of course, the better gift was the diamond necklace. It was appropriately special and honoured the mother properly. Every hand went up for her so-called "vote" of who saw it her way. Every hand, that is, except mine.

"Do you honestly think the mop and pail were the better gift, Kathleen?"

Muted snickers from classmates. Tension. Challenging authority in a Catholic school is virtually indistinguishable from challenging an ecclesiastical decree. But my answer impelled from a depth, dark but rich, that overcame the lump in my throat.

My logic was that the diamond necklace was an excessive waste of money that could have been spent on food. Besides, in the mother's social circle, she'd never have had the chance to wear the necklace, and it might even have been stolen because her home was shabby, insecure, violable. Perhaps during the crime she or her sons might even have been injured. The far better gift, I thought, was the mop and pail. First, it was a prudent choice that didn't unduly drain resources from the son's budget, leaving something for a rainy day. Second, every time she used it – which, by profession, would be often – she'd be reminded of her birthday and her loving son's thoughtfulness. Third, no one would want to steal it, so the family would be as safe as they ever were. In fact, they might be even better off if the mother's ability to clean improved the management of her daily tasks.

Three or four heads turned to look at me like I was an alien. Sister's stifled moral dilemma morphed into a venomous stillness as the only sound was the hard, hard thump of books being gathered into a neat pile at the front of the class. The ripples of stress were so acute that a sweet boy in our class wet himself, as he invariably did when anxious. He sat at the back, as he had since kindergarten, precisely because of this problem. As a result, he was my nearest seatmate, year after year.

It was so sad, that yellow puddle forming, winding a slow path around the legs of his chair and his desk as he began to cry. "Kathleen, go get the mop," Sister ordered. I'm not kidding.

Off we went down the hall, him to his hook in the primary locker room to get the spare pants that hung in waiting, me to the custodial cupboard to get the mop, a stringy thing with a worn wood handle – a skinny, smelly giant. "It's not your fault," he said, but we both knew that already. The catechism sister was just a mean woman. This would be the same sister who had used me one day in a twisted experiment in classroom management. If two mischievous boys talked, she promised, she'd hit *me* with a ruler. Of course they talked. After all, we were only seven. So I had to place my hands on her desk, palms up, while she struck me with one of those fifteen-inch metal rulers. By the time she counted to eighteen, though, the boys were crying and I was still staring at her in the eye, unmoved. As if this even hurt! I watched her arm swing towards those hands way down on that desk. No problem. That's when she got that look again, the look of someone who's encountered an unanticipated problem. So she stopped.

"It's okay," I said to him that day as we cleaned up together, taking up our regular routine, calmly as always. I truly didn't care. It was still well worth it to sit at the back. Besides, it gave me time to think, to memorialize the moment. To inscribe it psychically as I strive to do when I think I'm living something significant that I should try not to forget. For here were the two babysitting grandmothers rendered in print. The mop versus the necklace.

I guess that recording mechanism is automatic somehow, a multi-sensory imprinting of anything particularly potent – formed maybe because of my troubles. But I hear it as a supportive and steady voice, in English only, issuing basic instructions: "Remember this. Now listen. Now look." I think the non-technical word for it is "hearing voices," and there are wide-ranging opinions about this phenomenon. It's described in very different ways by spiritual leaders, drug addicts, survivors of near-death experiences, and the *Diagnostic and Statistical Manual of Mental Disorders*. But I frankly can't imagine having lived without that help, and I have no memory of myself without it. After all, it was the same source that counselled me to *run!* or to *hide!* – what I regarded as life-saving advice, to be followed immediately.

In any event, here I was running and hiding in the middle ground of my bicultural self – my selves. I was inside one cultural paradigm, my *English* Catholic school, yet even while there I remained inside my other cultural paradigm, my *French* Catholic mindset. I travelled easily from one set of views to another. Chose my allegiances and my values issue by issue, like at a cafeteria. Pretention versus humility? An easy choice. Besides, Sister's English Catholic idea of "scary" was laughable. It couldn't compare with my French Catholic version. So I wasn't afraid of her in the least. And I was beginning to be quite comfortable with my psychological duality, my existence as a *matryoshka* doll, this continuous inversion of inside and outside – my linguistic, cultural, and psychological ambivalence. My life as a human hyphen.

Etiology

«En fin d'compte,
c'est juste comme
un p'tit animal.»

"After all, it's just
like a small animal."
A familiar adult was
recently explaining
the motivation for a
toddler's actions —
the limitations of
not even a baby
but of a good, sound
mind of more than
two years of age.

That's the missing link
in the absurd causation
of the acts against me.
It wasn't enough to
accommodate *zeitgeist*:
misogyny, patriarchy,
sexuality, oligarchy,
pathology, criminality,
materiality, theology.
There was also a need
for *radical empiricism*.

The child as *tabula rasa*:
capable of nothing but
the feeble needs of flesh.

The child as a *subject*:
understanding very little,
remembering even less.

The child as a *primitive*:
a debased captive in the
rigid empire of adults.

The etiology of the acts
is a deviant philosophy.

18

RUPTURES

DES P'TITES POUPÉES

I headed off to school each day in those years at Marymount dressed like «une belle p'tite mademoiselle,» my hair pulled back tight with fabric flowers all around, a meadow halo. My mother would insist on that hairdo until I was twelve, impressing upon me the importance of always looking one's best. At school, the hemline was mercifully dictated – no more than two inches above the knee, measured on random check days. But out of school, my wardrobe consisted of excessively short dresses with matching frilly underwear well into my sixth or seventh year. From there, skirts remained skimpy (pants disallowed until age twelve), but the frills on the underpants were abandoned in favour of another triumph of modernity, artificial fabric: «p'tites culottes» in unbreathable acrylic or nylon.

It was «complètement normal» [completely normal] in the French-Canadian culture of the 1960s, where young girls were expected to be «des p'tites poupées» [little dolls] or «des p'tits bouts d'choux» [little bits of cabbage]. Both options delivered a compliant, coy female who was sure to make the uncles and father's work friends whistle. Making them whistle was supposed to be a good thing. Being invited to sit on their laps was apparently a good thing too.

That cynical conclusion of mine, according to kitchen table conversations with my mother, is just one more example of my prudishness, my «froideur d'une anglaise» [the coldness of an Englishwoman]. She means my sexual conservatism – my so-called anglo view of life by which I'm relatively more inhibited, as my granny was, or so I'm told. Her husband, my French-Canadian paternal grandfather, the soldier, apparently thought she was «très froide.» I don't know if my husbands thought me cold. Perhaps they did. But I did stay married to a man twenty years younger than me for seven years – something hard to do, one would think, if I were really repressed. Then again, he came from a relatively conservative Islamic culture. Maybe by his standards I was a wild thing, a sexual beast.

Does my sexuality depend, then, not just on the language I live and speak – with my words and with my body – but also on the language of my listener? Could it be that my sexuality isn't really my own at all, but a kind of product of dialogue? It's a strange idea, but maybe I'm always who – or whoever – I am because of who I'm with. And what I think of as one of my key personal attributes is actually created outside of me – in the space between what I speak (with my bilingual body) and what my listener (in his or her linguistic body) can hear? Is sexuality born on (in) a hyphen, too?

After all, this is the main analytical frame in the social sciences these days, "social constructivism," in a nutshell – and it's also what can be explained by it. The idea is that we exist in spaces where what we are and become is critically hinged on where we are and who we're with. Then again, this could be just another example of how my mother is right. She usually is. I'm more English than French in my sexuality, in my gendering. I do not, for example, find myself at all flattered by whistles on the street, though my mother still does. And I still avoid frilly things like the plague.

Years after the frilly underwear days, I found out that my brave auntie – the British one who was, according to the French females in the clan, «pas bin l'fun» [not much fun] – had called my mother after at least one family event to tell her that this way of displaying a daughter wasn't appropriate. Poor uncle, my parents thought: «C'pas bin drôle avoir une femme comme ça.» [It's not very funny to have a wife like that.] So the frilly underwear years went on until I outgrew the largest available size. I lost track of those years and most of those parties, except for memories of being grabbed by the butt by men whose laps I was asked to sit on, and having tongues forced down my throat when I was asked for a kiss on the cheek, always followed by howls of laughter. «Bin voyons-donc. Y'a rien là.» [Come on, now. There's nothing wrong with that.]

Why did I think my mother was so right if this didn't feel right at all? I suppose I resolved the matter like we all do, delaying a true understanding of our parents until we're old enough to see people as products of their times, no more nor less than we are. In this case, products of times when there was too much tolerated from the heads of households – those dear old patriarchs – and family myths remained relatively unbroken from previous centuries. When sexuality and pleasure were let loose following two great wars and a financial depression, leaving ordinary people in a celebratory mood for decades. And when little credit was given to the selfhood of children – their ability to have bodily and spiritual integrity as distinct beings, capable of learning and remembering from the get-go, even in utero.

At the very least, the paradox that I still consider my mother my main guide, despite openly resisting her guidance, speaks volumes for the myopic politics of the mother tongue. We see the world only through our mothers, and our mother tongues, from the start. More than a tongue, our first language is a set of eyes, a view on absolutely everything. We can't even see our way out except from here – and we can't understand our own stuckness except through this lens. Our nearsightedness becomes both our purported safety and our enforced limit. No wonder, then, that I resist my suffering in the same stroke – engage in a classic passive-aggressive relationship with my mother, and my mother tongue, in one fell swoop.

This is the origin of the sorrow so many others feel, too, when they endure language attrition. There's a profound sense of dislocation at being edged out of your place, even if you chose this alienation for yourself, for whatever reason. There's no stronger pull than a mother tongue, however troubled your life in it has been. It's a linguistic fate from which any effort to escape tempts calamitous outcomes. For if you refuse or reject it, the pain of being excluded will be yours forever. And the constant sorrow of exclusion is far harder to endure than the daily injustice of inclusion.

In a home barely five miles away, four French female cousins who attended religious school at the Ursulines* while I attended Marymount ran around the house routinely at bedtime while their father threatened to catch them, saying loudly, «M'a't'manger 'es p'tites fesses» [I'm going to eat your little butts]. One of those cousins would join me when we were eight and ten respectively in dressing up as Playboy bunnies, puffy tails sewed onto our ballet leotards, offering and lighting cigarettes at a casino-themed party one night at my home. Around the same time each night, at my British auntie's, three English female cousins got into flannel nighties and were tucked into bed with a story.

Trudeau once famously said that the government had no place in the bedrooms of the nation. But the truth is that in the politics of this nation – and of my family – English and French *have* been in the bedroom together.

HOW IS THIS ALL GOING TO TURN OUT?

I ran into Trudeau once, quite literally, when he was still prime minister. He had a home that backed onto Mount Royal Avenue, behind McGill, and I was in the habit of parking my car there, not really thinking that I was at the rear of his house. It must have been 1978, early spring, because of the boyfriend I was with – my invariable marker along my timeline. Trudeau came out of his rear gate, looking every bit like an ordinary professor up on the hill, maybe law or French literature.

We crashed into one another on the sidewalk, laughing and uttering niceties. I honestly can't remember if we spoke English or French. And there was nothing about it at all that seemed out of the ordinary or memorable. It was just another day in Montreal, where out of a sea of concrete rises more culture than can fit into the densest Mordecai Richler story. Back then, at least, you could easily bump into movie and rock stars while you were just out buying bagels.

Strangely, not more than six months later, the following summer, the collision incident almost repeated itself. This time I was in Quebec

---

* The Ursuline Convent in Old Quebec is organized by the French Roman Catholic Ursuline order. Founded in 1639, it is recognized as the oldest educational institution for women in North America.

City, and the bumpee was none other than René Lévesque, riding the high tide of popularity, just coming out of a bar on Grande Allée with his entourage. I was with a girlfriend who was easily six foot two, and the top of his head was barely at her chest. He laughed warmly, and again there was friendly chatter. Still, there was nothing unusual about it: just another day in a town where politicians outnumber restaurateurs, and everyone ends up at the bar sooner or later, elbow to elbow.

But the juxtaposition of those two events within less than a year suggests a growing sense of something gurgling, rising. Positions and ideologies about French and English weren't being formed far off in legislative halls in Quebec or Ottawa but on ordinary sidewalks, in ordinary bars, by people who'd grown up only a few miles from each other, knowing each other's languages, bumping into one another each and every day. And yet, they saw their home and heritage in such opposite ways.

And this language debate, as we'd come to name it, would soon shape the daily lives of individuals like me, as our bilingual identities would be re-formed and re-crafted into political entities – turning us into players in a dangerous game of "national vision" versus "authentic ethnicity." It would add a heavy social layer to the complex linguistic structure in which we already lived at the individual and family level.

In the space of the few short years that followed, we witnessed an earthquake that opened crevasses into which I and many others fell. I remember the October Crisis of 1970,* walking home from school to the sound of sirens. One of my English school friend's fathers was whisked off to a think tank somewhere, as if a bit of careful planning by English minds might settle the whole thing quickly – old tactics redeployed, a familiar pattern. But violence continued to pry into our social frames, bringing wave upon wave of civic clashes. Among the most notorious events was the death of Pierre Laporte, the deputy premier and minister of labour at the time, in whose honour the bridge by my home would be retitled. Symbols of discord began redefining, and renaming, the scene around us. Within six years, the PQ was elected to

---

* A social uprising centred mainly in Montreal, but with effects province wide due to the resulting imposition of the War Measures Act and the political backlash that followed.

lead the province, after which many anglo families took their children and their money to Toronto for good.

Changes came quickly from then on. With the momentous sign legislation,* the Greek souvlaki shop down the street had to be renamed in French only – along with just about every other business in major centres around Quebec where English and French had been trying to coexist until then. And routinely now, a new provincial-national institution, l'Office québécois de la langue française,† began issuing proclamations about ordinary language. For example, «une ride en van» – a common expression – was supposed to be «une randonnée en fourgonnette» from now on. It wasn't long, then, before we all began to feel like «des maudits colons» [damned colonists/uneducated subjects of an imperial power] who'd been speaking the improper language all along. Never mind English – even our patois was all wrong.

In the countryside, too, the transformations spread over the course of a single year. Huge billboards for Players Cigarettes and Coca-Cola gave way to signage for the «Zecs»‡ on the new landscape of the «francophonie.» The Marlboro man's giant American face was edged out by promotions for a local festival. And warnings about upcoming road construction became French only. If you didn't speak French, you'd never even understand about the new detour on the road ahead.

One of the billboards that disappeared in those days was a particularly familiar one, caution against careless campfires. It showed a huge brown bear running, his head turned towards drivers and his butt on fire. It was prominent along highways everywhere – along with his English warning, *Smokey says, "Watch out!"* or *Smokey says "Be careful!"* or something like that. I don't remember the exact wording, just the funny bear on fire. One of my father's brothers, another artist, had illustrated it for the province's park service, and it made a strong impression on me to see a painting I'd seen trial sketches for dominate the terrain like

* La Charte de la langue francaise [Charter of the French Language], also known as Bill 101, passed in 1977.
† The OLF is a language monitor and an agent of francization in Quebec – the most visible arm of Bill 101.
‡ Zone d'exploitation contrôllée, a provincial system for managing ecological resources since 1978.

that. But Smokey's English name, English slogan, and English butt got chased out of town. And within a few years, this uncle, who managed the *Quebec Chronicle Telegraph* for a few years – North America's oldest daily (since 1764), where I had my first-ever summer job at sixteen – took off too, like Smokey, to «les États.» There, he joined another paternal uncle, a Harvard business graduate who also decided to make «les États» his home. Their departure to English worlds was as much a sign of the times as the signs themselves.

There were so many shifts in a decade that at our family celebrations, even non-political types began to wonder, «Comment ça va tourner, toute ça?» [How is all this going to turn out?]. On any day, the situation in the province threatened to rip open, jeopardizing social relations on which we depended. For years we'd spoken the language in which we first made contact: English to bilingual school friends, French to bilingual family friends, French to one parent and English to the other, and so on. We'd never insisted on indivisible loyalties. But here we were now, talking about who was really French and who was English, and why it might matter. It was a strain that tore dangerously at the delicate balance in my own mind. I was walking gingerly, with a foot on each log, in a difficult but predictable river, when «t'din coup» [all of a sudden] the current of our everyday cultural politics changed completely.

My brother's best friend, a francophone, showed up one day at our English public high school (after I'd graduated) with a group from his French public high school. They were inflamed with péquiste fervour, as they staged a protest denouncing English schooling in Quebec. «Pas d'anglais au Québec!» the friend shouted from the sidewalk. As my brother watched from inside the building, his most valued childhood friendship – a decade of precious history – was excised from his heart. It left a deep, unmendable scar.

Meanwhile, one of my best friends for a decade got pregnant at fifteen. She was an anglophone neighbour sent to the French public school that adjoined her property, while I'd gone to the English private school that adjoined mine. Within weeks, she'd moved into the downtown core of Quebec, its most devoutly francophone quarter, with her péquiste boyfriend. A few months later, they set off for the country towards Kamouraska with their new baby. "You and your stupid gang," she said to me one day on a city bus, before they left. We wouldn't speak again for thirteen years. When we did, we were both in British Columbia.

In public and in private spaces, the fabric of so many intertwining lives had suddenly become undone, dangerously stretched, and then snapped, in relationships all over the sociolinguistic landscape. All this when, in fact, so little had been said between the people in question. Yet so much had been said around them, and to them. And so many words had died or disappeared in those days, leaving us with less and less to say that meant the same thing to each of us.

The casual discards from joual were immediately replaced with little emotion, like worn appliances, by remarkably similar words that were considered to be much better. Through this massive reno project, «d'la comprenure» [human understanding] was now «de la compréhension»; «une égrafignure» [a scratch] was now «une égratignure»; «un chanteux» [a singer] was now «un chanteur»; «un chicaneux» [a scrapper] was now «un chicaneur»; and «un conteux» [a storyteller] was now «un conteur.» And on and on. Each «nouveau mot» posed shamelessly as «son pareille» [its copy, mate, twin, same], as if the original would not be missed. But it was.

MAUDITDUPLESSIS

I reacted by detaching myself further, leaving the province for good in 1983, never returning except for brief visits. I lived in Manitoba for three years, and then went further west to British Columbia for fifteen years, where trees were as big as buildings and moss as thick as fur, and there was rain in every sky – the edge of the world. Then, just to be sure, I settled across the strait, a two-hour boat ride from the mainland. And even though I'd put myself in the most fragile tectonic region of Canada, where we felt tremors on a monthly basis that threatened to seal off and swallow much of Vancouver Island, I felt safer than I ever had in my life.

Meanwhile, retired since the early 1980s, my father ironically found comfort in little other than television: *Mutual of Omaha's Wild Kingdom* and Jacques Cousteau specials, worlds far distant. He sent me a Canadian passport application, and every time I called my mother (he and I rarely spoke directly), he prompted her to remind me to send in the application. By this point, his customary rant had evolved beyond «mauditduplessis» to «mauditpéquistes» [damned péquistes]. And he had a deep conviction, an obsession, really, that the province would be lost in his lifetime. I couldn't figure out what he meant. Would I be denied Canadian citizenship because I was a Quebecer? Would I be denied passage through a new Quebec? It didn't make sense to me.

Then again, in a profound way, my father understood perfectly. Deeply troubled himself, he'd absorbed and fused the disturbances around him, including the language debate. For even in those early years, it was becoming a convoluted mess. Irreconcilable linguistic selves, French and English had become like twins bound in too much history, engaged in a timeless metaphorical duel, holding selfhood for ransom. And using his own inimitable logic, my father had stumbled upon an emerging fact of considerable magnitude: language, identity, and location could be easily lost inside, and because of, one another.

Around 2006, at Pearson Airport in Toronto, I watched a family return to Turkey. They'd been here for about five years and we'd become close friends. The husband was kind and good-humoured; the three children, two girls and a boy, got along well with my three; and the wife was among the warmest, most sensitive people I've ever met. I cried as I watched them leave. I knew it would be forever. Why were they returning? Because somewhere in that confabulation of language, identity, and belonging, they felt they were losing their children. Increasingly fluent not just in English but in the lifestyle that accompanied the new language and country, these children – who were popular and happy at their public school – were becoming so different, too different in their eyes. They seemed to be diverging too much from the cousins back home, from the kind of people they'd been themselves as children, and from the children they'd hoped to raise: young minds and souls who could and would embrace their values.

They weren't the first family I knew that made the same choice. In 2004, I entirely missed the chance to go to the airport to do my crying because the departure came so suddenly. Another lovely family of five, Turks again. The father was a soft-spoken, moderate imam with a doctorate in religious studies and a full-time job as a taxi driver. The mother was a homemaker with a sprinkling of English from the few

LINC classes she attended when she wasn't tending to community work or teaching her heritage language.

The three children, two boys and a girl, were charming A+ students who were into soccer and social clubs at their public school. But there were too many days when the mother, a humble soul, was overwhelmingly sad that so much of the dialogue in the home among her children was moving out of her reach. She could hear it, but she couldn't understand it. Fast English, idioms flying past her – even the most polite ones – left her feeling edged out of motherhood. The decision was quick, taken over a weekend, a testament to the painful passion, the urgency, that informed the choice.

Two families not unlike my own. Not in the obvious way – considering the three children, or the co-location on the geographic and social panorama. But in the less obvious way, in that these parents were playing out right before my eyes, with their children, the decisions that had affected my parents and their children – my brother and me – so much. They were feeling in every cell of their bodies that their children were drifting away. That their children were changing from unwilling to willing exiles, adjusting to their new linguistic worlds by co-opting new psychological worlds. In the quiet purchase of five airplane tickets and a few second-hand suitcases, these parents resisted the drift. They sought and strained to pull their families back towards cohesion, collected the scattered pieces of the family image before it spread out too far to ever be mended.

EL MIROIR CASSÉ

In the mid-1960s, a popular art form invaded our home: broken mirror art. I don't know which matrilineal aunt started it, but it soon supplanted as the craft in vogue the spraying gold and silver of tree branches and driftwood. Re-casting a woman's power against religion and superstition, our households took to making something out of a broken mirror – «el miroir cassé» – other than a seven-year curse. If we didn't have any, we just broke a couple, putting them in a pillowcase tied with an elastic band, and smashing them with a hammer. Then we took the pieces and glued them tastefully onto black velvet stretched tight over plywood.

Sailboats and flowers were the customary themes. But far more consequential than the picture assembled by the shards was the picture broken by it. For everywhere around my home hung a piece of pre-postmodern art that, when I tried to look at it, made me see only my own face broken in a hundred jagged, uneven pieces. This was not at all like the sensation I had from time to time in front of mirrors, where I wondered if the face I saw was really mine, or whether that was really the colour my hair (wasn't it browner?). Those reflections on selfhood were internal – symptoms of fragmentation that could, at least, remain private. Instead, the reflection on the state of my self made by these mirror fragments – pieces deliberately broken and stuck with crunchy glue onto velvet banged hard onto stiffness – was brutally public.

In 1958, aged one: the first shard on the velvet landscape. *In the beginning, there was only darkness. There was no air and no animals. There was lots and lots of nothing. Empty. Then came liquid fire, pouring out of the earth. It was spitting up everywhere in that lonely darkness. And when it did that, you could see hard dry land between the cracks of red liquid fire. And the crusty dry land was broken up in deep cuts, scarred up with big earthquakes everywhere. Fire was coming up all over, like giant flame fountains, and the land was dead and empty. Nothing grew and no one was there. Only the fire was there, and the constant shaking of the ground, always breaking. And there was only heat and the spitting fire. The ground shook so hard. That's why the animals didn't come yet, I think. I don't know for sure. And that's how it was in the beginning.*

See how the Elder taught me well, taught an infant girl about the beginning. There, while he sat on the edge of the bed crying and quivering, and I lay there with no body, except a face, and no feeling of anything except a memory of *his* feelings – scared and regretful – and his sorrowful whimpering. He read bedtime stories to himself then. I got to listen – Genesis and Revelation, I know that now – his tears plopping on well-worn pages of his Old Testament. He was pious and pathetic.

But I liked stories then, still do. So I heard what he said and built a picture in my head, coded it as a kind of map of the world. It was an ordinary case of the primitive brain curiously recording an unconscious tracing in coloured pictures, printing it all to some place in the mind between the sense of smell and the sense of fear, in some ancient lobe that lets infants put away things that don't make much sense at the time, or at any time. It let me keep things that stayed buried in my psyche until my head broke open fifty years later. Dry and wretched, my memory spat sorrow like flowing fire as the deepest vacuums of my consciousness shifted, yielding a careful construct, mine from a time of absence. I found my old blueprint, this precious template of my life on which much was added from that first image, when the nothingness of empty space turned into living hell on earth. He was right. It was just the beginning.

In 1978, aged twenty: the final shard on the velvet landscape. «Bonne Année,» as they say. He has asked me to drive him home. Why me? It would take me fifty years to figure out why these events made me so tired. Why the Rivière Chaudière, there outside, called to me to jump in through the cracks of ice, head first, to start again downstream somewhere. Inside, voices were muffled as if through skin and thick dust. I should have been enjoying myself, but I couldn't. I saw accordions, laughter, singing, words. But something wouldn't let me relax here. (Do I ever relax?) A few canapés, pinched cheeks, «Bonjour ma belle.» I was done for another year. Four cousins gave me an apologetic look as I got my coat from the bedroom where they chatted, comparing lipsticks, adjusting minor complaints about a bra strap. I gave a quick kiss to all, and I was off to take this old priest home from the New Year's party.

Driving, twenty or thirty minutes passed. Silence mixed with questions about schooling. McGill, second year, biology, honours. I skipped the parts about the risky men, the drinking, the anorexia, the nervous breakdown, the amenorrhea, the recurring thoughts of suicide. I drove along the Trans-Canada, "the 20 East," from the party in Saint-Lambert-de-Lauzon towards Quebec City. Together we crossed over Pont Pierre Laporte – the bridge named after a soul caught up in a cycle of social violence. Myth and society merging with self, indissociable – the story of my life. A bit more driving from here, through the heart of the suburb of Sainte-Foy, right to the house where people like him live. People like him *do* live, you know: old priests with old housekeepers to cater to their old feet, their old sermons, their old pretensions.

It was a plain red-brown brick square, two storeys high, an ordinary house, 1940s style, absurdly normal. I'd never been inside. I stayed on the outside of everything, remote. I watched my life go by, just like now.

So I watched myself that day reach the front of the house and stop the car, a model I can't remember, with an interior colour I can't remember. Grey sky? Blue sky? No idea. My coat? I don't remember it at all. His coat? It must have been black. Everything about him was black except the thin white collar around his throat, a starched noose, and the rigid wrinkles under his thin-framed glasses. His look? Feigned nobility textured with self-absolution: arrogance, certainty, vanity, impunity, calm. His long right arm extended – gloved or not? I can't remember.

I just remember watching the breast below my left shoulder come under his large right hand, feel a squeeze, a hard squeeze. That's technique, I guess, going through layers of winter coat like that. I remember watching that hand on that long arm, and the breast, and seeing his eyes, fat bullets in a self-assured face, cold and confident, coming closer and closer. And then, his face stopping suddenly, a sharp change in affect. Surprise. Disappointment. Disabled rage in some faint register. Confusion, disbelief. Twisted amusement – almost.

If he said something then, I didn't hear it or don't remember. I watched myself sitting in the driver's seat. I watched myself say nothing. I watched the hand come off the breast, there on the left side of the body that is mine, and return to the right side of the body that is his. I watched him gather a bag on the car floor, shifting sideways. Then I watched him open the passenger door and get out. And I watched myself drive away.

I told no one about this except my Jewish boyfriend, a few days later, over sex and pot, when we had a good laugh about a decrepit Catholic pervert. It remained an isolated incident in my mind and my story, entirely disconnected from the shadowy memories I struggled to hold and understand – and, so often, to forget. But something deep inside tripped me up a bit, wouldn't quite let me settle on this version of things, of just a creepy old man trying his luck. I began to feel that I was lacking a critical piece. But what had I eclipsed here? Where else, when else, had I seen this man before, one of many of his kind appendaged to the family? The moment scratched its count on my prison wall.

Over time I cared less and less about the hand, the breast – and more and more about the eyes, the face, the tone, the look of presumptuous familiarity. Not a question, but a taking-it-for-granted conviction. A clear anticipation, as though I'd never think, nor even want, to deny him. As though sometime in a past I'd lost but he'd kept well, I had never denied him. As though he knew me as more than one of many who could have driven him that day. A day that seemed to be about something other than a hand, a breast, and a man obliterated for years who'd be filed in psychic oblivion for thirty more. A day about more than Père «Nom,» another completely forgettable man.

The broken pieces of my self, disjointed reflections scattered against a dark background, were hard to gather, challenging to reassemble into a whole. I heard but didn't listen to my father who, like other parents, worried about the fragmentation, the increasing irreconcilability of the emerging person. The dangerous rupture. Instead, I clenched my bleeding hands for decades around the shards I carried with me everywhere, hoping one day to reconstruct. With every breath I had left, I defended my ownership of those fragile, piercing bits of memory locked in the combined code of mother tongue and primal fear – that often threatened to become just a random bunch of bits.

Installation

It's a rough bath.
Two voices talk
beside me, dry –
away then closer –
not in the water.

One: slow, low, hoarse.
One: fast, quiet, bossy.

Scrubbed in a big rush.
Head, eyes all splashed.
Smoke round the tub.
Two sounds: La – Chine.
Again, again, again.
«Lachine? La Chine?»

«Vagin? Vagine?*»

---

* «Vagine» is rare old slang for "cunt," used in name-calling (or so the story goes) only among people with a very low level of education.

Another one, too.
A funny song?
Two step-counts.
Ends in «oune.»
«Baboune?*»
«Minoune?»
«Moumoune?»
«Toutoune?»
«Pitoune?»
«Foufounes?»
«Guidoune?»
«Zouzoune?»
«Bizoune?»

China and cheap slang
for sexuality are rolled up
together in my infant French.
But years later, I will
learn to speak English.

There will be much China
"this and that" at Granny's.
It's fancy stuff we put
on shiny dinner tables,
its name under everything.
I can read it when we scrub
the big plates so carefully.

*   The words in this stanza are all slang: baboune for "pout"; minoune for "mistress";
    moumoune for "a gay man"; toutoune for "a fat woman"; pitoune for "a slut" and
    also for "a little girl"; foufounes for "butt cheeks"; guidoune for "whore"; zouzoune
    for "vagina" and also a "female idiot"; and bizoune for "penis."

Made in China.
Made in China.
Everything comes
from this China.
Everything is signed
by this China.

It must be a great,
wide, huge place
full of fancy meals.
It sounds like vagina,
but it's not, you see.

In this language, English,
things are pretty, lovely,
handled only gently.
Not by rough hands.

In years to come,
I will even find
China on a map at
my brand new school –
and in a stamp collection.

And there will be dainty
China dolls to buy for gifts:
China and dignity
co-existing so politely
in my second language.

But I'll end up breaking
three China sets in all.
Child, I'll drop «par erreur
j'm'excuse bin beaucoup»*
two entire dolls' sets:
one my mother's,
one "my own."

Adult, moving, I'll drop
the "everyday" set
from my granny's.
The fourth, Granny's best,
lives in my furnace room.
I am afraid to touch it.

My sensuality entwines
my pathology. I'm still an
English China doll who once
bathed in «chinoiserie.»†

*   "By mistake; I'm very, very sorry."
†   Anything Chinese; also used colloquially in French to designate a jumble of
    information or an incomprehensible thing (physical or verbal), including mischief.

19

IMAGINARY COMPANIONS

PAPER PRINCESS

One of my very favourite possessions from childhood was a set of twelve wooden cubes, each about two inches across – a gift from my grand-maman Dumont. Four went sideways, and three went up and down. Each side of each block had a picture, one-twelfth of every story. If you flipped them just right, you could see six fairy tales spread across the blocks, one view at a time. Flip just one cube, and the picture became silly. Flip one whole row – very tricky – and you had a theatre scene change, stories merging. Turn them over all at once – almost impossible with small hands – and you could see a whole other story world underneath.

The set came with six small pictures showing the completed images, my blueprints. I remember Little Red Riding Hood: the woods, the girl, the bed, the granny, the wolf. I remember Snow White: the apple, the mirror, the girl, the dwarfs, the queen. I remember Hansel and Gretel: the woods, the trail, the candy, the father, the witch. I remember Cinderella: the mice, the ball, the girl, the clock, the godmother. And I remember the Three Little Pigs: the straw, the sticks, the bricks, the blowing, the wolf.

Why do I remember only five, no matter how hard I try to force up that last one from the deepest recesses of memory? I never find that sixth story – the missing pieces, the absent tale. I sometimes think I can picture it – wasn't there a donkey? Some beans? But not Jack-in-the-Beanstalk – I know that. Or do I? And then what bit I think I hold slips away again. Maybe I don't recall the pictures all that well after all. Maybe I've only fed a memory with repeated tellings of these classics, confused the present and the past. Switched sense and story – and vice versa?

Possibly, I've done just that. After all, the child's mind is porous, amorphous, generous even. It's free of the inconvenient boundaries of time and space. It knows no clear line between reality and fantasy – or between bedtime stories shared in books, and far-off stories shared in beds. That's why one may easily supplant the other as a substitution, a simple repetition. And that's how "fictions" about poisoned foods and magical kisses end up having exactly as much meaning as "truths" about how some things won't hurt at all, when they do – and how some things will feel good, when they don't.

This toy is so memorable for me, so infused with psychic history, that even though I lost it between dozens of moves, I was compelled to buy one like it at a yard sale in British Columbia in the late 1980s. It felt like a blessing just finding it. It's very much like my first one, made of wood with tightly pasted paper sides, and has six stories in all. I only have four of the accompanying images on well-worn paper – the previous owner(s) must have lost the other two. At any rate, I've put it in one of those pretty green boxes from Simons I love so much, and set it on my best bookshelf, among the works of my favourite scholars.* It holds more truth for me than anything they can ever write.

It's because this toy isn't a toy at all. It's a paper tapestry in six panels of the life I've led, a kaleidoscopic code in which tales spoke their plain lessons to me. Taught me that many people aren't what they appear to be, and you can never be careful enough to protect yourself when evil lurks in disguise. That the darkest woods can be safer than some homes that look perfectly normal from the outside. That a cave – a blanket, a big coat, a closet, or behind the curtains – can be a pretty good place to *hide!* if you're quick and quiet. That sleep can be very dangerous – how

---

* Simons is the most popular clothing retailer in Quebec City. It was founded in 1840, and its bright green packaging is iconic as «des boîtes de Simons.» The Simons family donated the 150-year-old Tourny fountain (from Bordeaux, Quebec's sister city) to celebrate the city's 400th anniversary in 2008.

can you get back? – and without any warning, you can meet wolves in your bed at night.

From twelve blocks of wood and paper, I discovered symbol-reading long before I knew the alphabet. I began to understand that every character in every scenario imaginable exists in multiple perspectives, on the surface and beneath, perpetually rotating and twisting, hidden and visible. To realize that coherent scenes of life are easily shattered, turned upside-down – flip, flip – so that days and stories get all mixed up. To examine every side of a story with a child's hands, a child's eyes, looking for meaning. To hope the missing tale is about a princess and a happy ending – and to dream of a noble rescue, a fairy godmother. To be a flippy block inside a small skin box.

ACCIDENTAL READING

I couldn't actually read when I first received *National Geographic Magazine* either, but I deciphered its meaning just fine. The magazine only started putting images on its covers in September 1959, but the timing couldn't have been better: it coincided exactly with the birth of my baby brother in October, when I was twenty-three months old – a huge event. Here was a tiny boy in a tiny bed – a storybook character. His body had other parts, things I didn't have – minor versions of monstrous ones I'd seen. So his was the birth of my perspective. Seems only fitting, then, that *National Geographic* started being readable for me right then. Prior to then, it featured only words – not so useful for my age group. But my brother's arrival perfectly announced the idea of an Other, and *National Geographic* delivered on it.

I had to grab my knowledge quickly to stay one step ahead of my mother's keen eye for dust out of alignment. Each issue lay around for only a few days before it went into a drawer or onto a high shelf. But what I found was astounding – treasures, dangers, wild chronicles, daring truths. It was all here. For starters, the hard projectiles that came at me – big and long and pointy – were explained in September 1959 and September 1965, when the covers showed some jets. And again, when a hummingbird (November 1960) and moth (June 1965) thrust their proboscises into flowers. I learned that other girls had their lower halves cut off – were numbed down below, sister mermaids. The October 1959 cover showed a girl snorkelling, her bottom entirely in the water, obviously a fish. In July 1966, there was a mermaid again – a girl splashing with her fish half safely submerged. Priceless data: evidently I had companions out there somewhere, sea people just like me.

From those precious covers, I also learned that others had issues with reflections, those strange moments in front of mirrors where maybe you couldn't recognize yourself, or didn't remember one of your features. Or the face seemed from another world, or time skipped a long beat while you looked. In October 1960, the cover featured a woman kneeling in front of the Taj Mahal, looking at its reflection in water. And March 1966's cover showed St Basil's Cathedral, another perfect reflection in water, with no one there even to think about it. No doubt about it – reflections were a world of their own.

Through my covers, I also learned that twinning was common. That eerie feeling of being two, voices stuck inside, a constant conversation. On the May 1961 issue, two similar-looking Indonesian women carried baskets, wore the same clothing, side-by-side, two in one. In December 1961, two similar medieval women ministered to others, their posture identical – side-by-side duals. In August 1963, two blond American girls that looked like me were together – one a bit in front, and one a bit in back, taking turns. In November 1963, two similar children looked at two similar deer – each pair side-by-side. In December 1964, identical doves. In January 1967, two similar Pakistani girls, face-to-face. Doubles were everywhere. It was just the way of things.

I even found maps a lot like the one in my head, that strange record I see when I *hide!* When all I see is only me. North, south, east, west: how I walked, faced, laid – was carried, taken, moved, pressed, turned. Directions others went: left to right, right to left, away, towards. Locations relative to each other: across, beside. Enough said. But on the cover of the November 1961 issue, here was Italy with icons. I had (have) icons too, sort of. Larger shapes: V-shaped indoor stairs, a left-side closet, a long hall with doors only on the right, a long window where I can only see the tops of trees, a sparkly ceiling, green paisley linoleum, a red wooden swing on chains, a pink bathtub, a dark vanity by a curtained window, a piano. And smaller shapes: a cane, a pipe, a wooden spoon, a small glass full of red liquid, swishing yellow tassles, a powder puff, a dark tool box. But enough said about that too. And here was another map in August 1962: Cape Cod with icons. We'd just been there with Granny. Did we go there because it was on the table? Or was it on the table because we went there? That was the beautiful, circular sense of safety that kept me going. Truth be told, it still does.

On the October 1966 cover was a man with binoculars. What gall, to tell it like it is! Brave, brave *National Geographic*! – my rescuer, my ally, my kin. Of course, it was frightening to see a "red-white man" front and centre, the sort I was most afraid of – still am, some ways, some days. But at least someone knew the truth. The problem was these old white girl-hunters, all pink and wrinkly. Sorry-looking, badly shaved Santa Clauses.

Of course, I'm telling this now using the big words of the big girl I became. The woman who doesn't believe in Santa has learned about the Taj Mahal and St Basil's, dated the family trip to Cape Cod through the baby book, and done painful inward looking to find a shattered self. Has figured out the difference between jets and hummingbirds, found old maps scratched inside her head, and remembered more than what is comfortable to say about a time that was profoundly uncomfortable to live. I have no words to tell, really, how it felt to figure this out in the winter of 2011, when my endopsychic perceptions came face to face with their doubles on those covers and I accidentally read my own mind. When I fugued into a curious space where the real "now" has never happened – and "then" is happening still, perpetually, suspended forever inside me. My psychic boomerang.

The shock sent my five-foot six-inch frame down to ninety-six pounds, triggered my eleventh bout of mononucleosis (after a twenty-two year hiatus), and prompted new apparitions of my old "smoke rats" – shadow creatures scurrying along the baseboards. Déjà vu: the cathecting of the present by the past. I wept my worst when I realized I was comforted not by story characters, fellow sufferers inside books whose full lives I could engage, but by flat, static, images where I picked up truth incidentally. Grabbed a fact here and there through illicit scanning, random glimpses. And started to believe, as I do now, that not only the unconscious speaks but the universe does too.

Once I conceived of these covers as symbols of reality, it wasn't much longer before I thought they could predict it – and I felt even safer inside my existence. On January 1960, there was an ox on the cover. In

November 1961, we moved to the suburbs right where an old farm road had passed. I could still see ruts leading from nowhere to nowhere, overgrown with grass. And not fifty feet from my back door, I found an ox skull. I took it as a sign of watchful grace – confirmed in October 1967 by another ox cover. That's how things started to make sense to me. Help the only way I had it, the way it was offered. And a real bargain too, at a dollar a copy.

For the first years of my life, these covers were my special "comm link," so to speak, to a place I had no location for. Kind of a pre-mother tongue. Their pictures registered in a part of the mind that seemed to come before or under my languages. Like fear, pain, love, wonder. Just to find them again flushed my entire being in a nanosecond. Nausea and sensory overload, ears popping, fever, systems voiding, forty years of an erased life returned in a flash. A labyrinth and a library. Raw seduction. I couldn't resist opening the door – and couldn't deny what I saw there. Material so difficult to remember, so impossible to forget. Reading as electroshock.

Yet through all those years in between, in fact, I *had* forgotten it. The covers, projectiles, reflections, twins, maps, girl-hunters. The archive had vanished, lost to me and lost in me. Throughout my twenties, thirties, and forties, I'd been buying old issues of *National Geographic* to use at school and home, for cutting up as second-hand goods, cheap. Through all those decades, I cared nothing either for the collection acquired by my father – the one who'd inadvertently taught me how to "read," inspecting every issue himself like a message from the front lines. So my mother gave them all away a few years ago – before my "revelation" and the flood of memories that returned their images to me. Neatly bound in leather and chronologically arranged, they went to a perfect stranger's house. A fitting end for them, I guess. Or, at least, one without a shred of meaning for me at the time.

But I get it now, my accidental reading. I see how materiality and fantasy combined, fused thought and image. Not in some muddling confusion, but in an all-sustaining symbiosis. Made it possible for a child to stare at pictures at eye-level and secure clarity and comfort. I read somewhere that this early habit of mine is a "delusion of reference" – finding meaning in everything around you. If that's so, I suggest the condition where people walk down the street with music or phone receivers in their ears, reading tiny screens as life, people, nature pass them by, be named a "delusion of occlusion" – finding meaning in nothing around you. It's like a new illness I recently read about, "white psychosis." Psychosis without symptoms. Seriously? Then, does the person who walks away from a terrifying car crash with only a scratch have "white paralysis"? Absurd. Every act of survival, however peculiar, shouldn't be named as an illness so easily. Some strange and wonderful human behaviours aren't just strange – they're also wonderful and human. In fact, I believe I owe much of my sanity, my quirky confidence, and my optimistic spirituality to the fluent symbolic language of those *National Geographic* covers. I'm grateful. In a childhood plagued by random pain and fear, at least hope and guidance showed up once a month.

These covers put bilingualism in a whole new light, too. I wasn't working with words, not yet, but my second language was already becoming a channel for information, an opening. And each issue of *National Geographic* was an emissary along this new trade route – a packaged set of objects from another mindscape and an entirely different frame of reference. Ideas that testified to an *Other* place – an elsewhere with realities I could join and share. Just the pictures from this other world were enough. And the images were rich, glorious, magnificent. So though I couldn't sound out a single word in English on those first covers, the mere arrival of that other language and its products triggered new possibilities. It invited my journey.

ALICE & CO.

From this point in my psychological history, it was a cinch to believe in the whole fantastic realm of fairy tales as fact. A simple matter of connecting the dots between what I heard and saw all around me, and what I felt and experienced inside myself. For starters, storybook characters were everywhere. Of course, there was my own brother, the miniature. Next, as a case in point, I performed as Bashful in the *Snow White* story in a school ballet when I was six. I was supposed to be Grumpy, but apparently I couldn't pull it off, so the class bully and I were switched at the last minute. And right around the same time, or a year or two before, I'm ashamed to say that provincial organizers put human dwarves on display at Expo Québec. The exhibit drew huge, enthusiastic crowds and their cameras.

The supposed "family" of dwarves was placed in a long hall-shaped house along the edge of a hill, one side wall made of glass flanked by a cordoned-off pathway. Visitors could snake by and gawk at a "typical day" in their lives, as three or four sat on miniature chairs eating at a miniature table from miniature cups and saucers. A miniature mother cooked food on a too-big stove and served it to her miniature children. I remember noticing how gigantic the daily paper, *Le Soleil*, looked in the father's hands as he sat in his miniature armchair by his miniature fireplace smoking a too-big pipe. *Poor toy people*, I thought at the time. *They can't just get on with their story. They're stuck inside this silly glass house.*

Meanwhile, Robin Hood was the emblem on the flour we bought for my mother's baking, and also on my archery set. Pinocchio was in a puppet show I saw one Saturday, and in the Eaton's Christmas window in Montreal. And Puss in Boots was on dozens of cans of pet food in our kitchen, for we had fourteen pet cats by then, courtesy of our highly fertile angora feline. These were well-oiled stories I lived in both my tongues. They offered characters that didn't necessarily become my imaginary companions, at least not consistently (though I do remember Maid Marian for a while). But they were all a big help because they gave me the key I'd need to survive, though I couldn't know it then. They presented me with a means of decryption, a gift of immeasurable worth.

And it was this: that the boundary between fantasy and reality was, is, permeable. It didn't matter whether I came away thinking that reality was as wild and exciting as a story. Or that fictional stories were actually biographies of unusual-looking beings. No doubt I believed both at once, or alternately, through the course of my early childhood – and beyond. The delightful truth was that there was no clear line between what was in my head, in my books, and in my world. So I could go from one to the other without worry, without difficulty, and without getting lost. Despite considerable evidence to the contrary, then, I *could* have a wide space of safety, a sense of my own creation, some kind of control. Of course, I already knew that from *National Geographic*. But the fact that storybook characters popped up in real life confirmed it perfectly. It was a marvellous lesson.

The same was true for whales, those beloved boundary swimmers. I already knew about Jonah and the Whale from some weird bedtime readings – scary stuff from the Bible read to me in the shadows of a smelly old coal stove and oppressive guilt. But when we moved to the suburbs, I found I could walk to the aquarium to see real whales. Actually, they were probably porpoises, but it was close enough for a young Linnean. I went again and again, alone or with friends, over the years. I stared at their pool from beyond the property gate, and made my way inside to press my nose against their big window.

Looking cautiously into my rupture, such delicate surgery, I learn that one particular dream became repetitive, installed. It was of a blue world where only whales existed. In one view, I was a whale myself, a free body on the surface of the sea, alone and searching for another whale that made a faint and distant cry, calling me. In another view, I was inside a whale, travelling like Jonah, with room enough for standing, ribs my bony floor, aware of sounds within my whale host's body. I could hear it speak to me, but I couldn't speak back to it. In one view and then the other, I rode on the oceans of the unconscious. I could flip from one whale to the other – be inside, or outside, my own big blue body. But then I already knew I could do that, look at things in two different ways – have two versions of my self. *National Geographic* had provided extensive coverage of twinning.

But in terms of sustained daydreams and useful imaginings, nothing surpassed the relationship I had with Alice. I don't remember how I first came upon her. My best guess is that Granny had the book in her collection and read it to me – but I'm not sure. It might have been at school, but that seems wrong because I feel as though I knew her long before kindergarten. Her story seemed to be inside me from the very start. So if it came from outside (and I understand rationally that it must have), I don't remember how.

Like the whale, Alice was both my imaginary companion and my self, through all of her adventures in Wonderland and through the looking glass. Going from fantasy to reality – story to life – Alice's stories embodied all of my most critical symbols: mirrors, inverted worlds, strange potions, distorted body imagery, suspensions of time, and deep holes where you could lose contact with the surface. And she looked so much like me, even – shoulder-length blond hair, my age – that my paternal artist-uncle had me pose as Alice to illustrate a new American edition of the book.

Alice was my twin in print, bringing me more messages to decipher the madness. She informed my entire conception of my self: a girl who kept her head, literally; exercised critical judgment and reflective, objective thinking; and came out at the end of a tough journey, sane and safe. I can't imagine how I would have managed without Alice's courage and intelligence. So I have Lewis Carroll, aka Charles Lutwidge Dodgson, to thank for my survival, too. He created my perfect hero. And moving from the pages into my psyche, my internalized Alice became more than the optimal model: she provided proof that my troubles were survivable.

The people in Alice's world were always trying to play tricks on her, saying or asking things that made no sense. Carroll managed to share a paramount secret of language here: that we need to "feel" what someone says. That's because the words on the surface are often a deception of intention, and our survival may hinge on what we understand and do next as a result. That's why the Cheshire Cat's poem really stuck: "'Twas brillig and ye slithy toves did gyre and gimble in ye wade." I could smell the evil of those toves as they waited in the wade, gyring and gimbling. I hated their slithiness as much as that ominous grin of the Cat, still glowing even in the dark.

But I loved Alice so much for being the girl who worked so hard to figure out what in the world was going on beneath and between the languages she heard, like me. Even unadorned phrases like «Viens-donc ici ma belle» [Come here, dear/my pretty] had a tricky meaning deep down. And the male voice that said it, a broad grin of his own that lingered in the dark.

Alice was my linguistic and psychoanalytic inspiration. From her I learned when I started to read that wisdom would still come from books. That beyond my pre-reading library of flippy blocks and *National Geographic* covers, there was a world of literature where the information I'd need might not be on the covers at all but *inside*, in and in-between the words and lines.

ONE FISH TWO FISH

I took my next expert, Dr Seuss, aka Theo Geissel, as an authority on Carroll's recommendation. I would not be disappointed. I had first met him thanks to the door-to-door salesman who left a sample copy of *The Cat in the Hat* all those years ago – the first book I remember owning so aptly being a serendipitous gift. But I soon found his work all over the library in my new English school.

I can easily understand why titles like *One Fish Two Fish Red Fish Blue Fish* were popular with teachers and librarians in the decades of phonics-as-programming that encompassed my primary school life. What the adults didn't know, though, was that Dr Seuss actually loved children and loved life – and wove joy, courage, and hope into his silly stories. Disguised his food inside his linguistic pedagogy. Healed me, let me live. For unlike the so-called «Docteur» who used real words that made no sense – lies, pleasantries, and facts all scrambled together (the one who delivered me and performed a few restorative services besides) – Dr Seuss used imaginary words that did make sense. I realized early on, then, that Dr Seuss was a real doctor, not just playing doctor like the rest.

His books of made-up words and nonsense rhymes were a school for thought par excellence. From this esteemed teacher, I learned that I could use both my languages, French and English, pretty much however I wanted. Language was something you could twist and turn, make your own. Seuss also taught me that the connection of thought and word was relative. I already knew that real words could signify fantasy – like «Viens ici ... j'te f'rai pas mal» [Come here ... I won't hurt you] – which turned out not to be true at all. But he showed me the reverse, too, that fantasy words could signify reality: the weirdness on Mulberry Street that really did happen; the incessant inner echoes of the Who, who turned out to exist; the Grinch, who actually did wreck the parties; and the hint that it was possible to have control over my life – *If I Ran the Circus* – even though my confidence was often about as hard to find as Solla Sollew.

So I lived with a rotating entourage that appeared whenever I felt those all-too familiar symptoms: ear clicks, racing heart, dizziness, muted hearing, pressed-in chest. And in the fine company of Sneetches,

Ooblecks, Zinn-a-zu birds, Things One and Two, and both the North-going and South-going Zaxes, I went to the land of green eggs and blue fish. What happened after that was irrelevant, because I was safe inside a story. Meanwhile, at school, things got even better. In the library, shelves of clues and new companions; in the classroom, precious Sally and her trusted pal, Spot. They spoke the language of my thoughts in open daylight – reality and fantasy, face-to-face, working together – *See Sally run! See Spot hide!*

But I can travel backwards even further in this regression – in this reverse chronology of my personal history of reading. Before Sally, Dr Seuss, and Alice – though after flippy blocks, covers, and fairy tales – there was Beatrix. I can't share this without shivering, actually, for I lived *entirely* in the world of Beatrix Potter for years – two? three? four? five? six? My granny must have read these to me, but I don't remember, because the world of Beatrix Potter was *always* mine. As if I wrote it, owned it, made it. Dear Peter Rabbit and his garden, innocence every-where. And the two for whom my heart still endures: Town Mouse and Country Mouse.

Potter breathed new life into Aesop's wondrous characters and ren-dered them in the most exquisite images of gentle nature. She painted watercolours where tiny, logical, sensible, polite characters managed their lives in a dignified, self-respecting fashion. And when Town Mouse and Country Mouse switched places, tried out each other's worlds, Beatrix showed me how to perform the skill that would most make a difference to my survival – to imagine myself in another frame entirely. *I owe her my life.*

I can't count how many times I saw myself with a red-and-white kerchief, tied in a tidy knot on the end of a decent stick, slung over my left shoulder. And I'd be on my way, outta here. That hobo gear became the single most prevalent image in my dreams for the duration of my childhood. I was still thinking it in waking dreams at age nine or ten. Sometimes a white mouse was my companion, and sometimes he was me. It was Beatrix who showed me how to be my own best friend *and* a character in my own story. And it was Beatrix who taught me to believe in a world full of loving, reasonable souls with a peaceful life, where threats were manageable and simple foods prevailed.

In fact, Beatrix showed me a perfect community of practice, and she invited me warmly to walk off the pages of my own life into her painted world. She taught me to believe in the possibility of being somewhere else, and she populated my imagination with illuminated pastel scenes of nature where I could lose myself as I befriended the kindly lot of animals living at the benevolent boundary of reality and fantasy. In this beautiful place, I let myself fall into silence, until all I could hear were crickets and birds, drowning out human words that faded easily into nothingness. Her stories let me reshape the sound of the harsh, insistent *Ssshhh!* in my ear until it was just a summer river trickling by, tall grass moving in the wind, a kindly rabbit hushing another.

Now here's the *really* crazy part: Beatrix Potter didn't exist in French. Of course, I understand that *Pierre Lapin* is alive and well today, along with about forty other multilingual clones. But when I needed him and his friends the most, they were completely untranslated, invisible, unborn, never even conceived in my mother tongue.

My second language, English, opened up not only the world of Beatrix Potter, Dr Seuss, and Lewis Carroll but an entire universe of authors. It multiplied without measure my access to literature I would otherwise never have known. And this new body of writing introduced texts that let me play with language, and play between my languages – the only games I ever enjoyed – seeing the nonsense of words and the worlds they inhabit. In short, my second language opened up new possibilities for my imagination: new constructs of reality, new points of view, even new fantasies.

It also showed me it was possible to have a wonderful life with entirely different kinds of people – friends, real love, even happiness. After all, here were my other perennial favourites, the Owl and the Pussycat, two divergent species who were so joyous together as they sailed away in their beautiful pea-green boat to places where life was so unlike home – a world full of bong-trees, piggy-wigs, and runcible spoons. Bilingualism took the narrow limits of my self and blew them wide open.

SSSHHH!

A broad, open door was precisely what I needed. A way to see, feel, and hear far beyond the harsh, insistent, male *Ssshhh* in my ear. Ah, *Ssshhh!* Where I begin and end. Not my first word, though. That was apparently «Papa» at six months, according to my baby book. It's an unusual first word for a baby to speak in my mother tongue. Statistically speaking, I should have said «Mama.» Maybe I did, and my mother was fudging the record a bit, to please my «père.» Or was I trying as hard as I could to snitch back then? Who knows. Another of my little clues went by, perhaps – just one more feeble and inadequate attempt at being understood.

Being unheard was just another kind of *Ssshhh!* And when I finally got to revisit the earliest sites of injury fifty-four years later, during the deepest psychological digging I've done to date, I found no words there at all. No sounds of any kind to go along with the weird snippets of pictures, bodily orientations, smells, sensations, and feelings. There was only silence except for one word, each time, in every scenario: *Ssshhh!* That *Ssshhh* was everywhere! Just like in the Bible: first there was the Word, and the Word was *Ssshhh.*

Here it is, for example, in 1959, on a day I spent with my older cousin. *I'm waving bye-bye with my right hand. Clown is in my left hand. In the car, my parents drive away. Snatch! I'm picked up fast. Clown drops. I'm up in tight big arms, crying. And Clown is down, far away on the grass. I'm carried in the big door, up the big stairs. I'm crying more now. «Ssshhh! Tu vas déranger 'es voisins!»* [Be quiet! You'll bother the neighbours!] *The door clicks. There's time and more time. Then there's hard laughing because I'm running now! I'm down the big stairs, around, around, out the big door. But there's no sun now. It's grey and dark, a different sky. And there's no Clown. I'm looking, but there's no Clown. I'm alone, with no Clown now.*

This moment defines sorrow for me – makes me weep in ways I can't easily stop. My grief is entirely contained in the constant shadow of that soft green clown with the plastic face who was about as tall as a wooden spoon, who disappeared from the front yard of our apartment building in the course of an afternoon not unlike many others. His loss is so intrinsic to my soul that it's immutable. His absence, my linchpin memory, my witness – the most loyal breadcrumb. As for that *Ssshhh*, it became permanent too – in my silencing, my forgetting, my being sworn to never tell anyone what I'm telling now.

And here's *Ssshhh* again, in 1960. *My downstairs neighbour and I sit on her bed. We face her kitchen doorway. My left ear is in her lap. Her right hand is on my right ear. I cry softly, on and on. She says Ssshhh, over and over. She pats my head slowly. I feel kindness in her palm. We crouch in front of a wide brown dresser. The top right corner has a big chip missing, from a dog bite, she says. She opens the bottom drawer. Look at that! Tiny coloured flowers on soft, white cotton. I can borrow one pair for today. I can change ...*

That moment defined mercy for me early on as an old woman, five foot three-ish, with short brown hair and a round olive face, who was a bit plump and had an accent (was it Polish? Russian?). Her permanence became my inner Angel, my Saviour, my security. And that particular *Ssshhh*? It became lodged forever inside me too, as comfort, guidance, healing, love. It would provide everything I was missing so well that I'd change nothing of the past, to be honest, if it risked losing what I received from her. My mother on the inside.

That *Ssshhh!* Not even a word – a non-word. But with so much to say. On board the human adventure from the start of our lives. Archaic. In fact, it seems that oral language – and that *Ssshhh* especially – is one of baby's first clues (along with light, air and temperature) that passage out of the womb has occurred. Baby's first reality check, one might say.

Then, in the months that follow birth, each bit of input from the outside world pulls us awake as adorable parasites completely dependent on our mothers into the world of family and society where we'll try to live as successful symbiotes, giving and receiving in complex webs of relationships. From our first cry, our need, and its first soothing response, *Ssshhh*, we begin language learning and learning about life too, simultaneously. That primary dialogue not only answers our call but also tells us that we're distinct beings – something we didn't know before and could only dream about, floating as we were in our pre-birth oceanic feeling. From here, the mother tongue enters like a Trojan horse, bringing culture along with milk. Making it seem equally essential to our existence.

Either our cry works and we're soothed with food, or it doesn't. Then, evolutionarily designed for development as we are, our cries become more complicated, varied for different needs. As they do so, we notice that the *Ssshhh* response becomes nuanced too – sometimes more or less patient, quick or slow, soft or loud, and so on. Our archaic language quickly gains a broad vocabulary of tone and pitch. And we learn by repetition how it serves us. It's a connection that never goes away, no matter how many languages we acquire. That's why the relationship between language and affect can explain things that the relationship between language and thought can only dream about, literally.

Did bilingualism change that primary relationship between language and emotion for me? How could it not? My pain and fear were embedded, embodied, in French. It was a powerful association of injury to the prosody of language so that the speech of key voices, then of voices that merely sounded like them, then of voices that used similar words, then of voices that spoke in similar places, became a spiralling vortex that gathered more and more momentum around it until my entire mother tongue was pulled into my trauma. I was living at the eye of a devastating storm, where all was quiet except for *Ssshhh*. And what about English, my new language? It was a perfectly sunny day over there.

CRYPTOMNESIA

I have a confession to make at this point. It's that sometimes I feel like I've stolen everything that I am. Maybe it's just one of those survivor complexes, something with a negative motivation underneath it, like guilt or aggression. I'm not sure. But everything about me seems to be second-hand, from somewhere else, like it's not entirely mine. After all, I made my Clown into my witness, and my next-door neighbour into my guardian angel. My understanding of my trouble came from story blocks and magazine covers. My imaginary friends, from books. My key self-concept, the twinning, from blue whales and white mice. My values, from nonsense rhymes. My emotions, from an archaic language. My origins, from French. My possibilities, from English.

My world was, is, a fabrication, a «bricolage» of half-truths, interminable hopes, random texts, convenient fugues, and magical thinking. I'll admit to that. I was a real little thief, a tiny perpetrator of cryptomnesia. Stealing memories from everyone and everything – recalling thoughts from everywhere as being my own. It was persistent, unabashed unconscious borrowing by which I fulfilled the single, solitary wish I had: to survive. For unlike older victims, I had no "pre-trauma" self to run back to, no life to "own again," no conception of myself at all before this trauma. I began my existence *in* it and *with* it. It was like starting from scratch after a catastrophic natural disaster – starting back at zero. I know zero. Zero is a solitary instant when there's no light, no objects, no time, no here. Zero is a single cognition-emotion-intuition-conviction – a death pulse. A buzzing silence loud enough to blow out your eardrums that says only this: *No one comes.* Then, somehow, something comes from inside you. Unspeakably mysterious, it's there. You continue. You should die, but you don't. That's the death-birth of zero.

I found my working models where I could. So be it. I fabricated an identity, hope, values, and faith not just inside both my languages – but beyond, before and between them. I collected resources not only in words but in non-words, too – emotions and their symbols – as I pulled in and transferred useful bits from people and their worlds to form a whole. Blended the phenomenal and the mythical, like stirring paint, concocting. The result? A whole that moved easily between English and French – and between the conscious and unconscious. A unitary being that monitored reality and fantasy to sense when it was time to cross – just like monitoring English and French to know which language to use. That attended to context and read input back and forth to register the tipping point, the moment requiring a choice of which mode to use. After a while the psyche became as porous as a cell membrane, words and symbols flowing in and out as needed. So passed my first decade – in the necessary crime of stealing my own story from my own life, and vice versa.

Maybe that's how my bilingualism really saved me. Maybe it gave a sense of normalcy to my inner duality, my sense of shifting – fuguing – between being and not being fully present. Maybe I thought that everyone with two languages felt like this inside – that it was a normal human business, this oscillation of valences of self. If so, that would have turned every bilingual human being I met or learned about into a model of normalcy. It would have entirely removed the stigma of my peculiarity. Bilingualism would have delivered the most life-affirming message ever: It's okay. Maybe that was it after all. Because somehow, I got stronger, despite everything, despite regular ups and downs. I became independent and increasingly secure inside, regardless of the insecurity outside. And in that gracious envelope of a growing sense of ordinariness, I developed some early beliefs, like any child does, that sustained me to my core.

One of these rushes in still – a conviction perhaps born in a forest I walked along, or on the page of a treasured book. An easy trigger?

My first home on Boulevard René Lévesque (formerly St-Cyrille) at Holland Avenue. It still stands, second from the northwest corner, the sixplex with the angled door and narrow staircase window. A beautiful tree grows in the front yard where there used to be only grass. *Trees talk among themselves. You don't hear them, but they watch everything down below from up above. And if they see a problem, they tell each other to tell the angels to come and fix it right away.* I'm glad I learned to steal sense from the world around me – not just from English and French, but from the language of nature, of life, and of texts near and distant. For that tree thrives on the precise spot where once my Clown and tears were planted.

I can visit that spot. Every time I go home to Quebec, I find a way to do a drive-by. I go along René Lévesque or Holland in one direction or another, and as I near the corner, I slow down. I have a quick look at that door, say a little prayer for myself – for that little girl – feel thankful I'm alive, and keep right on driving. I do all of this thinking and praying in English. Even my *looking*, my drive-by, is in English. That's what my second language does: it lets me keep a safe distance from my past, a seat in the car on the road just outside my trauma.

In December 2010, though, I did something I'd never done on a visit home before. I parked the car. I didn't even get out, just parked in front of that house for a minute. Or was it fifteen? Thirty? I looked at it for a while, thought of Clown (my eternal testifier) and that memorable afternoon. And there I was again in the waking dreams that victims know too well. Not asleep, but not in the present either. Somewhere over there, back there. The imaginal at the forefront instead of being below or behind. For me, those memories happen in French. There's the tense voice, the rush around the stairs. And the French shushing. It stabs right through my patois, cheapens and degrades it brutally. And the French laughing. The cruel ridiculing of a little girl who thought only of her Clown through it all. The harshness-disguised-as-humour of a man who cared so little about me that he would not stoop to pick up a tiny cotton body that meant the world to me.

I'll skip ahead an hour or so, past the grief and terror that made it impossible to budge, to the grocery store where I took myself to re-ground, as I always do, driving and finding one, as I always do. That, or a second-hand store. Mismatched goods, colours, textures, looks, sizes, words, pictures. And everyone too busy to notice the depth of sadness, the quiet madness, the internal rupture. Anonymity as a space of healing.

«C'est-qu't'étais?» [Where were you?], my mother asked when I returned an hour and a half late from a simple errand. I fudged the truth a bit myself this time, making up a fib that I was at Value Village. Seems I end up there a lot on trips home.

Where was I really? I was back in my mother tongue. And I only made it back from my mother tongue to my mother's house that night for dinner, to my lovely children who would know nothing of the moment, by getting into English and driving away. «Mon Dieu, t'es vraiment allergique à poussière, ehn? Gar'-donc tes yeux!» [My God, you really are allergic to the dust (in those stores), aren't you? Look at your eyes!]

Yes, I really am allergic to the dust of the past that infuses the atmosphere in my mother tongue. In English, there's air for me to breathe. A journey from the imaginal to the providential. That's bilingualism for me. Life.

Partridges

A funny story.

If you shoot one
on the top branch
of a tree with many,
the ones below
just watch it fall,
and don't even
try to fly away.

Every autumn,
my mother hunted
for small game
with my father.
Once, she killed
five partridges
in a single tree.

Laughing, she tells
how each bird
watched its family
be fired on and die,
tumbling right past
its open eyes,
and did not think
to move at all.

Moronic birds,
she says: *Des idiots,*
des espèces de
stupides dums-dums.*
Imagine watching
violence happen,
harm approaching,
and doing nothing.

Imagine.

*   Idiots – stupid, moronic species (creatures).

20

ON THE WINGS OF GEESE

MEA CULPA

Sometime during my early years, I started writing «un nouveau roman» in my little broken head. Clearly, to make up such an outrageous tale – an epic of courage and survival tellable to myself – another voice was needed. A language that wasn't my mother's or my neighbourhood's. One where I could think from my secret location about angels and fairy-tale characters getting me safely from one sign to another – a type of Mille Bornes game of the mind.* It was fortunate that English was hanging around the edges of my cultural world, because I could've easily ended up speaking the more difficult languages of delusion instead. At any rate, rather than pass through my culture properly, seems I by-passed it through the entirely undiagnosed, off-the-radar experience of infantile psychosis.

Talk about a story that can't ever be told – the absolutely unnarratable: a toddler with a psychic split. But I always sensed my injury. And now I see the soft, raggedy edges of my old wound, dare to name it: «une psychose transitoire» or «une psychose passagère,» the literature calls it – ironically, so beautifully. A psychosis I journeyed through, then

* This was a popular game found in most households in Quebec in the 1950s and '60s. It was invented in France in 1954, but the version we owned was distributed by Parker Brothers in 1962 in a small, light-green box. It's a card game involving road travel between stone markers, featuring hazards, remedies, and safeties.

arrived from. A psychosis on which I rode for a while, like on a boat, a train, or a horse – like my beloved Gumby rode on trusty Pokey. A psychosis in which I was «une passagère» in transit from infancy to puberty. Quiet, calm, automatic, alive only in my mind. The accident was apparently unnoticed, other than frequent commentaries punctuating even my earliest years that I was, I am, «pas démonstrative.» A trait that would, ironically, become attributable to my becoming "English." True enough, what emerged – the sequelae embodied – was someone who looked askance at her maternal family from across a broad chasm. From the place of mental repatriation I migrated to when my intimate space in French erupted, leaving only ashes.

It is 1961 or '62. I go to Paris – the Cinéma de Paris, to be exact, in Carré d'Youville, just beyond the stone gate on rue Saint-Jean. I carry a white, lacey plastic purse – «une p'tite bourse dent'lée» – where you can put des «p'tites niais'ries» [little nothings]. It's moon-shaped with two round handles that fit snugly around my wrist, and there's probably an orange two-dollar bill in it. It's a classic look for a pre-schooler, I'm sure – all the rage for «une p'tite mad'moiselle» spending the afternoon with the charming Elder. Isn't he helpful, when a father must work, and a mother must do the books at his shop, and Bébé is sleeping with Grand-maman, and I must be kept «occupée»? What better than a Disney movie on a Saturday afternoon and some Chinese food afterwards?

And that, I'll realize some fifty years later, is why I always time-travel when I drive along la Côte d'Abraham to la Basse-Ville – the lower-town area it leads to. Along «les rues d'la Tourelle, d'la Couronne, Dupont, Saint-Joseph, pis Saint-Vallier est» – formerly all part of «el vieux Quartier chinois.» Here was the Elder's previous home area and favourite haunt – though I'm quite sure he couldn't even have put China on a map. But it was a quick walk from the cinema, so I'll forever register China as the centre of the natural world. The issue of its most important symbol – the precise point that splits the universe into evil and good, dark and light, dualities seen and unseen – the *yinyang*. The place where it's decided whether you'll perish or be saved. Because somewhere between the fresh chop suey and the dry cleaner's kindness, I was pulled back from the abyss of a consuming fire. China as purgatory. Where children go when they die.

Inside the cinema, there are slips in memory where I can be in the past and present simultaneously, yet be absent from the scene – above it, not as me. In these spaces that are neither here nor ever gone, are five Disney movies, all released in the late 1950s and early '60s: *Bambi* (1957), *Cinderella* (1957), *Snow White* (1958), *Dumbo* (1959), and *Pinocchio* (1962). I don't remember them at all. Instead, what I've kept is of a divergent psychic texture entirely, so that their symbols are part of my inner world, informing my theories of mind and my notions of right and wrong – just like street noises and Chinese food have become code for "salvation." Dumbo, whose story I can never keep straight. Bambi, whose picture makes me cry even now. And Pinocchio, the Rosetta Stone that explains how things get harder and longer with lies. From the wide world of Disney, then, comes the fractured world of me.

There'll be sleepiness, and I'll miss part or most of the movie. There'll be disgusting smells, indelible and non-negotiable despite the intervening decades: nicotine, tobacco smoke, wet polyester, fishiness, dusty oil, cold mold. And there'll be the clear sense of something in my mouth that feels like a banana outside with a hard inside. It pushes my teeth until it feels like they'll all fall out and I'll have just a set of bumpy gums. It's a sensation that'll haunt the rest of my life – soft teeth breaking for no reason, swallowing teeth, teeth being pushed into the wrong places, smashed teeth. And another, of not being able to find my teeth, of losing them. There'll also be the visceral imprint of being on the lap of someone big who's on the toilet, facing the same way he does, something dangling below into the basin. Of spinning like a tipping bobble on top of something hard and pointy, like a very big pencil. And of having a long drip of slow, hot liquid run down my right inner thigh, recalled as black mercury burning a trail in my skin as it fades at the knee. There'll be no new charms for those events on the jingly silver bracelet I'll wear for a decade – another fad of the «p'tites demoiselles» of my era.

This bit in the toilet will become over-determined, repeated often on days I'll not bother to count, when the Elder – ever gracious – takes me shopping around the neighbourhood. «Y f'sa' toute pour aider.» [He did everything to help (everyone) out.] Ah yes, a real hero. On a familiar street, my hand in his, I'll need to use the bathroom again. Seems I always need to. Asking clerks to use the stockroom toilet: «Ma p'tite fille peut pas attend'» [My little girl can't wait]. «Mais oui, monsieur.» I'll see messy shelving and stacks of different kinds of boxes – shoes, gadgets, who knows what – on different days. Relief, as always, is only in the safety of the outside world and its strangers.

So incoherence becomes my only guarantee in those days when things happen to me that don't happen in speech – those years of living the inexplicable, the untellable. Back home, discomfort is negated by warm, innocent hugs. The stench in my nose is overlaid by rising bread. The Elder oils a creaky door hinge. And I'm rushed off to join cousins for supper. If there was ever a time to speak of it, it passed years ago. Seems it's a routine by now, hardly worth reporting. Besides, my thoughts are easily drowned out by the gaiety of four generations of women putting «du beurre mou pis a'salière» [soft butter and the salt shaker] on the table as they talk about whose husband «court la galipote» [runs around (cheats)] and whose is «binque trop branlant» [too hesitant (lacking ambition)]. Learning about the speed of men is key here. Prey talking about their predators. The kitchen as the war room. If there's another way to be a little girl, I don't know it yet.

But somewhere in there – between the laughter and the thunderous bells across the road – I'll fall out of rhythm with my own people into a disconnection akin to autism, through so many moments I'll never lose and yet never find. The lesson I extract from it is simple enough: «Y'a bin des genres de monde dans l'monde.» [There are lots of different kinds of people in this world.] So we have two choices. Everyone does. Become a suffering soul, saying «'mande-moi pas c'q'm'a faire a'ec ça» [don't ask me what I'm going to do with this knowledge, problem, etc.]. Or, «fa' queq' chose pour t'aider» [do something to help yourself]. It's just that we're born into a long line of thoughts that eventually becomes a long line of ways. It's called culture. And our job, as far as I can see then, is to survive it.

In your mother tongue, your mother teaches you about your culture – first at her breast, then on her knee, then in her kitchen. How does she learn it? From her mother, from precious tips found «dans l'fin fond d'une boîte» [at the very bottom of some random box]. It's a bit like putting on lipstick and your best dress when you feel like crap, only a little more complicated. But only a little. And how does your mother know exactly how you feel? Because the Elder knows her, too – just as his elders knew hers. Because it goes on and on and on. And I'm afraid that out of due respect for the living, I've already said too much.

But the art of forgetting sexual abuse here will make «des chef-d'oeuvres» [masterpieces] out of «des p'tites oubliettes» [little lapses]. Of course, the family Elder's been witnessed with his fingers up little girls' vaginas, and with girls on his lap while his pants are open. But he works so hard – and at least «c'pas un courailleux» [he isn't an adulterer] ... And of course, the priests fondle everyone they can get their hands on, but they're a harmless joke, really – «rien q'des m'mères» [only whiny, feminized men] ... And of course, big boys like to experiment, they're just trying out their manhood – «c'est normal» ... In my Quebec at mid-century, such unpleasantness from older males was a mere ritual of childhood – «une bebelle» [a trinket] in the grand scheme of things.

So my "aha moment" arrives in the fact that there's no "aha" here at all. Everyone merely learned how to get along «dans l'temps qu'les hommes f'sa' bin s'qu'y voula'» [in the time when men did what they liked]. First, we know no better. Later, it's a given. Even later, it's forgotten. It isn't talked about simply because it's so terribly ordinary. That's how trauma becomes culturally relative.

So it's my internal narrator that's off somehow, causing me to misread cultural memory. Making me stand up and say, "Hey, wait a minute!" It's not the early sex or the secret that makes me unique. Like I said, there's nothing special here. It's that it feels to me like something to be explained rather than forgotten. That I still need to talk about it.

POUR TOI QUE J'AIME

In Montmagny each year, countless people come to see the geese fly overhead along their traditional flightways. It's known as the "snow goose capital of the world." Most people take photographs or have picnics as they watch. In season, some take out their guns, permits in hand, and kill a few. I remember on many occasions my father, accompanied by my brother or mother, dragging in three or four by the neck. There were also days with five or six dead ducks from La Beauce; a bag full of bloody rabbits from Baie St-Paul; and dead partridge, my mother's favourite, from around the cabin in the Parc des Laurentides. I hated it. Hunting remained one of the great ethical discords of our family – «On est une famille qui colle ensemb', pis qui fait toute ensemb'. Mais toi, bin évidemment, ej sais qu't'as d'aut'idées.» [We're a family that sticks together and does everything together. But you, really obviously, I know you have other ideas.] My mother, right as always.

I really shouldn't be so sure about holding the moral high ground, though. I have my own guilty handling of my obligations to the living. For I let my children grow up without any connection to the French language, French culture, or Quebec. They looked at me between 2008 and 2010, my nose in a book by de Montaigne, or working on my side project, a 180-page description of the patois and its grammar, *El Patois Saintongeais à Québec astheure* – and wondered what I was on about. They took to calling it "Mom's *patois* book" with a forced, pretentious sort of an accent, in regular displays of good-humoured teasing.

After all, why should they care? Having had only the prescribed forty minutes of French per day (or less) from Grade 4 to Grade 9, between British Columbia and Ontario, years ago now, they can barely read the homework I bring home from my elementary students in French immersion. And the blame is entirely on my shoulders.

For I demonstrated a clear distancing from French – an open refusal of my home language and culture – during the most formative years of their lives, in the 1980s and '90s. I have almost guaranteed that any dear little grandchildren who might come along in the future will be raised in anglophone homes by my children and their (highly likely) anglophone partners. As a result, they will likely know and value virtually nothing of the French roots that, in a strictly genetic assay, would amount to at least 75 per cent of my own origins. In the short span of barely one generation, I've managed to asphyxiate French inside my own family line.

Language death is a serious concern around the world, with researchers tracking how many become extinct each year. Like endangered species, hundreds of languages have only a handful of elderly speakers left, and local newspapers chronicle the tragic day when the last one dies, ending a linguistic lineage that was vibrant for thousands of years. In hindsight, then, it might have been more ethical for me to get a hunting licence and right along with the rest of my family chase down those geese, ducks, partridges, and rabbits. Instead, for those two key decades of my children's collective youth, I took up a much deadlier kind of hunting against my own heritage: I became a language killer.

One of my maternal aunts who lives in Montmagny has achieved considerable fame for herself as a painter of the magnificent geese. She creates astounding images of these birds against the sky, canvases of light and grace that sell for a thousand dollars or more. I own a small one she gave me many years ago, with a tiny brass plaque on the frame: «Pour toi que j'aime» [For you whom I love]. Words that have never felt like me. How could she have known my angst even then? But there's something in the flight of those birds against the sky that's completely me.

There's something special about this aunt too. Dignity incarnate, she's well over six feet tall, mannered like an aristocrat. She has clear opinions that she articulates in immaculate French, to match her political inclinations. She was well known for resenting my father's being «un maudit anglais» [a damned English person] – and he always resented her for being «une maudite séparatiste» [a damned separatist]. But between the champagne and trivialities, and his frequent abstentions, family events went off without fists flying.

The other memory I have of her is a complete contrast. One evening she came to our home, popping in to say hello on her way through town, and she needed to use the washroom. I was in the bath, about ten years old, but she came in to use the toilet anyway. «Y'a rien là,» she said [There's nothing to worry about here]. «On est toutes des p'tites filles. Pis c'est juste un p'tit pipi en fin d'compte.» [We're all little girls. And it's just a little pee, after all.] And while I couldn't see her body across the half wall between us, I was aware of her Frenchness there on the toilet, chatting me up – unpretentious, disarmed, unself-conscious. I, on the other hand, struggled to gather bubble bath to hide my body – shocked, scandalized, my Englishness showing through the vanishing foam. I felt so embarrassed that she'd come here to do this while I was there. She laughed at my awkwardness, not unkindly, and left. *I must remember to lock both of the doors to this bathroom next time,* I told myself – in English.

A GOOD GAME OF SLINGSHOT

When does it begin, this gap, this chasm, between language worlds? Between language selves? I'm not sure exactly. But it seemed that for the longest time, my two languages were just like children, good friends, playing side by side. Yet somewhere along the way they stopped "playing nice" and started living by different rules. Then they took to separate playgrounds where they could barely observe each other's games from a distance, and eventually they didn't bother to look.

Most days of my early childhood, for example, my next-door neighbour and I went for walks in the woods behind our homes. There are too many anecdotes to share, so I'll stick with one. One afternoon when we were both seven, she shook an apple tree hard so a few would fall for us to eat. But something more than apples came loose from those branches. In an instant we were covered in bright green caterpillars that worked their way into our ears and noses, strands of hair wrapping around squished carcasses, leaving bits of legs here and there, and sticky sap.

It took our mothers hours to pull them from our hair, longer because they were both laughing about it, and we almost were too. But within five years of that memorable day, my best buddy and I would no longer even be talking. She'd become sensitized to nationalistic politics, and she stuck to her friends from French school. I stuck to my friends from English school. There was less than fifty feet between our front doors, but it might as well have been fifty miles.

Another favourite early game was for a group of us to walk the block from our street to the railroad track. We'd travel a mile or so in either direction alongside it, looking for pussywillows, cattails, frogs, and random treasures. We might be three, or six, on bikes or not, ranging in age from about four to twelve. If we went west, we could step off the tracks near l'Aquarium du Québec. It was almost new back then, just built. We grabbed and clawed our way along about a hundred feet of cliff, a sheer rock face right by Le Pont de Québec, so we could sneak under the wooden railing near the outdoor fish tank and get onto the grounds for free. We checked out the marine life for a while, and we watched from our vantage point as they built the new bridge alongside the old one. Then we walked back home and had dinner. That was the substance of an ordinary life in the undeveloped suburbs.

We enjoyed this activity from about 1961 to 1970. After that, it seemed that we never went to the tracks anymore, and no one could look even at that bridge, Pont Pierre Laporte, without remembering the October Crisis. It was a gigantic, stark memorial with a 360-degree vista.* And when we did talk about it, or about anything around it, or about what defined «péquistes,» or what defined our families, or our grandparents, and so on, we were always getting into some kind of heated disagreement. Flags started flying on everything from cars to brasseries – flags of Quebec or Canada, as though a language choice entailed a national choice automatically.

Many bilingual francophones began refusing to speak English on principle, a tension that was palpable even at the corner store. Meanwhile, bilingual anglophones began refusing to speak French on principle, just to show they weren't buying in. Daily, weekly, old friends parted from each other essentially forever, cursing the ground the other had walked on. Francophones appropriated English just long enough to yell, "Yankee go home!" to bilingual former friends whom they knew perfectly well weren't Americans. And bilinguals yelled back, "Damned frogs!" though their own mothers or fathers were French too. It was patently absurd – a dangerous game in the hands of children.

But on a typical day, in the earliest years in the suburbs, I joined a dozen kids in a far safer game of war. Weapons usually included slingshots, and toy bows and arrows. We had two fields and the woods behind to divide and conquer. These weapons and lands were already firmly written into the folklore of the neighbourhood. The only thing up for grabs each time was the make-up of the teams.

At this point in Quebec's history, an average street like ours included two or three anglophone-bilingual homes to about fifteen monolingual

---

* The new bridge was built between 1966 and 1970. When the provincial vice-premier Pierre Laporte was murdered during the October Crisis, it was given his name instead of the planned name, Pont Frontenac. It's the longest main-span suspension bridge in Canada and the longest non-tolled suspension bridge in the world.

francophone homes, although a few neighbourhoods had more anglophones – especially where there were «des bin grandes maisons» [really
big houses] – and many neighbourhoods had none. Ours was, then,
a typical street where the patois was the lingua franca. English kids
had to work their way into groups, asking permission to play, as parents were beginning to filter their political convictions down through
their children. The «pure» francophones were dominant in number,
and the two or three oldest got to pick their members and allegiances
for the games.

My younger brother had a reserved seat on the francophone team. I
guess he was deemed less indoctrinated by school, but it could also be
because he was best friends with the ringleader's brother, and a hell of
a fine shot besides. His French team chose to be the Americans every
time. This meant the bilingual kids, including me and anyone who
spoke any English at all (other than my brother), had to be Germans,
along with whoever else they put on our team – usually the terribly un-
spartan toddlers. And no matter how much we argued that this didn't
make sense because we spoke English and they didn't, the francophones
wouldn't budge. Because it was also written into the folklore that the
Americans would win every time.

One day, when I was seven or eight, we were preparing for war, as
usual, but that day there were no other bilinguals. There was only me
and seven or eight francophones, and an innovative strategy involving
a different battlefield on some adjoining streets. The ringleader had
made up the two teams, as he always did, and I wanted to play, to join
them in this game. But everyone was beginning to disperse already, and
I was the only one who hadn't been picked. I stood on a patch of grass
between this triangle of streets – Valmont, Matapédia, La Rochelle,
names that haunt the soul for centuries, as if war had never left, as
though the land of the past and the present were the same. I called out
in French, «Eh, moi aussi j'veux jouer» [Hey! I want to play too].

Everyone stopped. Time stopped. The ringleader then turned to me
and said, I swear, «Bin, dans quelle langue tu penses, toé?» [So, what
language do you think in, you?] It didn't even occur to me at the time
that this was an incredibly sophisticated idea for a child aged no more
than thirteen to articulate. Still a decade shy of the Official Languages

Act, it seemed that its unofficial enforcement had already begun.* But ever lacking the confidence of the bold, I couldn't return a snide remark and run to join them anyway. Instead, I remember pondering this question for the first time. I thought a few thoughts (about what, I can't remember), then I asked myself honestly what language I'd just done it in. I took his instructions seriously enough to realize, in that moment, that I was thinking in English – something I wasn't aware of doing until that point.

«En anglais,» I finally answered.

«Bin, tu peux pas jouer dans c'cas là. On veut pas d'anglais dans c'jeu-là.» [Well, in that case, you can't play. We don't want any English people in this game.] And off they went to play war, in French only – a re-enactment of the Second World War in which half were Germans and half were "Americans." The irony struck me even as I watched them fade into the horizon, my brother with them. A group divided unto themselves. Playing roles they actually hated equally. It wasn't even fantasy anymore. It was a toxic soup.

That moment changed things between my brother and me. It was an otherwise ordinary day, but it became the precise instant in history when paths diverge. Poor soul: he was only six and he just wanted to play. But I was no less devastated than if I'd seen all those I loved the most get on a boat and sail away without me.

L'ACCORD FÉMININ

What happened that day is that I'd suddenly been made conscious of my difference in a way I hadn't been before. The verdict: I was cultural-ly impure. From then on, I retreated from the land of common ground to where I was banished, and I built myself a new castle there. That's just the way life is. Some things just happen. Like caterpillars falling on your head, and other things beside. But if you believe in some kind of

---

* La Loi sur la langue officielle [Official Languages Act] of 1974, which made French the official language of the province of Quebec, affecting commercial and business transactions, education, and justice.

solution, however odd it might seem to others, your prognosis is much, much better. So I empowered myself with the tools I had.

My new world offered me things that my old world couldn't. First, it was a relatively clean affective space. I didn't keep bumping into loaded words that set off old fear instincts and made coping with my chronic anxiety virtually impossible. Instead, it was almost a fresh start – enough of a one, at least, to give me room to breathe. I could exercise a bit of control over old bodily patterns that persevered like habits left unattended. That's what reinforced pathways do – that's what defines them. But I got to turn the tables a little in English. To have a small conversation, and then a few days and years, and eventually an entire life that didn't leave me constantly (only occasionally) hostage to the automatic *click-click-click* of those all-too-familiar triggers – *Run! Hide!*

Second, in English, I was able to salvage at least a bit of a sense of humour from what seemed, often enough, to be fairly unfunny times. That's because my new tongue gave a wonderful twist to old, familiar words. And it took my favourite game, word play, to a whole new level. Now a «pissenlit» [dandelion] was a "piss-in-your-bed." A «crapeau» [toad] was a "crap-on-the-water." A «phoque» [seal] was … well, you get the idea. English was amusing even on its own. There were crazy felines running around everywhere: *cat*fish («des barbottes»), *cat*tails («des quenouilles»), *pussy*willows («des saules à chatons»), dande*lions* («des pissenlits,» again), and *tiger* lilies («des lys»). I loved this game and I played it constantly to memorize new words. I ran funny twists on morphemes through my head, making up combinations with individual pieces of words that were just as silly as the little flippy book I was becoming – the head of an owl on the butt of a chick.

Even better, this game was a great way to learn about the difference between appearance and reality. Take, for example, «un cochon d'inde» [a guinea pig], a common pet. If you spoke only French, you'd assume the adorable furry guy's roots were in India, of course. But in English, you'd be led to think that his ancestors were actually from Africa. Which should you believe? You couldn't be sure. You needed to keep checking one against the other, stay sharp. Understand that these words that passed for truth in one tongue might not be considered true at all in the other. Keep bringing evidence from one frame of thought, one world, into the other. Become a smarter player.

It was the same for «une nuit blanche» [a white night]. The meaning nowadays is of an all-night arts festival. But it wasn't always so – this expression has changed fairly recently. A far more ancient French idiom represents the most common meaning of the phrase. If you say, «j'ai passé une nuit blanche,» it means that you couldn't sleep at all because you were worried about a horrid problem. Or you spent the night at the emergency ward, or something equally calamitous, and that's why you couldn't settle. You weren't attending a party – you were attending to a catastrophe. In English, though, the "white knight" who comes to give a perfunctory kiss to the sleeping damsel, to wake her up – and maybe take her to an all-night arts festival – sounds exactly like a "white night." So the word game becomes a reality check, again. Is the "white k/night" – «la nuit blanche» – a saviour or a tragedy? You can't be sure.

And this shift in meaning isn't just for objects, but for the feelings people have, too. Take, «un cœur gros,» a big heart. In French, you're terribly sad, on the verge of crying – but in English, you're generous and kind. Meanwhile, if something is "formidable" in English, you're likely going to feel some anxiety about dealing with it – awe mixed with dread. But in French, if something is «formidable,» you're going to look forward to it without reservation. There are hundreds, quite possibly thousands, of examples like this between French and English – relative truths that keep you on your toes. Other sets of languages have more, or fewer, of these contrasting pairs, words that look the same but don't mean the same at all. Noticing these tricky differences hones your ability to attend carefully to input from the outside world. To monitor what makes sense and what's true – or not. In other words, it promotes constant reality checking, helping you sharpen a fine spear tip that's very useful, whatever your psychological make-up. But one that's especially vital when you need to defend a fragile self from more internal damage.

Best of all, in English, I didn't have to worry anymore about the uncomfortable business of gender. About my femininity and my core identity. It was a complicated subject at the best of times. The abuse permeated my sexuality and made it problematic in ways that were more or less apparent, just like those word contrasts, depending on the day, mood, partner. I was often, as the word says so perfectly in both my languages, ambivalent about sexuality. But in English, the "he said, she said" business inside sentences could be easily fixed by using "they" and stating things in the plural instead. Speaking in generalities instead of requiring a commitment about gender. And a boy and a girl could be equally nice (instead of «gentil» or «gentille»), or equally interesting (instead of «intéressant» or «intéressante») – and so on. In English, there was no functional difference between «un ami» and «une amie» – or between «un idiot» and «une idiote.» A word, a thought, was free of the body, the sexuality, of its speaker or owner. And adjectives, pronouns, and articles were completely free of their nouns. The whole business of language was released from the machinery of sexuality, liberated.

Not like in French, where «l'accord féminin,» feminine agreement, was such a big deal. To add, or not to add, an «e» at the end of a word: that was the question, after all. It went miles beyond proper grammatical agreement to far broader considerations of «l'accord féminin» within the culture – women knowing their place, and agreeing to it. Accepting their lot. Moving within the bounds set by men, religion, and the norms of silence erected to maintain families and their peculiar religio-cultural myths. For in French-Canadian society in the 1950s and '60s, women were expected not just to get along with men but to tag along. To make their social and sexual accompaniment of men, their "feminine accord," the central paradigm of their existence.

That was a major problem for me for two reasons. First, I'd skipped French school entirely, so I'd failed to learn enough about the finer aspects of «l'accord féminin.» As a result, I'd struggle with its grammar all my life when writing anything but common constructions. Second, through the deviant "after-school program" the French men in my milieu had operated, I'd acquired far too much knowledge about «l'accord féminin,» the sexual accompaniment of men. And what I'd learned is that it hurts a lot, inside and out.

A SUFFICIENT LIFE

The pain of belonging-not-belonging had started in early games I played against my full consent in dark places. And it spread right across the years, and onto the streets, to games I played willingly in broad daylight. In those first days of bilingualism, of course, I wasn't aware that language was a tangible thing; it was just something I could do. I could talk in one or another tongue and mostly be understood. It was only later, as I got older, that I realized that speech was something people could examine, embody, judge, accept, reject, embrace, refuse. And the way I learned this – the way language was excised from my head and thrown down hard onto the road – became a trauma unto itself.

For in all those years since that day when I was shut out of that game of slingshot because of my language choice, I've felt abandoned by my culture. It was «un jour impossible» when I was forced to declare a singular allegiance to French, but couldn't. I imagined myself to be a traitor, «une indésirable,» and I withdrew further. In time, this sense of betrayal became a two-way street in which I generated at least as much sorrow as I endured. For in learning "to think in English," I challenged, even shattered, my mother's understandable expectations that I'd be «une bonne fille» who'd respect her unconditionally and duplicate her values. Instead, I became «une maudite anglaise.»

Perhaps we all disappoint our mothers. Or did my bilingualism make me the worst of children? I think I know my mother's answer to this question, but I dare not say it. What I will say is that if she could take back my English education, I believe she would. As for me, I can only give my answer slowly, and it's "No." True, I became a tiny migrant, the prodigal daughter who learned that the foreign land has many wonders, and never returned to the ancestral hearth. My new language had put something into my head that wasn't there before. Does a new language ever not do that?

«'Mande-moi pas c'qu'al'a ent'les deux oreilles!» [Don't ask me what she has between her ears!] It's a common expression in Quebec. You use it when you don't understand what in the world is in someone's head, when you're in shock about bad decisions or generally problematic conduct. This idiom gets a lot of mileage on the streets, and I spent many years wondering what was, in fact, between my own two ears. I questioned not just those languages of mine, English and French, and my flowing back and forth between them – I could easily believe that – but also those memory fragments, shipwreck debris drifting between consciousness and unconsciousness. I couldn't believe that – it was not permitted. «Bin voyons donc!» The "best" of its adults being its worst? The "worst" of its children possibly not being as bad as all that? Please!

Be serious now! In this narrative frame of reference, it was understandably easy for the «maudit(e)» and the «bon(ne)» to become confused.

In Quebec, there's a new, ongoing discussion these days about «La Grande noirceur» having been the symbolic mother of «La Révolution tranquille.» The theory is that great darkness instills resistance and the desire for change. Is this one of those idiomatic truths about necessity and invention? That we need a motive to act on the present, something to propel our rebellions against fate? Was my personal darkness the symbolic mother of my revolution against my own silence? Did my trauma engender my reason for reclaiming my voice in another language? Perhaps changing tongues simply meant changing cultural and emotional scripts, transmuting my reactions, my roles, my realities. Using whatever chance I had to achieve the typical objective of most revolutions: long-term peace.

In fact, I could say that this peace held for life, in one way or another. As the years went by, my two languages remained in perpetual, paradoxical tension – as if managed through a carefully negotiated truce – swirling, mixing, yielding, crossing. Sustaining a highly functional state of contradiction and ambiguity between the language of origin, and the language of safety. The language of core, and of ego. Of destiny, and of agency. Of roots, and of shoots.

Pick any paradigm – the fundamental truth of my bilingualism was the same. And it was that each of my languages had, and has, an inherent value and an insurmountable problem all its own. Something that makes it irreplaceable, and something that makes it insufficient. That's why my languages aren't the two irreconcilable solitudes Canadian politicians often make them out to be. Rather, they're the flexible contours of a psychological space stretched out before me where I enact a most sufficient life not just upon it but because of it. For in the topography of my bilingual mind, English and French are the shores of the syncretic sea I inhabit – the essence in which I turn and return.

Avalanche

Life with childhood trauma
is life in avalanche country.
Memory is a rock face of sheer ice,
entirely unassailable.
You don't dare step too hard,
or cry too loudly.
You fear the ground will give.

You dread your own primal
screams, learn stillness,
doubt every step,
tread only on the surface,
and forget, over time,
about what lies beneath.
You embody your compliance.

Momentary light triggers
temporary thaws, becoming
shifts that open tiny passages.
But these close up again too soon —
these tectonic promises
of a cataclysm to come.
Who knows when ...

Sudden whispers set off
quick fault lines in the
thick crust of remembrance,
mass gathers murderous speed,
shatters tension with its thunder,
smashes internal mountains
into powdered crumble.

By the time you're strong enough
to stick your head out,
and catch your breath,
the terrain has changed completely,
revealing caverns you left behind
and entire landscapes
you forgot you owned.

It takes a while to steady feet,
chart a new course for yourself,
when there's no mountain left to climb –
when the avalanche is finally over,
so that silence is not required,
and you no longer fear
your own echoes.

21

THE GIFTS I KEEP

RECOUVRANCE

There's a famous tree on rue St-Louis, about two blocks in from one of the gates to the Old City, on the south side. A cannonball is stuck in its roots, from that day in 1759 when the fateful battle took place between English and French, after which the French surrendered primary ownership of the land. The tree has become an amusing anomaly for tourists to Quebec City. For me, it's a potent monument, in plain sight, to the difficult days that initiated my own tug of war between those same two languages, after which French surrendered primary ownership of my identity. Like that tree, my life continued around my wound. It took a minor detour, splitting around that gaping hole for a while, then found its balance, pulling itself together and sending up one strong stem that encased the site of injury, and then kept growing.

When I worked in the Old City as a tour guide, as I did for six summers, I took up embroidery during my breaks and unwittingly reproduced a version of that very tree. The trunk is brown and wide, with a large circular hole. Inside that hole, I stitched the colours of the rainbow vertically. The coloured threads work their way up the stem, side by side, to yield multi-coloured leaves – from greens to yellows to reds, left to right across an eight-inch oval. And there it was again, the language of imagery accidentally coming through, my hands speaking while my eyes failed to listen.

It would turn out to be the last summer I'd spend in the city of my birth. Sitting on my bedroom shelf today in a small glass frame, that tiny tapestry has moved twenty-seven times with me. It's a profound reminder of the connection between my internal constitution and the soil of my home, between my solutions and my symbols. I dared to dream in colour, even when the mind was dark. It wasn't that I was delusional, or ridiculously optimistic; it was merely a matter of life continuing, like that tree – enduring. And like me too, by the time that tree had moved far enough along in years, that skirmish for power between the two languages had been settled. It was then that was revealed the rooted primacy of French in its identity, against all odds.

From the cannonball tree, my memory walks about three blocks east, further into «le Vieux Québec,» and turns left (roughly north) onto Rue du Trésor. Here, painters and illustrators hang their works up and down both sides, on hooks, boards, and clotheslines. As a young girl, I remember going there with my granny to visit my American artist-uncle (her brother) and another artist-uncle (one of her sons, my father's brother) several times, as they each sold their stunning watercolours of Quebec and did quick sketches for a few dollars.

At the end of this incomparable road of grey-black cobblestones, worn smooth over four hundred years, is the Basilique Notre-Dame de Québec, the largest and most ornate church in the city. It's good to have a look inside and outside, but visitors today can't see all there really is, or was. Before its current form (dated early twentieth century), here stood the Basilique de Québec (late nineteenth); before that, l'Église-Cathédrale de Québec (mid-eighteenth); before that, l'Église Notre-Dame-de-l'Immaculée-Conception (late seventeenth); before that, l'Église Notre-Dame-de-la-Paix (mid-seventeenth); and before that, la Chapelle Notre-Dame-de-la-Recouvrance, built in 1633 by Samuel de Champlain, borrowing a name which, before that, belonged to a chapel in Orne, France, where «Notre Dame» had been worshipped since the ninth century.

The structure visible today is a layered reconstruction that's survived three major fires (in 1640, 1759, and 1922) and the furious shelling of 1759, when its destruction became a symbol of the English conquest. Its current solidity hides its migration from Old World to New World, its uncomfortable transitions from one shape to another, its months of flame and ruin, and its years of laboured recovery. It isn't just a splendid basilica but an extraordinary metaphor of how a fixed exterior can embody a complex history. Another perfect symbol on the soil of home.

UNE BELLE P'TITE BLONDE

Reconstructing from my own flames and ruin, disguising my own personal history within a solid shell, I survived in English an elaborate crime enacted in French. I sought refuge in English, and I recalled what I could of the incidents in English. In fact, English became the vehicle of memory to such an extent that when I hit puberty – by which point I considered myself dominantly English – I created a conveniently compacted picture of the crimes against me, fully narrated in English only. French had lost its meaning, its truth, its story.

My picture was an elaborate composite of my memories, nightmares, waking dreams, fugues, fears, allergies, scars, illnesses, emotions, habits, intuitions, deductions and ongoing problems. In short, it was the product of every instrument I had at my disposal. And in executing my masterpiece, I painted my father dead centre inside a frame I hung to hide the deep gash on the wall behind. So it was that all who knew me then knew only of my problems with him – and not of any of my problems with the rest. My ironic mask over my private self. And so it was, too, that I flew home with my baby for my father's funeral in 1994 only out of a thinly worn sense of filial obligation. His passing ensured his continuing silence, so the principal guilt just stuck to him more easily after that. Meanwhile, the real details of the sexual abuse remained submerged in my deeply constricted French identity, right off my own radar. Absolved in absentia – that hauntingly quiet confessional where the one most to blame never showed up at all. And sixteen more years went by.

"It's a damned good thing Dad didn't know before he died," my brother said recently. "It would have killed him, or else he'd have done something … I don't know what … Jesus!" My mother holds an opposite opinion about this which seems astounding in its own right: «C'est d'valeur qu'on l'sava' pas. Y s'd'manda' t'jours comment ça qu'ça marcha' pas ent'vous deux. Eh, Mon Dieu.» [It's too bad we didn't know then (while he was still alive). He was always asking himself why things went so badly all the time between the two of you. Oh, my God.]

And what do I think? I think this is a cave of sorrows I'll have to leave to the ages. I can't enter it. Not yet.

Nonetheless, my picture provided such a practical re-transcription of events that I returned to it regularly as my viable theory, my road map through history. Over time, then, I repressed even further the actual story and its perpetrators. I couldn't see that, unlike the aesthetic integrity of the composite I crafted so carefully to try to make sense of it all, the assaults upon me had been a messy hodgepodge of men, opportunities, and events that made no sense. In English, I put a lot of effort into controlling, taming, my traumatic past. And so for years at a time, I forgot almost everything except my symptoms: itchy-crawly skin and the rest of a largely invisible collection of highly personal memorials. In French, I had not even a hope of control – «pas d'espoir pantoute.»

It would take the first-ever visit to my home in Ontario by my mother, my brother, his wife, and his son in early August 2010 – nine years after I moved here with my three children – to wake up my dormant self, knock on the closed door deep inside me. It was a simple family dinner on a Saturday night that went on a bit late. A few objective comments shared by my brother about my father. An opening of genuine kindness. A curious anecdote shared by my sister-in-law about a male in the extended family. And somehow, a tiny, tiny, tiny light went on, imperceptibly. A flickering candle in the farthest reaches of an old castle long thought abandoned, along corridors of echoes. After they returned to Quebec the next day, my brother and I began to exchange emails. And the rest, I've told. Bruce Cockburn sings that you've "got to kick at the darkness 'til it bleeds daylight." But you have to be ready for a long project sometimes. Maybe ten years. Maybe twenty. Maybe fifty.

One of my tormentors, the Priest, was actually a quasi-famous philologist, a Franciscan who wrote French dictionaries. «Ah, y nous tanna' donc bin quand y v'na' pour souper chez-nous, lui-là. Y nous talonna' pour el bon mot pour ci pis ça, a'ec son dictionnaire s'a tab' de cuisine. Ah, qu'on aima' pas ça quand q'y v'na'.» [Oh, that one annoyed us so much when he came to dinner (at the boarding house). He'd bother us with his questions about the right word for this and that, with his dictionary on the kitchen table. Oh, we (sisters) didn't like it when he came.] It's an ominous story my mother shared with me only recently. How can the truth stare at us in the face and still elude us? And dictionaries – my fascination, my instrument. How much of our tormentors do we absorb into our being? How much of my own thinking has been shaped by his beliefs?

For his part, my main offender, the Elder, always struggled to avoid me at family gatherings, no doubt fearing he'd trigger a recollection, a link to the unconscious state in which he was all too familiar to me. Yet feeling his rejection while others were hugged and talked to, and grasping for an explanation, I assumed he disliked me because of my escalating betrayal of «la patrie,» and took it as hard proof that I was becoming English. Given that cultural identity depends on recognition, the feeling that you belong, I wonder if I'd have "left French" as readily if he hadn't made me feel like I already had. «Vaut mieux pas savoir,» my mother always says – best to think we shouldn't know since we can't. From the practical to the parable, that's the heritage of my «patrie» too.

Between these two men – the Elder and the Priest, the first and last shards of the broken mirror, the patriarchy and oligarchy, the culture and religion, the alpha and omega of my troubles – much happened that need not be told in further detail. Unlike preposterous claims about how sin begins, the crime was distinctly unoriginal. It's been a long time, though, since I was «une belle p'tite blonde» [a pretty little blonde], words that spit like venom. In the interim, I've not only endured in English but thrived. I'm a reinvention of myself, a relatively safe, successful "me."

Objectively, I know the horrific scope of what occurred. Yet in English, I can state calmly that I was toyed with and forced into an unspeakable submission of my body, opportunistically, during a span of many years. Unethical acts? The matter of ethics is omitted, irrelevant, here. Inhumane acts? No. Humanity is thoroughly complicit in every gesture of a twisted mouth, hand, passion. And that's about as far as I can take the explanations at this point. For the Elder himself was surely a victim of a similar crime, in similar hands, in his own time's version of men in dark cloaks spewing words purporting to be holier than another's. And the Priest, training as an altar boy – working his own way up by moving way down – surely suffered likewise himself. Even the hangers-on to the scene, apprentices, were scarred this way and that, accumulating their own grievances.

And what of those silent women, not just witnesses but the real Silly Putty of the era? Those who placed all their bets on perfunctory penances and their own obedient incantations of the Pater Noster, «Notre Père»? Their pain precedes, maybe exceeds, mine. Aloud or alone, they prayed, «Que ta volonté soit fait sur la Terre.» [May your will be done on Earth.] And so went the rule of their world to the will of the fathers.

All were survivors of a social world where people discretely categorized accounts of sexual transgressions as "minor" or "major" – like music scales or parted vaginas – and then let their mental division satisfy them, release them of human obligations. Descartes would have been proud. Such mechanics of mind produced a sturdy, rusty chain that bound its innocents into hierarchies. A multi-purpose twist of sexual and psychological knots, one linking the other, ad nauseum. The transgenerational transmission of horror in the name of something beyond reproach. Automatic, systemic absolution.

In the case of my life in Quebec, it just happened to be «au nom du Père, du Fils, et du Saint-Esprit.» And holy ghosts, it surely left behind. So I am now the result: the girl who looks at the girl who suffered. It's only in French that memories are salient, haunting, and insistent. In French, I carry scars that speak to my absence from a sociocultural sphere that was no longer viable. In English, I keep a safe orbit.

But my act of identity has come at a price, one paid not only by me but by my family. And now we can't take it back. We can't make me into a girl who doesn't go to university and takes on the family business, like my cousins. And we can't make me into a daughter who stays close to home and entrusts her mother tongue to the next generation, like the rest. I go away to school because I've always gone away to school. And I move away to English cities because I've always repositioned myself in English spaces. English is the land of my personal migration, my purchase of distance. I am that rude child in the library, escaping a mother's reach. This is what I became, and this is who I am.

I recall my father setting traps during hunting season every year, close behind the fishing camp he purchased when I was twelve. One morning, I found a sprung trap with a rabbit's foot in it. The foot was chewed off just above the lowest joint. "What happened to it?" I asked my father back at the camp, when I relayed what I'd seen. "It chewed its own leg off," he explained matter-of-factly. "It understood it was stuck, so it chewed the leg off to get away. Rabbits can do that." That story gives a heart-wrenching spin to the whole idea of a lucky rabbit's foot.

HAVE I GOT THE PROPORTIONS RIGHT?

Of course, in the context of the times, Catholicism offered a neat cover for the acts committed against me, but predation on children and women isn't unique to any religion, region, culture, or time. Pedophilia infects every society, and the incest taboo exists in ritual more than in actual rights. In a real way, then, every child is born not only into his or her mother tongue but also into its cultural version of silence. Emerging as bounded selves, we're all hostages of our own sociocultural paradigms – nested or trapped, take your pick. But a cold fact remains: if I'm deprived of my voice and my positionality in my mother tongue, it's only because I can bear the separation more easily than the reverberations.

Feeling myself so disconnected from early childhood, I read *Anne of Green Gables* three times to find out how orphans survived and overcame. I read it once around age eight, again at seventeen or eighteen during a depression, and again in my mid-twenties. There was something about Anne, and the blood-red soil on which she managed to find strong footing, that made her one of the most important peers I had, especially in adulthood. With Anne by my side, I orphaned myself psychologically, leaving my mother and mother tongue behind as I got myself adopted by this other language, this other culture. But there was a consequence for disowning myself, for my linguistic crossing over: it was the bond with my mother, my competencies in my mother tongue, and my roots in the land where my grandmothers and their grandmothers have been settled for four hundred years.

«Ah, Kathy, a'erviendra jama' à Québec» [Ah, Kathy, she'll never come back (to live) in Quebec], my mother has forecasted, cursed, around the kitchen table many times. She's been known to speak of me in the third person like this, even as I sit right there in front of her. She isn't being unkind. It's as though I've already left. As though, in a palpable way, I'm always absent. I am.

I've been gone for decades from «el foyer,» the hearth of my mother tongue. And curiously, while I was away, it changed too, withdrew, yielded to the greater power of the standard French. Its mother? I abandoned my patois just as I did the tiny girl inside me, and in much the same condition too – assaulted, without recourse, rendered mute – for it was endangered as much as I/she was in those years. Strange to think you're so tied up in a tongue that you live parallel lives.

And that's how I became a survivor not only of a complex sexual trauma but of an equally layered psycholinguistic and sociocultural trauma that's even harder to heal. I honestly wonder which is the deeper loss: the dangerous violation of dignity, or the disorienting alienation from home. That I hold these two sorrows as equal, so that I'm unable to choose the main tragedy, says much about the potency of our bonds with the first language we hear and utter. It's a harrowing pain whose words have been taken so that one can hardly even remember or speak of it – an inaccessible, incurable loss.

So what have I concocted from French and English after all? Is it the right balance of heart and mind? It sounds easy to do, like cooking. And easy to verify – just taste it. Have I got it right? How would the proportions have turned out without the trauma? I'll never know. But as I ended the first draft of this text, another of my father's brothers died, just past eighty. We gathered at home from points distant, and between the wine, sandwiches, and family albums, had the most wonderful time together. Folks spoke French to others who answered in English, and vice versa, as listeners joined in whichever language suited them. Others translated lovingly for the aunt from Baie Saint-Paul who's not perfectly fluent in English, or for an uncle's American wife with francophone roots who's lost some, but not all, of her French.

There was no clear line here between English and French, no set mark between words, no rules we consciously followed about where a switch from one language to the other could or couldn't be done. We just found the best way to say what we wanted to say, whatever the language. Tapping into all of our resources like this, we were way past thinking about so-called code-switching. The switch *was* the code as we negotiated meaning within our wide expanse of possibilities in both directions. Bilingualism still thriving, in all its beautiful asymmetries and imperfections, nearly one hundred years after that young English girl made her first home with a French rail worker in the backwoods of Quebec.

Child of an anglophone war bride and a francophone war hero, my now-deceased uncle, himself a decorated World War II veteran, would have been happy to see his French-dominant children host an Irish-style wake in the heart of Quebec City on this stunning fall day – between seasons, between life and death, between our linguistic worlds. Bilingualism offering its multivarious pathways for living. More than just language choices: rather, a nuancing of being. Subtleties of meaning, tone, affect, belonging, selfhood.

RIBBONS ALONG A RIVER

It was a healing weekend, as I realized how much I enjoy choosing which language to use. It felt like therapy, like I could breathe more deeply. There and back, airline personnel addressed me in English (if they didn't see my last name), or in French (if they did), as I flew between my languages. Yet something tipped my wings a little. Through the tiny window by my seat, the ground below me shifted.

There's an invisible line somewhere around Cornwall as you fly east. It's a place where land shaped like rectangles yields to land shaped like thick, colourful ribbons in greens and browns, embracing each other side by side, dipping one end into the St Lawrence River, el Fleuve Saint-Laurent. It's the legacy of my ancestors, the seigneurial system under which my great-grandmothers lived, land subdivided with only one thing in mind – access to water. From the air, it's breathtaking, defining, transforming. For me it's the ultimate confirmation of my location, my origins.

Every time I fly home, I watch for it, this glimpse of old land grants from the air. And when it's time to go again, that's what I hold onto as my last look as clouds move in. This familiar landscape of multicoloured bands across a stretch of the world where my people have been, and still are, means something to me in a way that the neat farms of Ontario, the Maritimes, the Prairies, or British Columbia – lovely as they are – do not. For after all of my odysseys, risking all that was known for the safety of the unknown, something calls to me from here in a voice like no other. That's the paradox I experience each day, forging an existence through which what I present on the outside remains in tension with what's broken and hidden on the inside – and through which what draws and eludes me are one and the same. Life as a constant pulse of engagement and withdrawal.

A few weeks after that trip home for the funeral, a card arrived for my birthday from a maternal aunt who wished me «des paniers de ‹je t'aime'›» [baskets of "I love you"]. My losses are still so obvious to everyone that they can be perceived even at a distance. For in every sense, mine is a typical narrative of exile: pushed forward by forces that couldn't be prevented, yet pulled back by forces that can't be dispelled. A tragedy precipitates the migrant's urge to find shelter somewhere, anywhere.

So though there are actually twenty-eight ways to ask "where" in the patois,* I don't have any answers. I have no idea exactly where I am, ever, except that I'm continuously suspended somewhere between my two linguistic worlds. Strategically alternating my position within two semantic and cultural fields that never have, nor ever will, overlap precisely. And though I can choose which language I use, I can't fully control the effect my mother tongue has on me. That's a matter entirely outside of choice, in the unspoken depths of the psyche, the prelinguistic self – in attachments nascent in the womb and the earliest days of life, long before identity forms and presents itself to the world.

As for my "troubles," I'm far clearer now about the "who," the "what" and the "when" than I ever was – or than it was ever possible to be before. Caught up in silences, events were erased for so long. If a problem is never talked about, the words for it are never learned, never exist. Not spoken, it doesn't happen. It's like a missing paper trail, only it's a missing trail of phrases somewhere between babyhood and culture. Quickly, then, we reach another telling bilingual mismatch be-

---

* «C'est qu', iyou, iyousse, iyousse que, iyousse que c'est, iyousse que c'est que, ouas, ouasque, ouasque c'est, ouasque c'est que, où c'est, où c'est que, où c'est que c'est que, où est-ce, où est-ce que, où est-ce que c'est que, où c'que, où que, où que c'est que, ousse, ousse que c'est, ousse que c'est que, you, yousse, yousse que, yousse'est que, yousse que c'est que, où.»

tween those semantic fields, different measures of what constitutes a statement. In French, a «phrase» is a whole sentence, but in English, it's only a few words, a partial thought. As for the "why," that's the single question I've worked hardest to answer, to address, to locate.

Grasping for coordinates, I think about my life and what I might make of the past and future. I turn things over, this way and that, as I strain to see the best of what occurred and who I became because of it. I locate this powerful lens in a box of tools deep within me, in the heritage of my mother tongue culture that I haven't lost. Looking through it, it seems I manage to see blessings even in the inevitable and find grace in even the most ordinary things.

I was born under the promise of modernism that the decade of my birth assured, but I ended up with a profoundly postmodern existence instead. I am, I have, a fragmented, fluctuating collection of traits by which my identity is hybrid and elusive, shaped by acts of agency that have let me appropriate what I can of this world, within and despite it. And though my original identity was obscured – the *sans trauma* person I might have been – I've used language as well as I could to animate a new version of myself. My instruction in English became an education in promise and possibility, one that's endured for a half-century and enabled me to be productive despite a difficult trajectory through an irreplaceable childhood I experienced primarily in French, the reservoir of my soul.

In the end, my story of moving from my first language to my second is a simple chronicle of survival. It's past and present, nothing and everything, private and public, emotional and political, mute and multilingual, trauma and hope. It's both, every time. So I finally realize something as I end this narrative: that I've been perseverating with a critical figure-ground illusion all along. Stuck on one view, again. The flag of my home is four white «fleur de lys» on a blue background divided by a white cross. That's true. But it's not only that. It also has four blue birds cut out, flying free in every quadrant of the sky. From beak to tail feathers, wing tip to wing tip, each one embodies the only genuine benediction I've ever needed: liberty. Chalk up another "aha" moment of my double life.

Closing my tale, I reflect on my favourite photograph of "home." Another one of those small black-and-white Kodak prints, it's of my brother and me, aged two and four, smiling ear to ear as we squat in scruffy shoes in the hay outside an aunt's farmhouse in Saint-Isidore de Dorchester. Our hair, skin, noses, eyes and smiles are identical in that small window of years. There's no sign here of what will soon separate us – the injuries and anguish that will propel me to take the languages we were both offered to slowly run away, one word at a time. There's only evidence of what keeps us joined: an unending love of place, even in dangerous times.

So while Quebec remains a home I had to leave, it's the home that never leaves me. I'm woven from these ribbons along the river – forever textured by my mother tongue. And that is where my story begins.

Libellule   Dragonfly

Une lune enflée	A moon swollen
de lumière	with light,
et nourissante	and nourishing,
recouvre l'ombre	covers the shadows
du monde.	of the world.
Elle se retrouve,	She finds herself
éclatante de joie,	bursting with joy,
car c'est la nuit	for it is the night
de la liberté,	of liberty,
des escapades dans	of flights into
les champs de lavande	fields of lavender
sans bornes,	without bounds,
des gouts délicieux	of delicious tastes
et pétillants sur la langue,	sparkling on the tongue,
du vent doux qui danse	of the soft wind dancing
entre des antennes perchées	between antennas perched
sur un visage	on a face
caressé de curiosité.	caressed in curiosity.
La réflection des étoiles	The reflection of stars
joue légèrement sur	plays lightly on
une peau mauve-verte,	purple-green skin,
particule de l'aurore attendue.	particles of the waiting dawn.
En état de grace accomplie,	In a state of assured grace,
elle s'épanouie et se jette	she opens and throws herself
vers la terre abandonnée,	towards abandoned earth,
seuil de ses mémoires,	hearth of her memories,
et revient vers le ciel	then returns towards the sky
qui l'invite vers l'éther.	that invites her to ether.
Sa vie est désormée	Her life from here is forever
dans l'air,	in the air,
où le fil du temps,	where the thread of time,
se déroulant,	unraveling,
charte une nouvelle route,	charts a new route,

chemin précieux parmi les astres, treasured road among heavenly bodies,
qui dévoile silencieusement that unveils silently
un destin aussi ouvert a destiny as open
que ses ailes, as her wings,
et tout aussi translucent. and just as translucent.

EPILOGUE

«J'en'rviens pas comme t'as 'ne bonne mémoére, toé-là» [I can't believe what a good memory you have], my mother recently said, not without irony, as we reminisced about an aunt's life. My brother concurred. Seems I've been recategorized from family oddball to family historian, for our first two decades anyhow. Yet with all due respect to their opinion, which does matter, it's my own view of myself that's having the biggest impact on my life these days. Because ever since my sexual abuse was confirmed, I've realized that I held on to core beliefs about my convoluted world against some powerful odds. And that's the critical affirmation that gives me the courage to set down my burden, these words.

Throughout my twenties, and possibly a bit before or after, I dreamed I was at a precipice, or in the middle of an empty field. And I'd open my mouth and just scream and scream and scream. I'd wake up every time with the same conviction: that if I actually did that, somehow everything would be better. That I'd be better. I dreamed it over and over, but I couldn't figure out what it meant. By then, I'd long forgotten about having once been a raging baby. And I'd even outgrown that «maudite belle p'tite fille» – damned to mutism as she was.

I hadn't even thought of this dream in decades, but I had it again right after finishing the final draft of this text. It was an agonizing reminder of what it was like to be at the scene of the accident that was me. And upon waking, to know that I'd managed to walk away with my scratches, that I'm no longer there. To know, too, why screaming and screaming – the wild release of trapped sounds – would feel better. Because it does.

I do understand that there was a huge hole in my bucket all these years. A void, an immeasurable mass of stillness without clear contours right in the centre of my self. Through that hole, I kept some things and watched others drip away, just like dear Élise-Liza. But after much mystery about my own constitution, I finally get that I have an English valence of identity as a sturdy layer, a fix atop a complex personal profile. It's what makes it possible for me to pick up my bucket and go about my daily business. It's a fairly decent repair job, too. My exterior looks reasonably strong, though more than half a century has passed since the first rupture of its original integrity, its body, its bucket-ness.

But I don't want to keep looking back. Even just reading this narrative throws me for a reverse loop that's hurtful testimony to how far I've come – of how language education delivered my personal liberty, my psychological emancipation. Besides, reality testing tells me my homeland is safe for me now and my world is no longer closing down around me. After travelling all that time and distance, I discovered that my voice was waiting where I left it. And that my bilingualism provided the greatest security I ever had – my state of mind.

So I've come full circle from intending an *apologia* to refusing altogether to apologize for my journey – my linguistic drifting, my sociocultural distancing, my "self-othering." After all, I survived in no small part because of it.

The last time I saw my mother inside the writing frame of this book, we took time for a special outing that had been awaiting my next visit home. We went together to a renowned «restauratrice» on Avenue Maguire to have the tear in the *Madonna* painting fixed, after all these years, more than twenty now. It was promising to be expensive, almost $400, but my mother held dearly to doing it: «Ej sais q'c'est bin spéciale pour toé, ç'ta peinture-là.» [I know it's very special for you, this painting.] By then, both she and my brother had reviewed a partial draft. «Y'a des bouts qui sont bin dur à lire,» she'd told me. [There are parts that are very hard to read.] They were hard to write, too.

We wrapped the painting carefully in a clean sheet for safe transport, and we somehow got a parking spot right in front of the shop, on one of the most popular streets in Quebec – a lively hustle of caféterrasses and specialty stores – on a Saturday, the busiest day of the week. It was a necessary miracle, for the years are wearing heavily on my mother's body, secrets and disclosures both taking their toll. But as we described the painting for its official record on the invoice, my mother and I were each stumped for the French word for "halo." «Bin, c't'une couronne, en fin d'compte» [Well, it's a crown, after all], she insisted. Yet I didn't think so: «Non, c'pas 'n couronne. Ej sais ça. Mais el bon mot m'échappe» [No. It's not a crown. I know that. But the right word escapes me]. Old age and psychological distance manifesting the same symptoms.

It would be late that night when my sister-in-law would furnish the right word, «une auréole,» while we waited for the Elton John concert on the grounds of the Festival d'Été – still hanging out «s'es Plaines.» And until I woke up the next morning, she had me blissfully, delightfully confused. The same word for a bird and a halo? That seemed perfect. But no, the bird was an «oriole» and the halo was an «auréole,» the online translation dictionary brutally announced at daylight. In truth, I was happier in between somehow, lost between my languages, between blurred possibilities.

I was happier until I remembered later that the area around a woman's nipple is a close word, too, «l'aréole» – in English, "an aureole." In both languages, that word's also used for the moon's luminous corona and the circle around infectious skin rashes. How quickly that reassuring ambiguity of bird-and-halo became uncomfortable: bird, nipple, moon, disease, and halo. If I speak of my *Madonna* in French, then, as having an «auréole,» I cultivate the beautiful allusion to a bird. But other meanings I don't care for – reminders of infection, bright flashing lights, a naked female body – come rushing into the semantic field, and I can't stop them. On the other hand, if I speak of her in English as having a "halo" (rather than an "aureole"), she's pure and plainly good. Stripped of depth, maybe, but stripped of dangers, too. Small difference on the tongue, big difference on the ground – and on the psyche. Bilingualism is just that.

My mother sat in the car looking strangely peaceful that afternoon. Seems she was satisfied about finding something we could mend easily, even after all these years. But still no «ej (je) t'aime» from my end – and still no «pauv' p'tite» [poor little one] from hers. We're at a verbal impasse – a *impass*able point we can't overcome and which is, so the word itself tells us, awfully close to what is effectively *impos*sible. Before writing this book, I'd never thought of it as our tacit social contract. But it strikes me now that this is precisely what it's been all along, and that fifty-four years is a very long period of precedent-setting. So it is that silence continues its double duty – in the service of peace, in the service of violence.

Rereading, of course I realize how cold and detached this all sounds. So damned English?

We drove away, leaving behind us along Chemin St-Louis the nearly adjoining cemeteries overlooking the Saint-Laurent where are buried my grandfather St-Onge, my granny St-Onge, my paternal great uncle-artist, two of my father's brothers, my own father, and the eldest of my brother's two sons, who died in infancy. Yet we were a long distance – a lifetime away – from the cemetery where lay my grand-papa Dumont, my grand-maman Dumont, my grand-grand-maman Blais dit Raisin, plus countless other elders and priests from those days in that first neighbourhood of Saint-Sacrement.

My *Madonna* will be delivered to my mother's home a few days later, when I'm safely back in Ontario, adding to my already cluttered re-frigerator door a few souvenirs from another typical visit "back home." One day driving in, two (maybe three) days there, one day driving out: I reach my practical limit. There's chatty breakfasts, family dinners, a restaurant meal, a cultural event, the inevitable half-day shopping «din' cent' d'achats» [at the malls]. And somewhere in there, an indispens-able drive into the Old City – usually alone. My kids have definitely got a "been there, done that" feeling about that piece of the trip by now.

I come up from down below, along Boulevard Champlain (to the south) or Boulevard Charest (to the north), and head up the steep rock face. Or, depending on the traffic and my mood, I come as straight as an arrow down Grande Allée through La Porte Saint-Louis. But the destination is always the same: the statue of Samuel de Champlain on that point of land that juts out boldly into the Fleuve Saint-Laurent, the absolute edge of my world. I park if there's room – if not, I just slow down. I look around the whole square, from La Rue du Trésor to Le Château Frontenac, and out onto the water that points to the «Pont d'l'Île d'Orléans,» and beyond, to the open ocean. I take a deep, deep breath. And I say a quiet greeting to Samuel. Maybe it's a prayer, but I don't know for sure – and I don't know for whom either, exactly. Just life, really.

I admit that lately my eyes well up more than they used to, doing this. But I only linger briefly, then drive away. My trip to Quebec feels done then and there, every time. Climaxed. I'm incapable of being home, or leaving again, without paying my respects like this. Without having «un p'tit bout d'journée dans l'Vieux» – a part of a day in, among, the Old. That's what's left now. Bits of time. Snapshots of ancient history.

What'll I do from here on in, with my self in mid-restoration – that refinished bucket? I'm not sure. But I've begun filling it with art pencils, the whole glorious range from 4H to 4B, and I'm contemplating taking it to a drawing class. I still find my favourite subject-objects among my old friends at the treasured borderland between reality and fantasy: baby animals, birds, and bugs of all kinds, especially dragonflies. Creatures like the dear crawler I had for a pet as a toddler that was a story (and a universe) all on its own. I search for them in books, or in the grass near my home. I like trying to sketch their homes, too – trees and flowers of all kinds.

And I've also started my PhD, part-time, to explore the therapeutic potential of language education. How is it possible, psychologically, for this kind of internal rescue to happen? How can you imagine yourself as a survivor, and then become one? It's research as a different kind of art, a different kind of blurring of reality and fantasy. Seems I'm safe at school again.

"Are they all like this, your drawings? So soft and innocent?" a colleague recently asked. I hadn't really thought of them like that before, but perhaps they are. Then again, why shouldn't they be? Psychological theft isn't at all like physical theft. In a fundamental way, I still own everything that was taken from me.

From being bilingual to *bilingual being*. Not just one view or possibility for existence, but many. Not just an identity in translation, but a profound reinvention. Not just enduring, but living.

Bilingual, paint from different language brushes layers specks of many colours upon the canvas of the self. And in the end, it's good enough. «En fin d'compte, c't'assez.»

ACKNOWLEDGMENTS

I'm a linguist and language teacher who's focused on bilingual education – ESL and FSL – for over twenty-five years. Language is my passion. Recently, that interest prompted me to interrogate my life as a bilingual Canadian. I was curious about my linguistic and cultural drifting – away from French, towards English – following a decade of sexual abuse as a child. I found myself reflecting on how my education in English created an alternative social space where I made a new life for myself, one so different from that inscribed by my hereditary French setting. Learning a new tongue gave me a new voice as a bilingual being. It's a story centred on Quebec, Canada, French and English, and Catholicism, but I trust it's a story that goes beyond its location to become a tale about the power of language and culture over the self – and the reciprocal power of the self over both. It's because having a choice of tongues translates into having a broader choice of lives. And in that wide expanse of possibility between language worlds, there's the opportunity – the invitation, even – to overcome the past and embody a new identity.

Before closing, I'd like to express my gratitude to York University's Faculty of Education – my new grounding in a shaky world – and specifically, to Lisa Farley, Jen Gilbert, Colette Granger, Alison Griffith, Karen Krasny, Razika Sanaoui, Sandra Schecter, and Belarie Zatzman. Special thanks to Mario DiPaolantonio, my first instructor after a twenty-five-year gap, whose warmth secured my engagement; Heather Lotherington, who first encouraged me to tell this story; Carol

Anne Wien, who nurtured its initial stage; and Karen Hardtke, my therapist at York's CDS. And to three outstanding individuals for their support, and for ideas now inseparable from my psyche: Deborah Britzman (the emotional world of education); Alice Pitt (the hide and seek of learning); and Daniel Yon (the messiness of identity). I'm also grateful that decades ago, there was another university where I felt safe and supported: McGill. Here, I thank Myrna Gopnik, Michel Paradis, and Vicki Zack. And my deep appreciation for McGill continues, in particular for Mark Abley, of McGill-Queen's University Press. He graciously reviewed my manuscript and persevered with me for over a year, providing thoughtful critiques and comments that sustained my courage.

I also have intellectual debts to a number of writers whose work changed my life. Ariel Dorfman, author of the first language memoir I ever read, who confirmed my "double life." Eva Hoffman, for her reflections on life between English and Polish – the best representative of the genre. Sandra G. Kouritzin, for her wrenching study of language attrition. Aneta Pavlenko, who interrogates the connection between language, emotion, and identity. Kathleen Dean Moore, an environmental philosopher who is Beatrix Potter for my adult life. Donald W. Winnicott, a psychoanalyst, for his ideas about false selves, the work of play, and the good-enough mother. The two most esteemed folklorists of Quebec, Jean-Claude Dupont and Luc Lacourcière, who connect me viscerally to my inheritance of the heart. And the inimitable philosospher, Jacques Derrida, my adoptive father «en théorie.»

I'm especially indebted to Sigmund Freud. For most of my life, I confess I held the usual stereotypes about Freud. But during months of working through the mysteries that secretly steered my existence for half a century, I revised my opinion entirely. In the legal field, a "chain of custody" denotes the chronological flow of evidence – its possession, transfer, seizure, disposition, and (in)security. Testimony hinges on it, especially when the goods are susceptible to trickery. As I conducted my "personal investigation," Freud explained the convoluted transport of memories, affective shards, and personality formations from the past to the present. He provided the instruments I needed to become a reliable witness in my own life and to begin to account for the whole of my story.

On a more personal note, I thank T., for everything, as well as my Granny St-Onge – Gladys Louise Garland. In her dying days, she entrusted me with her memoir, from which I've drawn many references. And John L. St-Onge, my father's brother, a retired professor with a penchant for history about my Grandfather St-Onge. But more than anything, I'm thankful to my three children, Sarah, Jacob, and Peter, for more than I can put into words. They're unique, kind, brilliant and successful adults who offer everything from love to feedback to comic relief. I hope that I've not embarrassed them and that they'll be a little closer to understanding the questions they ask of themselves as anglophone Canadians, such as "Why does Mom care about her French heritage so much?" And its companion query, "Why didn't we go to French school?" Good questions indeed.

In fact, I shunned my mother tongue and my French Canadian heritage almost all of my life – leaving my mother, Thérèse Dumont, and my home behind as I othered myself, bit by bit, into English. My mother considers this the trauma that changed everything for her, much as a different trauma changed everything for me. I thank her, for every child's story is also a mother's story. In relating family narratives, I render all of my mother's words in the so-called joual of Quebec City, my hometown. I can't fathom trying to capture her world without using the authentic tongue into which I was born. This often disparaged (yet still ubiquitous) patois, rather than standard French, is my real mother tongue.

This book is a series of narrative essays around common themes. But the French rather than the English meaning of the word is the one I intend. «Un essai» adds the sense of "an attempt," and this is nothing more than my effort to tell a story – one necessarily infused with my point of view. It's a «mélange» of ethnography, reflections, and secrets that can be told anywhere now, but for more than fifty years could be told nowhere at all. Yet a single drop of water falls, again and again, and a mountain eventually crumbles. Silence is a weak pact against the forces of nature.

The twenty-four poems are crafted from the therapy journal I wrote in the months following the confirmation of my trauma on 29 August 2010. Each has travelled an arduous journey from the unconscious to the conscious, to a formless sea of more than five hundred pages of tiny-fonted print, to poetry, to here. I hope you'll forgive their intrusion from another mental space entirely, and allow the child reporter to have a word inside the story the adult writer is trying to tell. My tale wouldn't be complete (or mine) without them.

I offer this book in loving memory of my deceased maternal cousin, Sonya Poulin, who was my elder by about two years. I further dedicate it to my sister-in-law, Julie Blouin, whose astute listening on the bridge between my brother and mother throughout the summer of 2010 broke my personal history wide open, delivering air. And to my brother, Richard (Rick) – my only sibling. Were it not for his keen memory of odd details and his willingness to indulge annoying questions from a sister who'd long felt estranged, I'd still be in the dark about why I traded language ships and sailed away. Siblings surviving diaspora: a tale of hope. Or so I hope it is.